D0559235

Smart

Is the New

Rich

Smart
Is the New
Rich

If You Can't Afford It,
Put It Down

CHRISTINE ROMANS

WILEY

John Wiley & Sons, Inc.

Published by John Wiley & Sons, Inc., Hoboken, New Jersey.
Published simultaneously in Canada.

For general information on our other products and services or for technical support, please
contact our Customer Care Department within the United States at (800) 762-2974, outside
the United States at (317) 572-3993 or fax (317) 572-4002.

Wiley also publishes its books in a variety of electronic formats. Some content that appears in
print may not be available in electronic books. For more information about Wiley products,
visit our web site at www.wiley.com.

Library of Congress Cataloging-in-Publication Data:
Romans, Christine, 1971-
 Smart is the new rich : if you can't afford it, put it down / Christine Romans.
  p. cm.
 Includes index.
 ISBN 978-0-470-64206-1 (cloth); ISBN 978-0-470-92565-2 (ebk);
 ISBN 979-0-470-92566-9 (ebk); ISBN 978-0-470-92567-6 (ebk)
 1. Budgets, Personal. 2. Finance, Personal. I. Title.
 HG179.R633   2010
 332.024—dc22
                                                          2010024725

Printed in the United States of America

10 9 8 7 6 5 4 3 2 1

To Ed,
the smartest person I know, who
makes life rich beyond all imagination.

Contents

Foreword

Before I get into complimenting Christine Romans on having the decency to write a smart, charming, easy-to-read book on something that gives most of us heart palpitations, namely money and what to do with it, I want to compliment you for picking it up. Now I don't know if you've already bought it, or if you're standing in the bookstore thinking about it, or reading the first three chapters on your iPad or Kindle. But I do know this: Money makes people crazy and you're trying to feel sane about it.

There are tons of books out there about money, and all of them seem to vacillate between investment schemes that read like a lotto ad and fear-mongering manifestos from the "dismantle the Fed or we'll all be in work camps" crowd. Today it seems people hunger for dramatic extremes. Many people think it's our high-tech, coffee-driven society and our constant need for distraction. And it very well may be. It might also be that we have grown lazy—not because we are bad people, but because we have been tortured by an idea that money is a mysterious uncontrollable force that must be handled by someone else, and that feeling has made us numb to it. We know when we want it, and we certainly know when we need it. Many of us know how to get it, but a lot of us don't know how to keep it . . . so we freeze. At worst we do nothing, and at best we hand our money over to someone and hope for the best. But where has that gotten us? Stuck. Fearful. Confused. Broke in many cases.

You've probably made past attempts at fixing your money woes before and you may have been lectured by others about it. They've told you and you told yourself that you need one thing. And if you had that one thing you'd be able to get command of your financial situation. What is that one thing? It isn't information. That's everywhere, and most of the time it seems there's too much of it to get a grasp on any of it. Ironically, it isn't more money, either, at least not yet, because if you had it right now without a new way of dealing with it, it would be gone like all the rest of it. No, the word we're looking for is one of the most celebrated and feared words in our society. That's right. Discipline. Yikes! I know. Everybody wants it. Nobody you know has it. Not really, but that's what everyone thinks will solve the problem. Discipline—a word just like money that fills us with hope and apprehension at the same time.

I'd like to give you a new word, one that I'd like you to replace the word *discipline* with and one that will help you as you apply the very smart things Christine prescribes here in this book. That word is *consistency*. Discipline is nearly impossible, but we can all practice consistency. Just go through the book with consistency. Be consistent with the application of what you learn, and when people congratulate you for all the discipline you have, you'll know that all you did was read this book page by page and follow the ideas bit by bit. And you'll look back on the good habits you formed and the security you've created and it'll amaze even you.

Rats! I've run out of room! Okay, real quick: I met Christine at CNN on *Your Money* and was immediately aware that—with all due respect to those working on the show—she was the sharpest, steadiest, and most caring person there by far. In a room full of very intelligent people I call her "The Smart One." She's the reason I never pass up a chance to do that show, because I always know that not only will I learn something useful from Christine Romans, but I'll enjoy the process. Now . . . keep reading.

HAL SPARKS
September 2010

Preface

There I was in a radio booth at CNN in New York, taking phone calls, e-mail, and Facebook messages about money. More came in during the hour than my producers and I could keep up with.

"How do I raise my credit score?"

"I lost my job six months ago and I need to start my own business to start bringing in some income."

"I want to buy a house but I need to save a little more money for the down payment. Should I raid my 401(k)?"

And then, a call that went something like this:

"I saved for my kid's college and now have lost one year of tuition. I saved for my retirement, and I lost a third of that. I am underwater on my house, because two neighbors have foreclosed. We drive two cars, neither new, and my husband's office just announced they are cutting 10 percent across the board. I thought I was smart about my money, but it doesn't seem to matter."

This book is for you.

I hear from so many of you who played by the rules during the boom when common sense took second place to maxing out risk and credit. And now you're wondering what the new rules are to start building your wealth again. This book explains how the new rules aren't so new at all—they are really retro rules that were lost. Your time will come again.

Whether you read this book cover-to-cover, or pick and choose the money topics that interest you, the material in these pages is meant to help guide you through the New Normal and reassure you that, yes, smart decisions today *will* help you build and prepare for retirement.

These pages explore everything from health-care reform, to taxes, to job-hunting to debt, and what it means for you. The material is diverse for a reason.

Because "you" are a diverse lot: "you" are running small businesses, "you" are stay-at-home moms. "You" are college students who want the right major and not a ball and chain of student debt. "You" are young married couples who want your first home, and "you" are job changers and job seekers who need to sell yours.

"You" want to retire with enough money for your health-care needs in the last 10 years of your life, but "you" also want to put your kids through college so they have the right start.

Statistics that matter to your bottom line—called Romans' Numerals—are signposts to guide you down the different paths the book takes. I've written it (I hope) in a way that allows you to follow the path as it winds through, or you can steer off the road and jump ahead to the Romans' Numeral that means the most for your money—how you earn it, save it, spend it, and retire on it.

Like apps, there's a Numeral for just about everything. Take credit card debt. How long would it take to pay off $10,000 in credit card debt by only paying the minimum? Would you believe 46 years? See Chapter 5 for strategies to pay off that debt and become "Debt-Free in Three."

There is enough in just Chapter 3 to help you rethink your relationship with your career, recharge your job search, and revise your strategies for success at work. This chapter is meant to apply to every worker out there—whether you have a job you love, you are stuck in a job you barely tolerate, or you need a job *today*.

Chapter 6, "Home Sweet Home," examines important assumptions and mistakes for the biggest asset you will ever own—which is also the biggest debt most of us will ever assume.

I found myself spending the most time writing this book immersed in these two subjects—jobs and houses. We live in one and hope that it provides for our retirement. We need the other to provide the paycheck that powers our personal economy. These are the two assets most important to the vast majority of the middle class. It's the meat of your personal finances and the meat of this book.

The chapter I had the most fun writing—and put most of my personal experience and advice in—is Chapter 8, "Family Money." This chapter is for everyone—no matter where you are on the financial arc of earnings, savings, spending, investing, and retiring. I hope it provokes discussion—even debate!—around the dinner table. Many families don't talk about money enough. It's either bad manners, embarrassing or for some odd reason inconsequential. I could not disagree more. After reading Chapter 8, I hope everyone is inspired to talk to grandma about a living will, the grandkids about which major to choose and the ensuing college debt, and Generation Y about savings and paying their bills on time. And remember, money habits start young. Your kids learn from you.

Here's a tease (as we call it in television news) for this chapter: "How making your kids take out the trash could make them rich! And avoiding debt can keep you married! Coming up in Chapter 8!"

Each chapter features links to helpful mortgage, student debt, and credit card interest rate calculators and tables. But I encourage everyone to use the additional resources at CNNMoney.com. It's a treasure trove of free and up-to-the-minute tools for investing and retiring.

Okay, you are not interested in spending a half-hour reading chapters about kids and money, small business, taxes, or the difference between good and bad debt. For you I have included at the end of each chapter something called "The Payoff" for a quick read if you want the salient facts, best advice, and sharp perspective quickly.

My hope is that this book doesn't end for you on the last page, but instead starts a running conversation between you and your spouse, your kids, and your parents about how to smartly prepare for a rich future.

CHRISTINE ROMANS

September 2010

Acknowledgments

I'm so fortunate to be surrounded by curious and talented journalists who are always willing to dig deep into the economic data with me and tell the stories of the people behind the numbers. First and foremost, the CNN teams behind *Your $$$$$* and *Your Bottom Line*; the bright-eyed crew of *American Morning*; my producer in the wee hours of the morning Karina Frayter; the many journalists who fan out with me to gather the facts and talk to the people whose stories show what the numbers really mean— Jennifer Haley, Erica Fink, Hussein Saddique, Juliet Fuisz, Sara Lane, Stephanie Genkin, Jennifer Bragg, Jennifer Icklan, Joanna DiGeronimo, Kristina Yates, Ben Tinker, Adam Thomas, Alyssa Zahler, Julian Cummings, Vivienne Foley, Elise Zeiger, Adam Reiss, Ronni Berke; to Jessie Opoien for her keen copyediting, and the people who encourage me to tell these stories on air every day and provide a platform for me to interview everyone from the Treasury Secretary to the CEO of Goldman Sachs to Serena Williams to Gene Simmons—Michael Kane, Gene Bloch, Jamie Kraft, Darius Walker, Bart Feder, Ken Jautz, and Jon Klein (who had the bright idea to present my wonky love of numbers as "Romans' Numerals").

Andrew Rubin from NYU for all his guidance on health-care reform; Certified Financial Planners Ryan Mack from Optimum Capital Management and Doug Flynn from Flynn Zito who teach me more about money each time I interview them on *Your $$$$$*; Greg McBride, senior financial analyst at Bankrate.com; Jeanne Sahadi and the phenomenal reporters and editors of CNNMoney.com; and of course, my co-anchor Ali Velshi.

A special thanks to the folks at John Wiley & Sons and to Christine Pietz, Carolyn Disbrow, and Christa Robinson; Adam Leibner and Paul

Fedorko at NS Bienstock who did not think it at all unusual that I would write my first book while raising two toddlers, pregnant with another baby, and working my day job. (Thank you for the encouragement.) And mostly, to my parents who taught me the value of a dollar, and to my husband, without whose patience, sharp editing, and encouragement I could never have written a single word.

Reset, Repair, Recover

$111,000

ROMANS'
NUMERAL

Cost of the average high-end kitchen renovation—twice the median household income.

There's smart. And there's rich. For much of the past 15 years, you could be one and not the other. And vice versa.

It's over. The next 15 years, you'll need to be especially smart about money before you'll ever be rich again.

The "rich" of the 1990s and 2000s was an imaginary rich, anyway.

We all know someone who made a killing in the bubble, flipping houses, or moving up into a bigger house with no money down and an adjustable rate mortgage. It seemed like everyone was into it and the "smart" thing to do was double down on credit, acquire big debt, and live like a king. The credit card offers were flying (2.9 percent for six months!), there were new ways every day to drain the money (real and hypothetical) out of your house, and condos were changing hands at 20 percent, 30 percent, 40 percent higher prices before ground had even broken.

The average price for a high-end kitchen renovation topped $111,000,[1] more than twice what most families make in a year, and we built houses with more bedrooms than people to sleep in them, bought more cars than drivers in the household, and somehow thought that living within our means meant living within our (ever-expanding) credit card limit.

The risk takers inherited the earth while the smart and fiscally fit were left behind, scratching their heads. Smart borrowers just never understood how a NINJA loan ever made sense. (*No Income No Job No Assets*. Really?!) But yes, it's true. The economic brainiacs, Congress, the banks—they all believed it was a new world of ever-rising living standards, rising home prices, and rock-bottom interest rates. Homeownership reached record levels, the treasury secretary said never before in his entire business career had the global economy been better,[2] and the Fed chairman said never-you-mind those nagging little concerns about subprime mortgages.[3] The housing market is so big and vibrant, the Fed chief told us, any problem with risky borrowers would not affect the rest of the economy.

POP!

The bubble more than popped. It exploded and spewed toxic mortgage assets like a mushroom cloud raining economic radiation around the world, hurting everyone—even the smart and the careful. Nearly $7 trillion in U.S. household wealth was wiped out during the recession. It's a number too big to fathom. But you can probably quantify all too well how much you lost—probably a big chunk out of your 401(k), for sure. And if you were a smart planner with a taxable stock or mutual fund account, you got hit there, too. There are tens of thousands of smart parents who planned ahead and saved money in a 529 only to see a semester or even a year of college tuition vanish. More than 8.4 million people lost their jobs, almost 3 million have lost their homes and millions more lost the home equity line of credit they were using as a rainy-day fund.

You may never have had a crazy exotic home loan. You may never have drained all of the money out of your house. You don't have a kitchen that cost more than a law school degree. You lived within your means. And you're angry. At the mortgage outfits that cooked up these crazy loans, the brokers who told millions of people they could afford loans they clearly could not, the banks who bought them, packaged them up in securities and sold them like legitimate investments, and the investment banks that found ways to make money off selling them to other investors and at the same time investing in bets that the investments they were selling would sour. Since the early

1990s, the savers and the planners and the risk-averse were left behind. All the traditional metrics of personal finance were out the door. Why pay off student loans when it made more sense to take on mortgage debt and flip the house? It was tax deductible, plus, home prices kept rising. By 2004, personal finance experts said the 30-year fixed-rate mortgages were obsolete. You could afford a bigger home with interest-only loans, and for anyone more conservative, an adjustable rate loan would do just fine.

A credit bubble fueled the housing bubble and that created an entitlement bubble. Somehow millions of Americans believed (with the enthusiastic approval of their elected officials, credit card issuers, and the Wall Street wizards) that we could spend more, consume more, save less, and live better in perpetuity. So soon after the dot-com bust, we *again* believed there was some sort of new economy out there, sustained by an ever-rising housing market that would more than make up for weakness elsewhere in the economy. Economists said trade deficits didn't matter—they were simply a reflection of a powerful U.S. consumer. They said low savings rates didn't matter either. Instead, they said again and again that the "wealth effect" of ever-increasing value in home prices made up for the lack of actual cash on hand for U.S. households. Somehow a $3,000 flat-screen TV for Christmas for every middle-class family became a national right, like having electricity on the farm in the 1920s. Think of it: This country went from flat-screens for Christmas in 2007 to foreclosures for Christmas just 12 months later.

The most rational levelheaded people were all caught up in the same line of thinking. Of course, in hindsight, it all looks like bubble talk. But at the time, everybody was making money. The builders, the flippers, the mortgage brokers, the Wall Street banks, the debt rating agencies, the appraisers, the real estate agents, the real estate lawyers, the contractors, the speculators at every level. . . . It's an endless list.

So now the bubble has burst and here we are standing in the wreckage of, in the words of former Federal Reserve chairman and current Obama Administration advisor Paul Volcker, "the mother of all financial crises."[4]

The "crisis" is over and we are left living in an upside-down world where more people are filing for unemployment than are buying their first home. A world where there are more people on food stamps than there are people in college. A world where 43 percent of workers have less than $10,000 saved for retirement, but the number of millionaires rises. On the same day the Employee Benefit Research Institute reported in its 2010 Retirement Confidence Survey that only 16 percent are confident they have enough money saved for retirement, another report from a group called Spectrem (which analyzes high-net-worth trends) declared that millionaires were making a comeback.[5] The number of U.S. millionaires in 2009 grew 16 percent to 7.8 million and the number of households worth $5 million or more soared 178 percent to 980,000.[6] Why? Because the stock market had roared back and people with money were more likely to have investments tied to markets. The middle class and upper middle class are more likely to have wealth tied up in their homes or other real estate, and their money and their financial security are closely tied to their jobs. So the already wealthy rode the stock and commodities markets higher, while the middle class and upper middle class were still reeling from a weak job and real estate market.

THE RETRO RESET

After two brutal years of recession, we're having a national reboot right now that favors the solvent, the confident, and the bold. We need to hit control-alt-delete on our goals, our expectations, and our plans for getting there. We're resetting to a more rational way of thinking about and living with our money: how we make it, spend it, save it, and invest it. We're saving more, spending less, and taking fewer risks with our money. We've gone from a national pastime of risking our money or living on borrowed money to protecting the money we have. The Great Recession has had a profound effect and will continue to do so, and it will provide opportunity. Twenty-nine million small business owners face an entirely new landscape—less availability to credit at the same time their customers and suppliers are reining in for a new more restrained reality. That means every business plan, every mission statement, and every personal retirement goal needs a reboot, too. Investing in the future will come from earnings and savings, and to a much-lesser degree, from credit. I like to call it "the awful Aughts"—those years of excess and disconnect and risk and froth. We will not make money the way we did in the "Aughts." With a nod to the old Smith Barney commercials, we'll make money the old-fashioned way: We'll earn it.

In many ways, we're starting over and resetting our expectations for where we work, how much we earn, how we manage our money, how we spend it, and how we invest it. In "normal times" it's a healthy exercise for every family to rethink its relationship with money, whether the family lives paycheck to paycheck, is solidly middle class or working to build something to pass on to the children. Now it is more important than ever before. It's the American Dream to climb a rung of that ladder every generation, saving and earning and investing in ways to provide more for the kids than the parents were provided. For the first time in my lifetime, that assumption may be at risk. We have to be smarter than ever to assure our place in the U.S. economy and to ensure that our kids enjoy a better standard of living than their parents and grandparents.

What if it takes seven years to replace the 8.4 million jobs lost in the two years since the recession began?[7] What if that means you are less likely to get a raise or trade up to a higher-paying job? What if it means the short-term financing you relied on for your small business is not coming back? There is no question you and your children will need extra training and education to set yourself apart and stay in the middle class or move up during the next generation. How will you afford it and what should you study? These are the questions for the New Normal.

As the economy gingerly crawls out of this mess and begins to grow again, every smart move you make today ensures a better tomorrow.

REPAIR THE BALANCE SHEET

Now the hard work of repairing your personal balance sheets begins. In the chapters ahead, you will relearn how to do it. How well you repair after the hits of 2008 will be the basis for building wealth for your future and your family. People with money are playing offense again with their money. You should be, too. And that exercise begins today, with you, and a positive attitude and the commitment that you are going to understand your finances and begin the repair immediately.

First things first: Are you still living in a bubble? Grab a pencil and answer each of the following, circling yes or no.

Your Money Quiz

Assume the recession is over and you land $10,000 tax-free.

- Do you put all or some in the bank   **Y or N**
- Pay down credit cards   **Y or N**

- Invest in a traditional or Roth IRA **Y or N**
- You will spend less dining out than you did before the
  recession **Y or N**
- In the past year, have you checked your credit report? **Y or N**
- At this very moment, do you know your bank balance? **Y or N**

Add up the yes answers.

5–6	Overachiever
3–5	Frugalista
1–2	Bubble consumer
Zero?	Not smart. Not rich.

What is a balance sheet? Think of your family economics like a business—because it is. What's coming in, what's going out? What is your cash on hand for emergencies? And what are you investing for the future? Smart households on a monthly basis know where they stand long term. During the go-go days of the 1990s and 2000s, the simple family exercise of planning a budget was passé. Saving a few dollars here and there and tracking the daily expenses was so, well, small-scale, when wealth was created for years by leveraging borrowed money. The family budget is back. So is living below your means. Smart families are lining up their assets and liabilities and finding places to save, squeeze, and invest so they will be comfortable if this storm takes much longer to blow away, or worse, another bubble comes rumbling across the horizon. Are your housing costs in line with your new income? Have you stopped investing in the future because you are just trying to cover your bills right now? Are you piling money away for your kids' or grandkids' college, but not saving enough for your own retirement? Are you not even sure what your balance sheet should look like? It's time to start.

The tools available today to help you do this are, quite simply, amazing. Your 401(k) balance and allocations are available with a click of the mouse. Automatic bill paying means you never need to miss a credit card payment deadline. Web sites like www.mint.com offer valuable tools to aggregate your entire financial life in one place. The smart money doesn't put the unopened 401(k) statement in a drawer. Smart money takes a quarterly or even (as I prefer) a monthly snapshot of where they stand.

Think of yourself as the household personal money manager. The strategies are different, but the results are the same. Spend the time to understand your outlook for your money, what you want it to do for you, and then figure out how to make it work for you. Depending on your personality and goals, the strategies can be quite different. Are you the type of person who is motivated by making lists and checking off the accomplishments? For you, the physical act of writing checks and balancing the checkbook by hand is a discipline that can't be replaced with high-tech personal finance tools online. For others, everything important in life— music, their friends' data, music, and videos—it's all organized by computer. If you're a tech-savvy "personal money manager," your money is as easy (and even more important) to manage, watch, and tweak as your music playlist.

No matter how you get there, the principles are the same. Follow the retro rules for your money that evaporated during the bubble to ensure the smartest and surest ways to repair your balance sheet today. A few quick questions to ask yourself about your money:

Does your money last as long as the month?

Are you spending more than 28 percent of your take-home pay on housing costs? (This includes maintenance, insurance, and taxes.)

Are you carrying a balance on your credit cards?

If so, how many months will it take you to be credit card debt free?

How old do you want to be when you retire?

Are you maxing out your 401(k) contributions?

Are you saving any money at all for retirement outside of your company-sponsored 401(k)?

We'll explore more fully these questions, how to answer them, and how to get there in the pages ahead, but repairing the balance sheet first means recognizing how far away you are from these goals. If you are on track, the next step is to build wealth.

RECOVER

The economy is recovering, but too many people are still out of work. So this "recovery" will be tricky. Is it a true recovery? Will the recovery fade? Will there be a "double-dip" recession where we fall back again later? No one knows. Even if you believe the recovery is real and lasting, it doesn't feel like it to the middle class.

One of President Obama's moneymen, Larry Summers, put it this way. We are in a "statistical recovery, but a human recession."

The government statistics tell us the economy has been recovering for several quarters. At the beginning of 2009, the most powerful economy in the world was shrinking—shrinking!—by more than 6 percent. That means homes, businesses, livelihoods, and dreams were vanishing at an alarming rate. It was sparked by a financial crisis that nearly destroyed the financial system. As Treasury Secretary Timothy Geithner explained it to me, "The rivets were coming off the submarine, people were saying 'I do not have confidence in anything' and when that happens, to go on, it is perilous and causes grave danger."[8]

But the United States averted a second Great Depression. And just three quarters later, by the end of 2009, the economy was growing vigorously—up 5.6 percent in the fourth quarter.[9] That's the fastest economic growth since 2003. The three-quarter swing in growth rates was the largest since 1981.[10] We went from real fears of another Great Depression to the fastest economic growth in six years. It may not feel like it yet, but for any one still solvent after the past two years, this is good for you. As you can see in Figure 1.1, the steep decline in economic growth that was felt in 2008 has turned. And for anyone determined and motivated to repair their finances and start growing again, it is certainly good for you, too.

Why is this happening? The stimulus and tax cuts and historic spending by the Federal Reserve Bank have flooded the economy with money, and that money is slowly nurturing the economy back to health. Is it real? How long will it last? What will the recovery look like? It's impossible to tell. Put half a dozen economists and academics in a room and they will have a dozen different forecasts.

Now what?

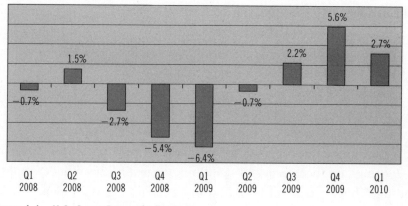

Figure 1.1   U.S. Gross Domestic Product

Now we wait for the jobs. They will likely be the last economic indicator to return to health. We can expect more bailout bashing and government mistrust and bank conspiracy theories. The farther we get from those "grave" moments when the rivets were popping off the submarine, as Geithner put it, and the longer it takes for jobs to return, the more the American people are angry and have every right to be so.

You and I can't make the jobs come back. You and I can't reform the banking system. You and I can't prevent a slip backward like the one in 1937 that took what looked like a recovery from a terrible recession and turned it into a Great Depression. But we *can* reset our goals, repair our personal balance sheets, and make smart choices to position for whatever comes next.

The system did not shut down, and for that, we are grateful. We will second-guess the bailouts, the stimulus, and the massive government spending for years. (And there will no doubt be some nasty unintended consequences to deal with, as well: maybe higher taxes, inflation, new kinds of credit card fees.) We will rail against waste, inside dealings, and fundamental unfairness of government intervention and how it plays into the pockets of the haves and infuriates the have-nots. Famous economists and Nobel laureates will argue that the country's historic financial rescue and economic stimulus was too big, too small, not targeted correctly. (Columnist, economist and Nobel laureate Paul Krugman worries we haven't spent *enough* money to prevent a slip backward in the economy.) Politicians will arm themselves with their talking points: We need more tax cuts, more regulation, less regulation, and less government intervention, and so on.

Some economists think higher interest rates are inevitable. Some fear inflation. Others say, no, the economy risks *deflation*.

Let them all argue and forecast. We can only take care of ourselves, and use this time to protect our money and get ready.

It's time to turn the Great Recession into the Great Inspiration.

The caution signs are flashing. But make no mistake—so much money is flooding into the system and there are so many opportunities created by the huge shifts in business landscape, that people are making money—a lot of it—right now, even with almost 10 percent unemployment.

Confidence, trust, and peace of mind are not back yet. But consider this—the economy *has* snapped back.

Economist Lakshman Achuthan studies business cycles for the Economic Cycle Research Institute and follows the natural swings in the economy. He calls what is happening today a "textbook recovery that is stronger than the last two. It might not feel like it yet, but things will get better," he says. He's as qualified as anyone to know: He correctly forecast the recession—and the recovery—long before either was apparent to the average Joe and Jane out there just trying to make the money last to the end of the month. So having predicted the recession and the rebound before most, what does Achuthan say we should do *right now* to reset, repair, and recover?

He says it's a good time to buy a home, with interest rates still low and home prices down 30 percent from the peak.[11] And it is a great time to be "proactive" in your job, Achuthan says.

"Look, now is the time to either upgrade or to get a job, because now the business cycle is your friend, right here right now. Before the hiring begins, your managers will be looking within for ideas and inspiration and hustle. Now's the time to get on an interesting project, propose the idea you've been sitting on to improve sales, offer to try anything," says Achuthan. His advice for you: "A lot of people have given up looking for work because they don't understand that unlike last year, 2010 will see a return to jobs growth. If you're looking to get ahead in your career this is the time to get proactive in order to get a jump on your competition."

THE PAYOFF

Money can't buy you happiness, of course. But it is the currency of life. Smart choices about earning it, spending it, saving it, growing it, and protecting it make life easier.

Your personal economic recovery is at hand. To get there, first comes the reset about your money. Then comes a period of repairing your budget, your retirement expectations, your job and career.

Only then does the wealth-building begin.

Sit down with your spouse or partner—or with your stack of bills—and ask yourself these questions.

Does the money last as long as the month?
Are my housing costs less than a third of my income?
How long will it take to get debt free on the credit cards?
How long must I work to comfortably retire?
Am I saving everything today I possibly can for retirement?
Should I be saving more *outside* of the company-sponsored 401(k)?

The goal of the next 10 chapters is to help make the answers to these questions more clear and attainable. It all starts with the only thing you can directly control—your spending.

2

Spending Your $$$$$

ROMANS' NUMERAL

71 percent

Americans who say they bought only what they needed in 2009, nothing more.[1]

Smart consumers don't live within their means. They live below them. Your home value, your job, your retirement accounts—all are in flux right now. With so many economic variables out of your control, the only thing you can directly manage is how you spend your money. And across every income level, the Great Recession has changed how you spend. Almost three quarters of Americans say they are making significant spending cuts, even if they don't have to, and most say they are so scarred by two years of economic upheaval, they won't go back to their old bubble ways.

In this chapter, you'll meet two office co-workers who are teaching an eight-year-old girl the value of growing vegetables, a mortgage broker in Dallas who is saving 20 percent of her pay, and a Depression-era survivor whose view of money was changed forever by the forced thrift of his childhood. Will the Great Recession have a similar lasting impact on us? You'll also hear what Treasury Secretary Timothy Geithner says are the three most important factors for American consumers, and learn five retro rules for how to spend your money.

Data from the Census Bureau show sweeping changes in U.S. daily life at home and at work. People are less likely to move, and when they do, they are buying smaller houses.[2] Homeownership rates have dropped. Fewer people are marrying[3]—yes, marrying! Demographers say it's because they want to be financially secure on their own first, or they just can't afford it. And fewer people are divorcing, either because they can't sell the house or because, as one study surmised, the recession drew people together.[4] The commute is getting a little longer because more people are carpooling or taking public transportation. City urban centers are looking more attractive after years of suburban and even exurban flight, and because rents are falling. According to real estate rental tracker Reis, rents in 2009 fell 3 percent nationwide and the vacancy rate was an astonishing 8 percent.[5]

GOING RETRO

Is it any wonder that people are spending their money differently? Amid these wrenching changes, the retail spending numbers show some surprises—retro consumers who above all else want to build their savings first, and then want value or an experience with their money, and who are more conscious of what that money can do for them.

Consumer Reports surveyed more than 1,000 consumers and found they learned big lessons from the Great Recession and vowed to permanently scale back their spending. A whopping 71 percent of Americans say they purchased only what they absolutely needed in 2009, 53 percent used credit cards less, and 39 percent said they put more money into savings. *Consumer Reports* calls this "intelligent thrift."

What are the things these smart, retro consumers are buying? Which categories of consumer spending delivered interesting little surprises? Seeds. Romance novels. High-end cosmetics. Canning supplies.[6] During the second summer of the Great Recession, search engine requests on Google for "canning recipes" rose 5,000 percent. Even more interesting, the numbers suggest that Americans are raising their kids differently: At the same time Americans were Googling more about canning, diaper sales were down 4 percent—retail analysts speculate that it's because newly frugal moms and dads prefer toilet training their toddlers a little earlier rather than pay 50 cents each for toddler diapers. Impulse buys are out, and poll after poll show shoppers are making up lists to keep them focused with their shopping carts.

Gallup Polls (and numerous others, frankly) show that Americans of all incomes are spending less of their money on "discretionary" purchases. While their housing costs and fixed expenses are rising, or their incomes falling, people are pulling back where they can. Yet here is the interesting twist: While frugalistas are buying cheaper store-brand foods, they are also splurging from time to time on $25 lipsticks. They are also going to the movies—for the first time since 2002, consumers are spending more money going to the movies than watching their video entertainment at home. Movies like *Avatar* and *Alice in Wonderland* set box office records, just as recession-weary consumers are beginning to fine-tune how they spend their money and find reasonably priced ways to enjoy themselves. The iPad sold 2 million units in two months and Americans dug deep to find ways to buy the next best gadget that will make their life easier or better. It shows that people will reach into their pockets for a value or experience that allows them to shake off the recession mentality but still be smart overall about their money.

The jobless and the distressed homeowner are the most obvious consumers to pull back, but everyone has changed his or her behavior. Even people who have jobs and can afford to spend like the early 2000s have wised up.

Where do you fit in on your pocket spending?

By February 2010, spending among upper-income Americans had dropped to the lowest level in at least two years, according to Gallup. Figure 2.1 shows just what Americans making at least $90,000 a year

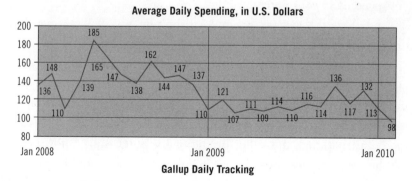

Figure 2.1   **Upper-Income Consumer Spending, January 2008–February 2010**
Source: Gallup, February 2010.

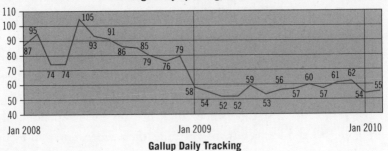

Figure 2.2   Middle- and Lower-Income Spending, January 2008–February 2010
Source: Gallup, February 2010.

spent in stores, restaurants, gas stations, and online in the month. Middle- and lower-income Americans spend about $40 dollars a day less than that. Figure 2.2 shows their daily spending has been cut in half since mid-2008.

Everyone is pulling back. Either because they have less money to spend or they want to protect and preserve what they've got left. Given the sheer amount of debt accrued by U.S. families during the bubble, pulling back is just smart.

For the unemployed, it's obvious. But a condition called "underemployment" makes it even worse. If you have a job, but are working fewer hours or for less money than you used to, you are pulling back even more. You are technically classified as employed, but you are not working up to your potential (because of the economy, not because of you) and that unease means you are not spending to your potential either.

In 2009, the average unemployment rate was 9.3 percent, but the underemployment rate was an astonishing 16.2 percent.

According to consumer polling by Gallup, such high rates of underemployment hold back spending. Table 2.1 shows how much less the underemployed consumer spends than someone with a full-time job in the same field. Average daily spending for someone with a job is $75 a day (for food, gas, parking, and other discretionary purchases). Someone with a job, but working below his or her potential, spends far less. In an economy two-thirds driven by consumer spending, the underemployment problem

Table 2.1   Daily Spending

Employed	$75
Underemployed	$48

Source: Gallup, January 2–31, 2010.

will remain a profound factor on how people think about and spend their money.

By choice or by necessity for the first time in a generation consumers are asking these questions:

Do I need this?

Will it make my family better, smarter, more prepared?

Can I even afford it?

The smart consumer is restrained and wants to repair a battered personal balance sheet and get back to building savings and wealth. We are spending less and saving more because it is the natural, visceral response to uncertainty and it is one of the only things we can really control. In many cases, there is no other choice: The credit spigot has been shut off forcing millions of people to live within their dwindling means.

In economics there is a condition called the "Paradox of Thrift," and we are experiencing it in all its textbook glory: This consumer-driven economy desperately needs consumer spending to recover. But Americans need to save some money, feel more secure in their jobs, and be able to pay their housing costs and taxes before they are confident enough to spend again. And if they are not spending, it could blunt any economic recovery. Bottom line, the economy needs everyone to go back to spendthrift ways to recover.

While this macroeconomic paradox plays out, best to let your neighbors do the spending to prop up the economy. Take care of your own economy first.

Treasury Secretary Timothy Geithner put it this way: "As people get themselves back to the point where they are living within their means and have less debt, and are less vulnerable in the future, that's a healthy process for the economy. But it means probably you'll see a slower recovery than we would normally see."[7]

Think of those three qualifiers: *living within your means*, *less debt*, and *less vulnerable*.

Too many people went too far, bought too much house, too many cars, too much stuff. Not necessarily because the country woke up one morning selfish or silly. Easy credit obscured real and troubling trends: stagnant wages for the middle class and a growing income gap between the rich and everybody else. Many financed the difference between what they earn and what it costs to live with low-interest, fee-rich credit card debt.

The fundamental question of family finance, "Can I afford this?" was replaced with "*How* can I afford this?"

With credit cards and home equity, it worked for a while. But we couldn't live beyond our means in perpetuity.

So what now? Instant gratification is out. Expecting value and "experience" with your money is in.

These changes are here to stay and we've only just begun.

There is a significant academic debate right now about whether at the first hint of recovery Americans start spending more than they earn once again. It may be that millions of Americans, when the all-clear bell sounds (or when they somehow get a higher limit on their credit cards) will go back to the old ways. But millions of others will never go back.

Those smart consumers will not be lured back into the 20-year crescendo of credit-card-fueled expenses. It's over.

Gail Cunningham has been a credit counselor for 24 years, through a handful of recessions, two big stock market crashes, and several recoveries. If the month lasts longer than the money, Cunningham says, "There are only three answers. Increase income, decrease expenses, or both."

So what kind of consumer will you be? There will be four categories in the new normal. Can you guess which is best for your family?

LIVING BEYOND THEIR MEANS

Easy credit and numerous credit cards meant that millions of people were living a middle-class lifestyle but they did not have the means to do that.

In all my reporting on the United States living beyond its means, Deepak Chopra, the best-selling author and spiritual guru put it to me best.

"First thing the consumer should learn to do is to stop spending money that they haven't earned to buy things they don't need to impress people they don't like," Chopra said. "We are buying stuff that we don't need with money that we still haven't earned just so we can keep up with the Joneses."

Those very people today are seeing their credit lines slashed, their home equity lines closed, and God forbid if they lost a job, they are pulling in wherever they can. That lasts into next year—2011. The "living-beyond-their-means" consumers have an $8,000 to $15,000 balance on their credit cards but the bank is cutting their credit lines so they can't spend more. These are people who used credit cards or home equity to pull themselves into the upper middle class, and the reality check for them is only just beginning. It will take in most cases many years to pay off the lifestyle they have already lived. (Still paying off the Viking range but nothing saved for a kid's college and an underfunded 401[k].) For them it means a sharply lower standard of living to make up the difference. They will spend less not because they want to, but because they have to.

THE VALUE CONSUMER

This is the smart consumer and the consumer you want to be. People with a financial cushion who *could* spend the money if they wanted to, but instead have decided to pay down debt, add to their cash savings, and save even more for retirement. These are also *values* consumers who ask: "Where was this product made? Will it enhance my family's standard of living or end up as junk in the basement? How does it fit into our family's worldview? Will this expenditure make us more prepared for the future?" These consumers are motivated less by price and more by the old adage "quality over quantity." These are the consumers who believe less is more in the toy box, who pay more for organic bananas, but skip the expensive coffee, who save money on store-brand staples, but splurge on healthful fresh vegetables.

These smart consumers never spent loads of money they didn't have, but they are still chastened. They've likely lost value in their homes and don't have a low-interest home equity line anymore. That "wealth effect" of ever-rising home prices—as economists called it for 10 years or so—made them more confident in how they spent money elsewhere for the last decade. That is gone.

These value consumers are returning, quite literally, to the home economics of their grandparents. I found some of these new consumers in my reporting of "Recession Gardens."

A growing number of Americans in cities and suburbs and rural towns are growing their own herbs, fruits, and vegetables. They are canning salsa and tomato sauce and bringing boxes of green beans into the office to share. You might have heard Federal Reserve Chairman Ben Bernanke quoted as saying there were "green shoots" growing in the economy. What he meant was that from the charred landscape after a recession, like a wildfire, small green shoots start to grow through the burned landscape. Bernanke is talking about figurative "green shoots." But millions of Americans are literally growing their own green shoots of economic recovery. More than 43 million Americans planted gardens in 2009, according to the American Horticultural Society, and 19 percent of those households were doing it for the first time.

Grisella Feliciano and her friend Karen Simonson are co-workers in Queens, New York, who decided to plant their first garden together, because between the two of them they didn't have a green thumb before the recession started.

With help from Simonson's daughter, Rebecca, they found abundance. "She's eight years old right now, and I thought it was a great activity for us to do together," Simonson says. To see Rebecca in the garden with her mom is to see a little girl who is thoroughly enjoying every minute—and every dollar—spent.

Across the country, families were tilling up their little patch of backyard to plant zucchini, potatoes, tomatoes, and cucumbers—8 million of them for the first time. It's the perfect "value consumer" enterprise. According to Burpee, the seed catalog company, a $100 investment in vegetable seeds yields $2,500 worth of produce.

"It's not that a vegetable is going to make you money. It's that you are not going to be spending that money in the produce section or the farmers' market or the supermarket," explained George Ball, Burpee's CEO. "That's money you could spend on your child's college fund, or buy something, or get the house down payment further advanced."

It's not anecdotal. The numbers bear out that Americans are becoming retro, value consumers. Sales of home canning supplies soared 30 percent two years into the Great Recession, either to be thrifty or to be green. Interestingly, these trends in the garden, at least, came at the same time and the recession fused them together. And consumer anthropologists say it's as much about savings as it is about being in control. It's impossible to know if this is a trend or a fad, but for millions (8 million new gardeners!) it's the new way smart consumers who want some control will live their lives. A reverse of the globalization that erased borders and gobbled up resources throughout the 1980s and 1990s, we may instead enter into coming decades of localization—sourcing goods and services close to home. Across the country, farmers' markets and grocery stores are slapping up signs to show which products are locally grown or raised to meet the new demands of consumers who are more selective with their money.

Americans are realizing that each dollar has a value in terms of what it buys, but also what it *does* and what it sustains. It's the value and values consumer. And retail strategists are taking note. This is the category they want to cater to and entice into spending more money.

THE RECESSION-WEARY

Even the responsible and the thrifty are getting a little tired of their newfound restraint. These consumers who are weary of the recession are willing to dig into their pockets for something that makes them feel like "normal."

Among the first and most durable purchases of this bunch of recession-weary shoppers is technology. Most everyone is spending less on pretty much everything, but Apple sold 3 million Mac computers in a single quarter of sales. Apple also logged its ten-billionth iTunes download to a customer in Georgia who bought Johnny Cash's "Guess Things Happen This Way." The iPad was a runaway success.

Gadgets that improve lifestyles and productivity, songs that cost as much as a lottery ticket but can be enjoyed much longer, a night at the movies or a new shade of Mac lipstick—these all add value in some way to the purchaser's life and as long as there is an income coming in, these are the things the recession-weary are finding the money to buy. This is still a smart consumer who is repairing the balance sheet first, and working toward a day when saving and investing are the top priority. But after a year or so of only buying what a consumer needs out of fear, the fear is passing and the purse strings are loosening. This is the consumer who looked a spate of wicked February winter storms in the eye and spent a little more in bars and restaurants, at furniture stores, and in the mall. It's okay to be recession-weary. Just be aware that the retailers would love for you to use this as the springboard for living beyond your means again.

THE CONSPICUOUS CONSUMER

You can understand the recession-weary. Even smart, value consumers are tired of the recession and willing to find the money for something that really matters to them. That's healthy. What's not healthy is raw conspicuous consumption.

Enter the Hummer—a 6.2-litre V8 engine in the modified body of a military vehicle. Only 875 were sold in 2000 and more than 71,000 were sold by the consumer peak in 2006. By 2010, it was dead.

Sales plunged 67 percent from 2008 to 2009 and as America downsized, the Hummer died. General Motors (GM) failed to find a buyer and that symbol of 2000s excess went to its grave and with it, many pundits said, the age of American conspicuous consumption. Not so fast. There is a great deal of debate about whether a sliver of a trend in consumer behavior emerges this year—a new conspicuous consumer. Call it the recession-weary with money and an unabashed love of excess. Already there is a fierce lobby to bring back the Hummer and to celebrate it for what it represents about the U.S. consumer's prowess.

Obviously this new post-bubble conspicuous consumer can't buy anything on borrowed money, but don't be surprised to see some people may put away their Great Recession black and start to party again.

A FOOL AND HIS MONEY

What kind of consumer will you be and will that change be permanent? The Depression survivors (the original Depression, of course) tightened their belts for the rest of their lives. And for millions, it marked their psyche. My grandfather was in college in Iowa during the worst of it in the mid-1930s. He often told a story about how he won a band competition and was awarded a $10 gold piece. So proud, and so flush, he walked to the corner market to buy groceries to share with his brother. Finally—meat to eat! The store owner just sadly shook his head—he couldn't change the gold piece. His cash register was empty. It was the same story at the movie theater and at the restaurant. My grandfather held that coin in his pocket for a day or two, careful not to flaunt it. No one could make change. No one had anything that valuable to sell. Finally, he went to the bursar's office and put it down toward his tuition bill for the next semester.

Imagine that experience and how it made men and women value the money in their pockets and truly understand its worth.

Until the day he died, a simple, off-handed question: "Grandpa are you hungry? Can I make you a sandwich?" would receive the same response every time: "I haven't been hungry since the Depression."

Chances are that all four of your grandparents knew exactly how many dollars and cents they had at the end of every day. Whether they were young men or children during the Depression, or their parents were, it changed how they thought about and spent money.

"A fool and his money are soon parted," they'd say.

Seventy years later, new generations are relearning the retro rule the hard way.

As the decades passed and the credit flowed, too many banks, home-owners, politicians, and consumers neglected to heed their warnings—warnings dismissed as old-fashioned clichés. What too many lived was instead, as my own grandmother liked to say, "A fool and his money are some *party*."

The worst part about it, even if you weren't the fool, the recession may have hurt you as well.

BE A GOOD STEWARD

"What is a reasonable, responsible person supposed to do right now in the face of all this uncertainty to protect my family and our future?"

In the midst of day after day of negative economic reports and increasingly dire news about job loss, a viewer sent this brief and compelling e-mail. It's a question I asked again and again as I canvassed experts, economists, credit counselors, Fed officials, two Treasury secretaries, money-smart moms and dads, and experienced business journalists for their thoughts.

The consensus: The first thing you can directly control is how you spend your money. As a country we need to spend less and save more. You can't hold up the whole country, of course, so you can only help your own family and your own situation.

Financial planner Ryan Mack is the president of Optimum Capital Management and frequent guest on CNN's money programs. He's a true believer that wealth comes from the daily decisions you make about your money. So how do we all become good stewards of that money? Mack explains.

> The good steward is my own mother who didn't have a lot of money to raise her two children but spent her days shopping at the thrift store, cutting coupons, and working her way off of subsidized living in a way that allowed her to purchase her first home. The good steward understands that it is never about how much money you make, it is all about what you do with the money that you make. It isn't about spending money to make an impression on others, it is all about spending money to make an impression on those personal goals and values that you find to be important to keep on your path to creating a financial legacy for future generations. The good steward takes risks, lives within his or her means, but most importantly when you analyze their online spending statement, you would see when he or she did decide to make purchases, *more often than not they purchased items that moved their household forward and didn't detract from its value.*

Part of being a good steward of your money is having a budget and sticking to it.

Does your spending move your household forward or hold it back? You might not know unless you prepare a family budget and keep track of your expenses and where they fit into your overall money strategy.

Mack's simple budget advice: "All of your bills should be listed, which should include a bill to *yourself* that puts monies into savings." The process to budget is simple. Put together an estimated budget—how much you think you will spend in one month on everything from housing costs, to cell phones, to groceries, gas, and tuition. Include everything. Then create a spending diary to monitor every single expense for 30 days.

No matter how small, write it down. Finally, circle back with an actual budget of what you spent.

There are numerous tools and calculators online. You can start with a simple worksheet that credit counselors use: http://www.nfcc.org/FinancialEducation/monthlyincome.cfm.

The goal here, Mack says, is not to make budgeting so onerous that you don't do it. Keep it simple. He recommends Quicken software if you are computer savvy, or the web site www.mint.com, if you want to track everything precisely. But it can be as simple and easy and low-tech as an accordion file with different envelopes, and literally putting money in envelopes for different expenses and drawing from them. Mack also recommends preparing a personal financial statement twice a year—once when you are doing your taxes and have all your annual paperwork in front of you and again six months later in October or November, just before the holidays, "as a reminder of not to spend as much money on shopping."

One viewer, Mary Jane in San Antonio, wrote to the CNN money team with her advice for spending and becoming debt free.

"I've been doing frugal February for years. I don't use my credit card for anything. I use my debit card for gas and food only." She chose February because it is the shortest month of the year but still close to the holidays to fix any overspending. But she recommends choosing your birthday month, too, because it is a gift, she says, to be debt free.

Whittling down a stubborn student loan I took out for a summer study-abroad program, I did a similar exercise—a post-college money diet, as I called it. I filled up the car with gas on Saturday, went to the grocery store on Sunday, and on Monday took $20 out of the ATM. With a loaded subway and bus pass and the rent paid, twice a year I challenged myself to see how long I could make that $20 last. Soon, many of my friends were joining me and we had a blast, exploring the city, finding free ways to have fun, and writing big checks to the student loan company at the end of the month.

RETRO SPENDING RULES

It's an exercise that translates no matter what stage of your life and it helps keep perspective on what money means to you and what it is doing for you.

After a generation where "me, more, now" was how we thought about our money, it's time to walk through these five retro rules when you are about to part with your money.

1. If you don't need it, don't buy it. If you can't afford it, put it down.

It's as simple as that. It's heartbreaking that for millions of Americans, this is not even a choice they can make—they don't answer the phone because a bill collector could be on the other end. The question of whether they can afford to buy something has already been made for them: their credit cards are over the limit and they can't spend money and the fees pile up. But for anyone with a little left over at the end of the month, every dollar has a purpose—to build for the future. Ask the three key questions before parting with your cash. "Do I need this?" "Will it make my family better, smarter, more prepared?" "Can I even afford it?" Only you know the answers to those questions. And just asking them gives you pause to evaluate whether the dollar buys you an experience and an investment in your family and your future.

2. Think of money like nutrition.

Is a purchase, whatever it is, something that is good for your body, or nothing more than a sugar rush? I'm often astonished when people spend so little attention to their spending, yet they are religious about their workouts and nutrition. Isn't it the same thing? You're only given one body and one life to live, and you want to treat it like a temple. Prolific and random spending is the money equivalent of eating junk food. It might feel good at the time, but it hurts you in the long run and then limits your options later in life.

3. Negotiate everything.

It seems gauche to call it haggling, so let's call it negotiating. Your cell phone company, cable provider, car rental company, and even your doctor need your business. Politely ask if there are discounts. For travel and leisure, inquire about a complimentary upgrade if they won't drop the price. (Vacations have never been more attainable—*if you can afford them*—this is a good time for breaks and discounts.) If you are polite and informed, you will be surprised.

The number of elective surgeries has fallen off in the past year and a half, either because it is not covered by insurance, or the co-pays are too high, or the patient doesn't want to be out of work. Make a deal with your doctor. Do the same with the dentist. Need a root canal? Ask about complimentary teeth bleaching. Dr. Jacques Moritz, director of gynecology at St. Luke's Roosevelt Hospital in New York, says you'd be surprised how much wiggle room you have at the doctor's office, especially if you don't have insurance. He suggests saying, "I'd like to pay the lowest rate you give an insurance company." The doctor appreciates knowing the check is coming right out of the patient's pocket. And the doc won't have to deal with the bureaucracy of the insurance companies.

"If you want plastic surgery this is the time to do it," Moritz says. "It's on sale. Also, when it comes to medical necessities you can ask, too. It's a service industry. Services are negotiable," Moritz says.

Plastic surgery, of course, is a luxury that won't fit in most family budgets, even with good planning. But more people put off elective surgeries of all sorts during the recession because they can't afford the out-of-pocket expenses. This is negotiable, too.

You can find savings in some of your biggest expenses—car insurance, medical bills, and travel. Where there will be no negotiating and no mercy—credit cards. New protections are in effect to save you from the most egregious card practices, but if you are charging things that you can't pay for, expect high interest rates. And as soon as you are late on two payments in a row, your protections vanish and the fees kick into high gear. Gone are the days of negotiating with the credit card supervisor at the other end of the phone line to erase a late fee "just this once."

4. Always save first.

For several years, the savings rate in this country was negative. That means month after month, quarter after quarter, year after year we spent more money than we put in the bank. (Economists justified this by saying the savings was in our house or in our stock accounts, not in the bank, and this was actually a sign of great progress for middle-class families. It was an economic assumption that proved wrong.) At the peak of our newfound thrift in 2009, we were saving around 5 to 6 percent of the money left over after we paid taxes. A few months into 2010, that savings rate was slipping a bit—more like 4 percent was going into the bank. Do you know how much you are saving? Look at your pay stub. Calculate how much money you bring home after taxes. Make sure you are saving at least 6 percent and hopefully 10 percent of that for your future. Save first.

One viewer, Brian in Florida, is conservative with his money (and his politics) and wants to take no chances relying on the government to help him in his old age. He budgets 20 percent of his gross annual pay to savings and retirement. "6–10 percent is the minimum. And not including Social Security or home equity."

Jennifer is a mortgage loan officer in Texas who can't see how anyone in their thirties and younger will be able to retire on Social Security, so she's saving 15 percent of her family's income for retirement. "We're assuming we won't have it or they'll phase it out for those who *do* have money in retirement funds. We're at 15 percent, but would love to be able to bump it up more! Gotta pad that college fund for the Girl before we bump it up to 20 percent, though." The girl, of course, is her elementary school-age daughter, and she observes the cardinal rule of personal finance—saving for her own retirement first before tackling the college fund.

5. Don't deny yourself.

Thankfully, this is not the Great Depression and we are not Depression consumers and don't have to be. We love to buy things: it's been a defining American trait for half a century. As confidence in the economy returns, the people who have the cushion to spend money will be critical to restore the economy. Every dollar spent at the pizza parlor, on video games, at the zoo sustains jobs. No one believes we are headed into a period of Post-Aughts Austerity, or that we should. Too much austerity and we choke off the economy and kill more jobs. But the bubble behavior—the wild, unchecked spending with borrowed money for big houses, piles of imported plastic consumer goods—has popped. Smart consumers don't live like it hasn't. They know the difference between needs and wants. For God's sake, don't buy something stupid. Even a $25 impulse buy is money that could grow in a 529 college fund.

The key is to know what you can live without.

The message for anyone struggling with money: The only thing you can control right this second is how the money leaves your hands.

Of course, one person's frivolous expense is another person's investment. It's why I am such a fan of making lists, setting targets, and marking them off. Every person's list will be different.

It's silly to say: "Ditch the Starbucks and you can save your way to financial security." If the Starbucks is a small expenditure that is part of your ritual that makes you happy and more efficient and focused at work, then by all means, keep it. If gourmet food-store lunches are an impulse buy, then get rid of them. You are allowed to have "wants" and not just "needs" on your shopping list. Make strategic sacrifices and you don't have to sacrifice too much in your standard of living.

 THE PAYOFF

My grandfather from time to time dropped an old gem that I find particularly relevant today: "Hunger is the best sauce." What he meant is that if we constantly indulge, we get no joy out of what we're consuming. But restraint and self-control mean the splurge when it comes, tastes oh so sweet, and means so much more. It took a Great Recession to reteach something our grandparents learned during the Great Depression.

- If you don't need it, don't buy it.
- If you can't afford it, put it down.
- Always save first.
- And finally, don't live within your means, live below them.

All of this, of course, depends on having money to spend. And that comes from your job. Read on for smart strategies if you have your job, you've lost it, or you're ready to advance in it.

CHAPTER 3

Your Job

5.5

There are 5.5 applicants for every job opening in the United States. It's not just a statistic—this is your competition for the job.

Unless you have a trust fund (lucky you!) or you are married to a millionaire, your job is the engine of your own personal economy. The job brings the paycheck, which pays the bills and fuels the savings and investments that will carry you through retirement. It's why nearly double-digit unemployment in the most powerful nation in the world is so profoundly unsettling. The 15 million people out of a job cannot live up to their potential as consumers, savers, and investors. Millions more are what economists call "underemployed," meaning that they are working part time but would like a full-time job. And hundreds of thousands more have simply dropped out of the workforce. They are ready, willing, and able to work but are discouraged from months of fruitless job searches.

In this chapter you'll meet a stay-at-home mom who is working hard to get back into the job market at the worst possible time. You'll meet a former Marine who is retraining from construction to physical therapy, and has quite good prospects for a six-figure income. You'll meet a telecom equipment manager whose job was sent to China, and a hotel manager who improved his prospects despite a near depression in his industry. We scrutinize a labor market unlike most of us have ever seen and take a hard look at what the job market will look like once it begins to recover. For some top performers, it means great new opportunities and even bidding wars for talent. For others it means less job security, fewer benefits, and longer periods between work. Still others will have to retrain to be relevant, or take a 30 percent pay cut to stay employed. And millions of people are sick and tired of their jobs but are stuck because the labor market isn't providing the opportunities it should.

Grim, yes. But part of making smart decisions about your job and career is to know what you are up against. Here's where you stand.

Pollyanna pundits and cocktail party economists sometimes trot out this reverse statistic: If 10 percent is out of work that means 90 percent of the public *is* working.

Wrong.

Just over 58 percent of the adult population is employed[1] compared with 64 percent 10 years ago (see Figure 3.1). That number is far too low for a developed economy. (It's on par with less efficient and less developed economies.) It's a startling statistic you will rarely hear, because labor economists instead prefer to measure the labor market as the people who have been *recently* working. But the fact is, the labor market has been shrinking. And too many people in our population are being left behind.

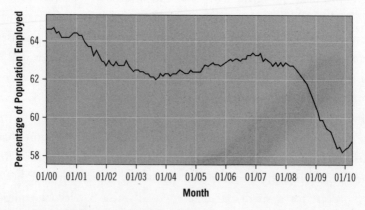

Figure 3.1   How Much of America Is Working?
Source: Bureau of Labor Statistics.

There are millions of Americans who are not officially in the labor market and not even counted among the unemployed, but are most certainly out there looking for jobs or waiting for the right moment to get in. They are stay-at-home moms who want to go back to work who are not now counted in the official labor market. Nor are early retirees who've lost up to a third of their retirement and need to work for a few more years. Some people are disabled and will never work. Others are full-time parents or in the military. Just over 1.5 million people are in state or federal prisons.

For the 153 million people who *are* included in the active labor market, the numbers are just as gruesome. Unemployment rose from 4.9 percent at the start of the recession in 2007, to 10 percent two years later. Double-digit unemployment is a condition last seen in 1983 when *Thriller* was released, Reagan was president, and the economy was in the grips of crippling "stagflation." It's a milestone no one ever wants to match. But we have.

The pain is obvious for those recently out of work: self-esteem, bills, stalled dreams. Millions of Americans feel like they are playing financial defense. The millions looking to reenter the workplace are paralyzed: How do you get back in, when there are so many other people out there qualified, motivated, and just as desperate? For those with a job comes insecurity and longer hours. All around, we see a jobs market operating well below the potential of this great country. Think of it—in the world's most powerful economy, the size of the out-of-work population is slightly more than that of New Jersey, South Carolina, and Illinois combined. A record number of Americans have been out of work for longer than six months, worrying economists and labor experts about degrading skills and flexibility in what should be the most dynamic labor market in the world. When will we know it is turning around? And when will we feel it?

This was no garden-variety recession and it will be no plain vanilla jobs recovery. Even as a recovery brews, millions of the jobs will be slow to return, and some whole sectors of the economy may never come back. *It will take more smarts than ever before to make sure you are on the right side of history.*

2010 and 2011 will be a transition away from the recession and toward the new phase, and a New Normal for job seekers. The economy is growing and mass layoffs will slow. Temporary hiring will pick up. It already has. The National Association for Business Economics (a trade group of business economists) forecasts jobs growth this year and into next. By the second half of 2010, these economists say that 103,000 new jobs will be created each month. That's the good news.

The bad news is that every worker with a job, every person who is unemployed, and every college graduate has to work harder than ever to get in and stay in the jobs market. Two years ago there were 1.6 job seekers for every opening. That's a healthy economy. By the beginning of 2010 there were 5½ applicants for every job opening. That tells us two things: It is incredibly important to hang onto the job you have and if you have lost that job, you will need to find a way to be better, smarter, and more interesting than the five other people applying for every position.

TURNING THE CORNER

Millions still feel left out in the cold, but the big jobs freeze is thawing. Economist and presidential adviser Christina Romer uses a different metaphor—she says the jobs market is "healing."[2] The horrible mass job losses of early 2008 are over. Companies are tiptoeing back in when they need workers. Open positions are being selectively filled. And in March 2010, we finally saw the most robust jobs growth in almost three years— 162,000 new jobs hailed by the president: "We are beginning to turn the corner," he told employees of a manufacturing plant in Charlotte, North Carolina. Census hiring kicked in later in the spring and in May 411,000 jobs were added to the economy.

Yet companies are still cautious. They are tiptoeing in, hiring contract workers or temps first. The hiring so far has not been enough to absorb the millions of people who still need a job. Worse, a record 46 percent[3] of the unemployed have been out of work for six months or longer— raising concern about who will be shut out of the jobs recovery. If this is the turning point, as the White House hopes, will it include millions of tech and manufacturing workers whose jobs have left for other countries? It's an infuriating middle ground between recession and recovery. If it sounds like in one breath I am saying things are getting better and in the other I say it still feels terrible for U.S. workers, well, it's true. On the one hand, the economy is growing, on the other hand, it will take a long time to grow our way out of the damage done over the past three years. It brings to mind the old quote from President Harry S. Truman: "Give me a one-handed economist," he said in frustration. "All my economists say, 'on the one hand . . . on the other.'"

When will the job market get back to normal, so many of you ask? When will I get my job back? Or my job security? Or at least some good opportunities again?

There is a deep concern that even though the recession is long over, things don't get back to "normal." Profound long-term shifts are under way (and have been for 20 years) and in the near term, the unemployment rate could remain stubbornly high. Remember, in February 2009, when Congress and President Obama pushed through the most massive domestic spending program since the Great Depression, we were told without it the unemployment rate could reach 8 percent. The jobless rate quickly rose above it anyway.

The risk for 2010 is that this is not the all-out recovery for jobs that some hope for. The jobs market is what economists call a "lagging indicator," and that means even when the economy recovers, the jobless rate can still rise. You will hear headlines of bank profits, economic growth, and the "road to recovery" but you will look around your neighborhood and say, "Not here." That's because Main Street is the last thing to recover, sadly, and this time is no different.

Here are more reasons why the jobless rate could remain a problem well into 2011. There are some 6^4 million Americans who are not looking for a job yet (those stay-at-home moms, retirees, discouraged workers), but will be when the headlines start to blare that hiring has resumed. When those people start looking, the jobless rate could rise. Companies may be slow to hire back workers until they are sure that their orders and businesses are going to continue to improve. Just like you and me, hiring managers are battle-scarred. They don't want to add workers they'll have to fire quickly again. They want to keep money in the bank and they aren't taking risks. And when fear of hiring because of uncertainty in the marketplace turns to fear of missing out on opportunities, that's when the jobs will really start to flow. But corporate profits are starting to improve, Until then, we are seeing a textbook response right now to uncertainty in the economy: temporary workers, consultants, and contract workers are hired first, until the recovery is entrenched. It is a sure sign that the huge battleship of a labor market is slowly, slowly starting to turn around.

You'll be hearing a lot about another "jobless" recovery, where it takes much longer to restore the jobs lost than it did to lose them. It happened after the 1990–1991 recession and again after 2001. The Federal Reserve in its official diagnosis at the end of 2009 said its brain trust "generally expected unemployment to remain elevated for some time."[5]

But there is also the notion that because this jobs crisis was so swift and deep, perhaps jobs will snap back faster than economists think. (After all, economists have been behind the curve on what will happen next for several years now.) Companies would have to hire back quickly and aggressively because they cut too deeply in the panic of 2008 and after.[6] Even as the Fed frets about "elevated" unemployment, there is still at least one theory that gives hope that opportunity is just around the corner.

"Nothing succeeds like success," says economist Lakshman Achuthan. "So as always it will take the return of job growth and a more sustained expansion before people feel better."

In the meantime, for top talent that opportunity is already presenting itself. Tig Gilliam, the CEO of employment company Adecco, says that there is already a war brewing for the best employees in highly skilled fields. This "war for talent," as he puts it, shows that at least one narrow slice of the gargantuan U.S. jobs market is starting to move again.

"Companies are clearly getting more confident about bringing people into their organization, but they are looking for the absolutely best talent inside the organization and out. So this is going to be a jobs recovery for the best and the brightest in their field, and I think what that means is you've got to be on top of your game every day," Gilliam says.

TOP OF YOUR GAME EVERY DAY

I've heard a variation of that theme for more than a year from economists, workplace experts, and money gurus. Herein lies the rub: You have to be on top of your game at the same time job satisfaction is deteriorating.

45 Percent

Only 45 percent are satisfied on the job, the lowest since the Conference Board began recording the numbers in 1987.[7]

It's a Great Recession version of survivors' guilt. If you *do* have a job, you're less likely to be happy doing it every day. Is it any wonder that happiness and security on the job are waning? If we have a job, we are afraid we'll lose it. Or we're doing even more work than before and we feel like our jobs aren't providing us the motivation and opportunity that they did just a few years ago. At the same time our bosses are getting more out of us every hour! Productivity—that is the amount of work we produce per person for each hour of work—keeps rising. But our pay is not, nor is our job security. For a country that loves to work, to make things, to start businesses and grow ideas, it's been a depressing few years.

My colleagues at CNNMoney.com said it best in a headline earlier this year: "Take This Job and Tolerate It."

There is a twist on this discontent, though, and it is something every single manager and employee should be ready for. When the economy really turns and jobs start coming back, the restless masses of the unhappily employed will be searching for new challenges, exciting jobs, and for the first time in a few years, some advancement. They are hungry for some satisfaction at work and they are ready to find new ideas, new markets, new ways to sell products, and new ways to innovate and compete in whatever this economy looks like next. Couple that with a thaw in the housing market so people can actually *move* again, and managers should be a little nervous, if you ask me.

Even as we savor these little signs of life in a moribund labor market, we know they are only a start, and we have a mountain of jobs to restore and a lot of work to do before these small glimmers of hope are felt more broadly.

Here's the math. The economy needs to add 100,000 to 150,000 new jobs every month just to keep up with growth in the working-age population. So even when jobs start growing, we'll need to see new jobs above and beyond 100,000 to 150,000 to start eating into the huge overhang of 8.4 million jobs lost during the recession. Just how big a task is that?

56 Months

How long it would take to restore 8.4 million lost jobs in the recession and absorb new workers in the economy, assuming 300,000 new jobs per month.

Imagine the economy begins to create 300,000 jobs each and every month. It would take another four or five years (56 months to be exact) of consistent (and very strong) job creation just to get us back to where we started before the recession. The country will need 100,000 to 150,000 new jobs every month just to keep up with new entrants to the workforce. You need significant jobs added above and beyond that to start restoring the jobs lost in the recession. It's why every worker with a job, every worker without a job, and every college graduate looking for a job has to be smarter than the next guy or gal.

This is the math facing Kathryn Gutowski. She knows she's in a sea of millions of job seekers and she is determined to elbow ahead of the 5½ others in line with her for a job, and so far, she's almost there. She's a lawyer by training, but a mother of four first—she spent the last 11 years home raising her kids. Now it's time to go back—in part to pay for the college educations of her children. Kathryn has made just about every right move. She's kept up her legal license. She has volunteered with a legal society. Now she's working with a law school program that helps professional moms reenter the workplace. After some classes and networking, she's interning at a law school admissions office. Most important, she radiates confidence and is unapologetic about her time out of the official labor market.

"What a lot of employers fail to realize is that a mother's brain does not stop functioning because she is raising children. In fact, the organization skills you acquire caring for four children under seven years old are transferable to any setting," she says.

She's just one of millions of moms trying to get back in at a rotten time. She's got smarts (keeping up with the industry while raising her children) and hustle (getting in on a program that trains her for reentry) and she's incredibly fortunate because she has the breathing space to do that because her husband (also a lawyer) makes a good living. But four kids headed for college, high property taxes, and falling home values will test any family's finances. Kathryn is determined to get back in.

Kathryn is not counted in the official unemployment rate. She has been out for a period of years, so she's not considered part of the labor pool. It's one reason why the jobless numbers are substantially understated.

Then there are the unhappily "underemployed," like Frank in Santa Cruz, California. He would like more hours and better pay, but is stuck in a job he hates—the night shift managing a hotel. Worse, he says his boss is a screamer who's cheating the workers out of overtime. He'd like to quit, he told me, but he needs the money. "I'm scared to lose my job in this economy but I'm also tired of being treated like this."

Some nights the boss is so horrible, Frank would rather go broke than work for her. "My boss said that if I take a day off I'm fired. I know that it's illegal but I feel like I have no other choice since I can't find a job anywhere else."

Frank was terrified to confront his awful boss after a co-worker did and was let go on the spot (and never paid for the last week of work). Working in customer service in the hotel industry, he knew dozens of people who had been let go and were out of work for months. He hung on and tolerated this bad boss for several months, and then he hatched a plan. He asked co-workers to bring him in on their projects. He watched and learned how his co-workers in other parts of the operation did their jobs. He had a perfect attendance record, a stellar reputation in customer service, and the admiration of his co-workers for putting up with the bad manager. He quietly put out feelers elsewhere in a terrible economy for the leisure industry, all the while imagining the boss's barbs just bouncing off his imaginary armor. The more ugly the situation got, the taller he stood. And wouldn't you know it, when a competitor needed one new worker Frank's reputation as cool-headed and flexible landed him the job.

Frank did what is difficult in an ailing job market. He managed to transfer out of a bad situation and into a better one. It can be done.

And there's Jayne in Detroit. She worked for a big bailed-out bank but lost her job like thousands of others. (She says her entire department was outsourced to India.) She was out of work for six months and replaced a growing feeling of hopelessness with an equal amount of hustle.

"You probably have heard that you need to know people at companies to get reviewed for any job openings," Jayne says. "I believe it to be true from what I've been through." A union job she heard about through contacts on LinkedIn was promising, but there were 500 other candidates. The financial job she ultimately landed "almost exactly six months from being severed!" she got through a friend who has worked for the rival bank for years. He helped her research open jobs at his bank, find the specific hiring manager, and get her resume placed in the right hands. She beat out five other candidates. "I am a success story, finally!" She says, but with a stark new starting point that millions of other job-finders are finding. "I am making about 30 percent less than at my previous job."

Jayne's experience is bittersweet. And all too common.

TAKE A PAY CUT?

Would you take such a drastic pay cut to get a new job? In the booming 1990s and early 2000s, the answer would be a resounding, "No!" But the vast numbers of unemployed workers today means employers don't have to pay more to attract talent. And you don't have many choices. The real risk is you may be taking a pay cut that resets your salary for every job that comes after it. After six months out of work, though, benefits and a steady paycheck start to become more critical than anything else. It's a cost-benefit analysis that only you can do. Can you afford the big pay cut? Can you afford not to take it?

During good times there is a rule of thumb that you shouldn't take the first job that comes along at lower pay, because then you are resetting the pay scale and taking a step back. Better to stay out of the market a month or two more, but ultimately get the higher paying job. It's advice that was sound in the 1990s and folly today. Why? Because many major sectors are not creating the jobs they used to, and, in fact, depending on what sector you work in, you could be seeing your industry shrink around you. I have asked economists, career counselors, human resources managers, consultants,

CEOs and even personal finance queen Suze Orman the same question: Should you take the pay cut or hold out for better?

Suze: "Don't be silly. You *must take the job.*"

Bill Rodgers, former chief economist in the Clinton Department of Labor: "Yes," take the pay cut, he says. A 20 to 25 percent "reemployment salary cut" is normal.

Lakshman Achuthan, economist at Economic Cycle Research Institute agrees. "You've got to be in the game and work from inside" to raise your salary and job profile from there.

With so many taking pay cuts to land new jobs, it's no wonder that the pay raises for current workers are so meager.

ROMANS' NUMERAL

2.7 Percent

The meager raise you can expect this year—if you get one.[8]

Welcome to the new American job market—where a good resume and impeccable employment history are not enough to get the job. In addition to all that, you need a PhD in hustle to beat out the others for the opening. And if you have a job, you're not getting much of a raise.

Why such long odds? The U.S. labor market is a rich and dynamic place—the most amazing and innovative in the world. But right now, the labor market is in flux. The usual rules don't work. That jobs boom of the 1990s when companies were hungry for workers and starting salaries were rising to attract them, well, it almost seems quaint now. The reality for the vast majority of workers is stagnant starting salaries, longer hours as companies squeeze higher productivity out of the workers they have, and give more responsibility to fewer people for the same or less pay.

And it is less pay. You've probably noticed that wages are not keeping up with life. From November 2008 to November 2009, average hourly earnings rose 2.2 percent. The Consumer Price Index is an index of what you pay for goods and it rose 2.3 percent. That means wages are not rising enough to compensate for the cost of living. The take-away for you: Your costs may well rise more than your pay in the weeks and months ahead. Plan for it.

Productivity gains mean companies are getting more for every hour of work out of their employees. And with almost 15 million people officially out of work (not counting the several million more not counted in the labor market but who want to work), employers do not need to pay up for a new hire. Unless you have a couple of offers in your back pocket, you don't have much negotiating room for pay. Even then, look around, budgets are tight. All you can do is get in there and do a great job and hope you can move up quickly within the company. Remember, some experts think that companies slashed so closely to the bone, when their business picks up they will have to hire back quickly as well. That's *if* you are in a growing industry.

According to workplace consultant Mercer, average base salary increases for 2010 will come in around 2.7 percent, versus 3.2 percent in 2008. Many companies are freezing salaries altogether—14 percent of companies surveyed by Mercer had freezes—but believe it or not, that's an improvement from the 30 percent of companies that locked their salaries down in the dark days of 2008. People working in consumer goods and high-tech industries can expect pay bumps of maybe 3 percent. The smallest raises, Mercer estimates, are in the industries where the economy is adding the most jobs—health care (2.2 percent raises) and education (2.4 percent raise). To put that in perspective, productivity is up 4 percent year over year, so that means you're delivering 4 percent more for that 2 or 3 percent raise.

SWITCHING CAREERS

New kinds of jobs will prosper, and old skills and education will need to be tweaked to fit new areas of growth. Being smart means staying nimble. First—where the jobs are *not*. It's not just the Great Recession. Consider this: From 1999 to 2009 the job market has morphed dramatically away from manufacturing and construction, autos and general trades. When the housing boom turned to a bust, construction jobs vanished. In manufacturing, aggressive competition from China's low-wage workers, cheap currency, and government-subsidized factory towns shut down factory after factory here. U.S. manufacturers simply could not pay U.S. wages, comply with U.S. environmental and safety rules and supply their products to Walmart and other companies and retailers as cheaply as Chinese factories could. So many manufacturers became importers of Chinese manufactured goods, moved offshore altogether, or they struggled. China pursued a brilliant national strategy of becoming the factory floor to the world, and succeeded. (In January 2010, China surpassed Germany as the world's second-largest exporter and was on the verge of replacing Japan as the world's second largest economy.) Look no further than the massive jobs lost in manufacturing for a sense of the shifting roles of global workers and the effects of rapid globalization. As the United States lost the lunch-bucket jobs that built the country after World War II, other countries picked up those jobs and began to elevate their own middle class.

Meanwhile, as the manufacturing-based middle class in this country struggles, there are new innovations sparking growth elsewhere: in computers and software and professional services. Jobs are also growing in sectors like the government, health care, education services, business services, mining and logging (see Tables 3.1 and 3.2).

Policy makers and economists for years have said that this country will shift away from manufacturing and toward services. There is great debate about the practical and personal impact of manufacturing's decline on our tax base. The economy is changing faster than displaced workers' skills can keep up. Are there enough service jobs to replace the manufacturing jobs and will they ever pay as much? Every lost manufacturing job supported a handful of other tangential industry jobs, a tax base, school districts, and consumer spending. How long before service jobs can pick up that slack? Is the U.S. public education system equipped to churn out high school graduates with the math and science fundamentals to compete in this new

Table 3.1 Lost Decade: Hardest Hit Industries 2000–2010

Manufacturing	5,700,000 jobs lost
Trade, transport, utilities	1,500,000 jobs lost
Construction	1,200,000 jobs lost
Retail Trade	780,000 jobs lost
Information	824,000 jobs lost

Source: Bureau of Labor Statistics.

Table 3.2   Lost Decade: Jobs Gained 2000–2010

Health care	2,900,000 jobs created
Government	1,900,000 jobs created
Leisure, hospitality	1,300,000 jobs created
Education	775,000 jobs created

Source: Bureau of Labor Statistics.

workforce? This is all still painfully playing out across the country, even as a jobs recovery rekindles. It's an unnerving time to be a manufacturing employee or construction worker.

It's no wonder that millions of you are asking where your job went, and when you'll get it back. Millions more are trapped in a job they don't like, deprived of the usual American opportunities to move and grow. But dig within the numbers, and there are opportunities and some important clues about where you can make your living next.

Meet Barry Hessinger, a former Marine in Lehigh, Pennsylvania, who lost his job as a carpenter.

"We were building more houses than we could handle three years ago and within a couple of months it totally died down," he says.

Now he's studying to be a physical therapist, his education paid for, in part, by the 2009 economic stimulus and local economic development programs. He thinks a career in health care will be more stable than waiting for construction and housing to return to health and it plays to his skills and talents—working with his hands.

"It just feels good to finally get into a career where I think I'll be working every day," he says. He has also chosen a field that will likely be in high demand as more Americans age and live longer. Government labor experts expect a 30 percent surge in physical therapist jobs over the next 10 years, much faster than the average for all other occupations. And unlike so many of the entry-level jobs in health care, his training puts him in a field that allows him to earn well above the median household income level. Median annual wages of physical therapists were $76,220 in 2009, according to the Bureau of Labor Statistics. If he really excels, he could earn well over $100,000.[9]

WHERE ARE THE JOBS?

The Department of Labor's own economists are clear about where the opportunities will be over the next decade (see Tables 3.3 and 3.4)—computer systems designers, biomedical engineers, nurses, and home health aides. Hospitals and health-care facilities will be hiring like crazy as the baby boomers age and more Americans need medical care. That means accountants, construction managers, insurance clerks, janitors, medical records managers, data analysis experts, and dozens of other job descriptions can be transferred to your local health-care system, to say nothing of the obvious need for doctors and nurses to treat patients.

Some of these growing fields are at much lower wages than those great manufacturing jobs that built the American middle class (and that the rest of the world is now trying to emulate to build their own middle classes). You will hear bullish prognostications of health-care jobs—and it's true there will

Table 3.3   Occupations with the Fastest Growth 2008–2018

Career	Growth Rate (%)	Wages ($)	Education/Training
Biomedical engineers	72	82,550	Bachelor's degree
Computer analysts	53	76,560	Bachelor's degree
Home health aides	50	21,620	On-the-job training
Personal/home care aides	46	20,280	On-the-job training
Financial examiners	41	79,070	Bachelor's degrees

Source: BLS Occupational Employment Statistics and Division of Occupational Outlook; BLS Occupational Employment and Wages, May 2010.

Table 3.4   Vanishing Jobs 2008–2018

Industry	Job Loss Forecast
Department stores	−159,000
Semiconductor manufacturing	−146,000
Car parts manufacturing	−101,000
Postal service	−98,000
Printing	−95,000

Source: BLS Occupational Employment Statistics and Division of Occupational Outlook.

Table 3.5   Fast-Growing, Good Pay, Some College

Career	Wages ($)	Education
Dental hygienists	66,570	Associate degree
Physical therapy assistants	46,140	Associate degree
Compliance officers	48,890	Long-term on-the-job training

Source: BLS Occupational Employment Statistics and Division of Occupational Outlook.

be tremendous jobs growth for entry-level health-care workers. But millions of these jobs are home health aides, often with no benefits and sometimes not even "on the books." Better-paying nursing jobs require at least some schooling. The Department of Labor says more than half of nurses have a bachelor's degree or higher, and 35 percent have an associate degree.[10] Dental hygienists and physical therapy assistants are also in demand and require less than a four-year degree (see Table 3.5).

By sheer numbers, health care dominates all the job growth forecasts. It is a diverse field with wide variations in pay and experience necessary, with some notable surprises: A survey of annual physicians' salaries found that some highly trained nurses make more money than doctors. Certified nurse anesthetists or CRNAs are advanced practice nurses trained and licensed to deliver anesthesia to patients. In 2009 they made on average $189,000 compared with $173,000 for family doctors.[11] Those doctors typically have four or five more years of schooling (and expenses) than CRNAs.

Kerry, a viewer and medical laboratory scientist from Chandler, Arizona, says that in medical labs across the country, the jobs crisis has been non-existent. "Physicians make 70 percent of their decisions based on lab results. We are needed! Phlebotemist, medical laboratory technician, cytologist, histologist and cytogenetic technologist are other positions in labs. We work in hospitals, clinics, reference labs, sales, and industry." Kerry has a bachelor's degree in clinical laboratory science and is an evangelist for lab jobs. "It's a great career for those who like science, want to help people but may not want to do direct patient care."

Chapter 9 has more information on health-care jobs and the opportunities for education and advancement.

It's imperative to look at growing fields through the prism of the best pay potential. CareerCast.com mashed the growing jobs categories with criteria like better-than-average pay, stress, and workplace satisfaction. The winner? Actuary. With an average income of about $85,000 a year, CareerCast.com[12] rated actuary "one of the least physically demanding jobs with little stress, a great outlook for employment and income growth, and a favorable work environment."

Best Jobs in 2010

1. Actuary
2. Software Engineer
3. Computer Systems Analyst
4. Biologist
5. Historian
6. Mathematician
7. Paralegal Assistant
8. Statistician
9. Accountant
10. Dental Hygienist

Worst Jobs in 2010

200. Roustabout
199. Lumberjack
198. Ironworker
197. Dairy Farmer
196. Welder
195. Garbage Collector
194. Taxi Driver
193. Construction Worker/Laborer
192. Meter Reader
191. Mail Carrier

There will most likely be exciting opportunities in data analysis, statistics, and anything having to do with looking at large volumes of information. Think of how much data companies and industries collect now about all aspects of their businesses. Strategic planning and analysis of that data is a nascent field that could provide great opportunities. There are no numbers or forecasts on this yet, but mastering vast amounts of information and making business decisions from it will be key to just about every field. Watch for stunning growth and interesting quirky jobs to develop there.

LOCATION, LOCATION, LOCATION

Former Marine Barry Hessinger was willing to retrain and refocus his skills to a growing industry—physical therapy. For many others, it might also be time to consider a move to another part of the country. Not everyone can do it. And I'm particularly sensitive when experts throw off this advice casually like every American worker is transplantable, with no strings attached. We are, after all, people, not just units of labor. I cringe when I hear the experts say that lifelong factory workers—unemployed for a few years and facing hard times in the Rust Belt—should pick up and move to another state. It just isn't as easy as that. We need to do a better job providing retraining and education and support to workers whose jobs have been outsourced or have become obsolete. Barry's story should be a model for other regions and professions. That said, if it truly takes four or five years, at a minimum, to get the jobs back we've lost, for many workers there will be no other choice but to move for better options.

2009 was the second worst year on record for the typical worker's ability and desire to move to new parts of the country to get a job, according to outplacement firm Challenger Gray and Christmas. With so few job opportunities and a crummy housing market, families are sitting tight more than ever before, taking fewer risks and chances in another part of the country instead staying where they have friends and family—"an established support network"—as outplacement expert John Challenger puts it.

It's harder than ever to move but the fact remains that job market conditions are different all over the country. North Dakota has only 4.4 percent unemployment. Texas is growing again. The West is still seeing more firing than hiring but there is net hiring in parts of the Midwest. Table 3.6 shows how it breaks down, according to polling by Gallup, who surveyed employees

Table 3.6   U.S. Job Market Conditions

Nationwide	Hiring 25%	Laying off 23%
South	Hiring 27	Laying off 22
Midwest	Hiring 25	Laying off 22
East	Hiring 24	Laying off 23
West	Hiring 22	Laying off 27

Source: Gallup, February 2010.

and asked them to look around their company and say whether there were jobs being added or cut.

As the jobs freeze begins to thaw, there will be opportunities for smart job seekers who are ready and able to jump. Parts of the South (Texas, in particular) are seeing jobs slowly coming back and with it, people moving in. Sunbelt states are seeing fewer new retirees moving in, and that may mean fewer service and health-care jobs growth in those areas. The opportunities, when they come, will come in some parts of the country sooner, depending on your skills and background and your willingness to move.

But wherever you are, the more education you have, the sooner those opportunities will arise.

EDUCATION

In May 2010, the jobless rate for high school graduates (no college) was 10.9 percent. It's less than half that for people with at least a bachelor's degree, only 4.4 percent! The message from those numbers is clear: The more education, the better. The job's recession has largely sidestepped people with

MORE EDUCATION, MORE PAY

2009 MEDIAN EARNINGS

No high school	$23,608
Only high school	$32,552
Bachelor's degree	$53,300
Advanced degree	$65,364

Source: BLS data, based on 52 weeks/year.

advanced degrees, and the more education, the lower the unemployment rate and the better the pay.

Tig Gilliam, the employment company CEO, says higher education is more important than ever. "Clearly if you are in the education system, you've got to stay."

Starting salaries for almost every kind of engineer promise to help you pay off those student loans and build a solid nest egg. According to the most recent data from the National Association of Colleges and Employers, 8 of the top ten 10 best-paid graduates of the class of 2010 will be engineers (see Table 3.7). Petroleum engineers make up less than one percent of bachelor's degrees, but earn one-and-a-half times the average starting salary for bachelor's degree job candidates.

Another survey by employment web site Payscale.com found lucrative mid-career salaries for engineers, as well as economists (see Table 3.8).

With apologies to Willie Nelson and Waylon Jennings, mommas don't let your babies grow up to be liberal arts majors. (This, grudgingly from the ultimate liberal arts major—double major Journalism and French.) I have always believed it's what you do with the degree, not necessarily how much

Table 3.7   Best-Paid Majors Class of 2010

Major	Average Salary Offer ($)
Petroleum engineering	86,220
Chemical engineering	65,142
Mining and mineral engineering	64,552
Computer science	61,205
Computer engineering	60,879
Electrical/electronics and communications engineering	59,074
Mechanical engineering	58,392
Industrial/manufacturing engineering	57,734
Aerospace/aeronautical/astronautical engineering	57,231
Information sciences and systems	54,038
Bachelors' candidates average	48,351

Source: Winter 2010 Salary Survey, National Association of Colleges and Employers. Data represent offers to bachelor's degree candidates where 10 or more offers were reported.

Table 3.8 College Degrees That Pay Off

Mid-Career Median Salary	
Aerospace engineering	$109,000
Chemical engineering	$107,000
Computer engineering	$105,000
Electrical engineering	$102,000
Economics	$101,000

Source: PayScale.com.

you pay for that education or what the actual degree is. But you might have to work harder to get where you want to go financially. Demand for liberal arts majors fell 11 percent in 2009. Study after study show on average certain liberal arts degrees pay less than their science and technology counterparts (see Table 3.9). The highest-paid English majors work as technical writers. The key is to translate the liberal arts education into the growing fields.

Statistics like these raise a whole host of questions about whether our public education system is preparing enough students to excel in these fields, if we are not valuing our teachers and social workers highly enough for their role in society, and so on. It's all valid discussion. But it won't get resolved in the next four years while millions are struggling to get back into the job market. The Obama Administration and Congress have reformed the law to make it easier for these lower-paying but important job categories to get affordable student loans and pay them off, yes. But if you are mid-career, out of work, thinking of retraining or you have a kid in college, I'd sit down with these statistics and

Table 3.9 College Degrees That Pay Less

Mid-Career Median Salary	
Spanish	$52,600
Music	$52,000
Theology	$51,500
Elementary education	$42,400
Social work	$41,600

Source: PayScale.com.

have a frank conversation about talents, interests, and opportunities. Especially if you are counseling a recent high school grad or college-bound student, discuss where they want to position themselves for the future.

GOOD PAY, NO DEGREE

There are, of course, dozens of career fields that with hard work, ambition, intellect, and on-the-job training, you can achieve the upper reaches of the middle class in this country. And the more training and certification, the higher you can climb. Did you know a top master plumber brings in $110,000 a year? A radiation therapist can make up to $101,000? A medical equipment repairman needs only on-the-job training and can make $95,000? An experienced court reporter can earn $113,000 and has great job security and benefits.

Many nursing fields start with at least an associate degree—that's two years of college—but pay more than the median wages for all bachelor's degrees.

Top air-traffic controllers earn well over six figures, and many have on-the-job training, not a traditional four-year degree. Keep in mind that new applicants from the general public most likely need a college degree to get these jobs. People with aviation experience at the Department of Defense or the Federal Aviation Administration do not need a degree, but do need relevant work experience, or they must complete an aviation-related program through the FAA's Air-Traffic-Collegiate Training Initiative.

The building trades (electrical and plumbing in particular) are excellent ladder jobs that can lead to owning a small business one day. What does "ladder job" mean? It's a job that may start out not paying well, but with a clear and straightforward ladder to climb higher each year until there is the possibility for owning your own business or being your own boss. It's why sometimes low-starting salaries can be misleading—ladder jobs can start out with below-average pay but the smart worker can move up quickly.

Police detectives and supervisors are paid well, often with excellent benefits.

The pay experts at Payscale.com say that it is less important to look at the starting wages of a career category and better to look at what the top 10 percent can earn with experience and continuing education. The breakdown in Table 3.10 shows the median pay of high-paying fields that do not require a

Table 3.10   Good Pay, No Degree

Job	Median Pay ($)	75th Percentile Pay ($)	90th Percentile Pay ($)
Radiation therapist	77,100	88,700	101,000
Construction superintendent	77,000	95,100	116,000
General sales manager (nonretail)	75,300	104,000	143,000
Fashion designer	74,800	100,000	131,000
Senior charge nurse	72,200	85,600	101,000
Journeyman lineman	72,000	92,700	120,000
Supermarket store manager	71,900	96,700	130,000
Intensive Care Unit (ICU) registered nurse	71,900	86,600	108,000
Semiconductor field service engineer	71,800	81,200	94,500
Vascular technologist	71,100	81,700	96,400
Cardiovascular technologist (cath lab)	69,800	80,500	92,200
Emergency room (ER) registered nurse	69,000	81,600	98,200
Magnetic resonance imaging (MRI) technologist	68,700	79,400	90,700
Medical equipment repairer	68,600	81,500	95,000
First-line supervisor/manager of police and detectives	68,100	87,700	110,000
Operating room (OR) registered nurse	67,800	78,500	92,000
Ultrasound technologist	66,700	77,600	91,200
Food and beverage director	65,100	83,500	105,000
Echocardiographer	65,100	75,700	89,400
Pipefitter	64,700	79,900	96,800
Millwright	64,600	81,900	109,000
First-line supervisor/manager of fire fighting and prevention workers	64,400	85,400	111,000
Owner/operator, small business	63,500	104,000	161,000
Construction and building inspector	63,300	84,300	118,000
Hotel executive chef	63,100	79,600	99,900
Court reporter	62,400	82,300	113,000
Estimator, construction	62,100	78,400	98,800
Master plumber	56,700	76,000	110,000

Source: Payscale.com 2010; copyright, Payscale Inc., 2010.

degree. That means half of all workers make more, half make less. The second column (75th Percentile Pay) means that these workers are in the middle of the top half of the pay heap. And the 90th Percentile Pay workers are basically the top earners.

More factory jobs used to be on this list. In fact, for much of the last century, the factory job was the stepping stone to the middle class, providing a decent living and a tax base for decent public schools. Factory workers' kids could go on to college and move up the ranks of the ever-more skilled economy, making more money and raising the standard of living for the next generation. That rung—in fact, the whole ladder—has been pulled out from under workers.

Now the factory job is the stepping stone to the middle class in *other* countries and policy makers are struggling here to figure out how to fill the void. What will replace it? Even if everyone magically could become a biomedical engineer, there would not be enough jobs to go around. And certainly not everyone can afford to go to the fancy schools and not everyone can sit through four or five years of engineering classes and succeed. Healthcare jobs? Hundreds of thousands of those jobs will not replace the benefits and wages of the lost factory jobs.

The jobs collapse of 2008–2009 hurt everyone, no question, but it hurt these noncollege graduates more than anyone else. Job security for college degree holders as a whole never deteriorated into critical condition like it did for everyone else. The trick for college-educated workers in the New Normal is making smart choices about your job and career. The trick for everyone else is getting into the middle class and staying in it.

Let's look at the Department of Labor's own data for a breakdown of median wages for careers that do not require four years of college (see Table 3.11).

Bear in mind, the more training, coursework, and certification you pursue, the more likely you are to end up in the top earners of one of these fields.

GREEN-COLLAR JOBS

Today there are more than just white-collar and blue-collar job categories. The buzz from Department of Labor officials and the president is that the

Table 3.11   Top-Earning Jobs Without a College Degree

Job	Median 2008 Earnings ($)	Education/Training
Air-traffic controller	111,870	Long-term on-the-job training
All other managers	90,230	Work experience in related field
Industrial production manager	83,290	Work experience in related field
Transportation, storage, and distribution managers	79,000	Work experience in related field
First-line supervisors/managers of police and detectives	75,490	Work experience in related field
Nuclear power reactor operators	73,320	Long-term on-the-job training
Sales reps, wholesale and manufacturing, technical and scientific products	70,200	Work experience in related field
Elevator installers and repairers	69,380	Long-term on-the-job training
Gaming managers	68,290	Work experience in related field
First-line supervisors/managers of nonretail sales workers	68,100	Work experience in related field
First-line supervisors/managers of fire fighters	67,440	Work experience in related field
Power distributors and dispatchers	65,890	Long-term on-the-job training
Commercial pilots	65,340	Postsecondary vocational award
Captains, mates, and pilots of water vessels	61,960	Work experience in related field
Electrical and electronics repairers	61,040	Postsecondary vocational award
Detectives and criminal investigators	60,910	Work experience in related field
Ship engineers	60,690	Work experience in related field

Source: Bureau of Labor Statistics data.

future is in green. Billions of taxpayer dollars are being plowed into weatherization programs and green retraining efforts. The president and his economic team often tout green technology as a source of future jobs.

This jobs category is still in its infancy and there are hundreds of different types of jobs that can be considered green collar. There are no official government statistics on how many green jobs there are, what they pay, or where they are located. The Department of Labor just now got the funding from Congress to start analyzing and counting green jobs and their potential. We don't expect any hard data on green jobs, their pay, or their availability until late 2011 at the earliest.

So far, the average green job, according to my colleagues at CNNMoney .com, pays around $12 an hour. That's because so much of the green work to date has been relatively low-skilled weatherization jobs. But if you count engineers, environmental scientists, and budding new fields of green technology, the pay scale starts to become much more attractive. Trouble is, labor economists say, this is a field for the future, and right now, right this minute, there are good people who need to feed their families who can't wait a generation for green technology to grow into a jobs category for millions of Americans.

Peter Morici is a former trade economist in the Clinton Administration and a professor at the University of Maryland who says green technology is no silver bullet for the massive loss of jobs we've just experienced.

Green energy investments, he says, "will create several thousand jobs, but not the millions that are needed. And those jobs will be slow in building out. Green energy is a new industry and it generally takes a full generation for a new industry to replace an old one. Whether it's stagecoaches for locomotives, the automobile for the train, what have you. Green energy projects [will not make up for] those jobs that we lost during the Great Recession. It will create jobs in the thousands when jobs in the millions have been lost. We need to rekindle those manufacturing jobs that were lost during the Great Recession and all those supportive jobs that go with them. In automobiles, steel, electronics, plastics, pharmaceuticals, and so forth."

Green may take a while. So what is the smart thing to do *right now*?

YOU'VE JUST LOST YOUR JOB

247 Days

ROMANS' NUMERAL

How long you can expect to be out of work after a Great Recession job loss.[13]

Welcome to a club of millions!

HOW MUCH MONEY HAVE YOU SAVED?

If you just lost your job, how long can you pay the mortgage or rent, car insurance, car payment, and grocery bill before running out?

Could you last 247 days—the average length of unemployment?

It's okay to feel disappointed and lost when the job disappears, it is only natural, and for many people it's simply unavoidable. Americans work hard and we define ourselves by our jobs and careers, our sales and successes. That job is the driver of our personal economy and when it's gone, so is economic security. A decade ago, six months out of work was the kiss of death on a resume.

If you lost your job 10 years ago, you could expect to be searching for about three months before finding a new job. What a difference a decade (and a financial crisis) makes. In June that wait is more than six months— 35.2 weeks or 247 days to be precise (see Figure 3.2).

The wait for a job is now longer than at any time since the 1980s. A few words here about the wait and the financial stress of being out of work. We are all a little more leveraged than we were back then (to say the least), so it means that many families don't have much breathing room. Even smart savers have found themselves short of cash. Personal finance experts for years used the same rule of thumb: three to six months of living expenses in savings. The

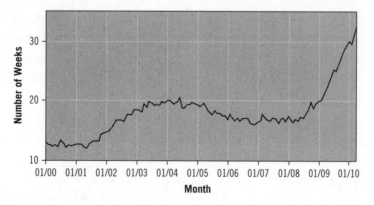

Figure 3.2   Average Number of Weeks Unemployed

Source: Bureau of Labor Statistics.

last couple of years have proven that even six months is too conservative, especially for older Americans, for whom it is taking even longer to get a job.

Hopefully, you'll find work sooner. Corporate profits have begun to improve and technically, it means hiring could pick up again later this year. That gap on the resume seems terrifying, but the good news is that with so many people out of work—and for so long—that gap on the resume looks slightly less alarming to hiring managers. Good, smart, qualified people are losing their jobs every day. If anything, it gives you a little cover. (Department of Labor statistics show a record 46 percent of the unemployed had been out of work for six months or longer.)[14] Congress moved to waive an employer's share of Social Security taxes on new hires for a year, to give companies an incentive to pick up these workers. As managers start hiring again, they are eager to pick up the best players who have been axed for no reason other than saving on labor costs. With a few simple, smart steps that can be you.

Here's how.

❑ Pick yourself up quickly.

There's much to be done. Treat the job search like it's a full-time job. Get active on Plaxo, LinkedIn, Facebook, or any other industry-specific social networking. (And for God's sake, get the pictures of the Caribbean cruise off there. Learn to use the privacy settings so your real friends and family can see you with a rum drink in Jamaica two years ago, but make sure no colleagues, clients, or bosses can! If you don't know how to use the privacy settings, find a 15-year-old to help you. Put this book down and do it now.) Along these lines, be careful of the groups you join and the causes you support. If you have colleagues, former bosses, and associates on your Facebook page or following you on Twitter, be wary of divisive opinions or rants. Imagine if an old colleague is looking to fill a job and thinks of you, pops onto your Facebook profile, and sees you ranting about health-care reform—one way or the other. Or worse, the old colleague Googles you and finds a blog posting with all your innermost—and opinionated—thoughts about politics. You have your First Amendment rights. Just remember that everything you write online is available forever for just about everyone to see. Imagine this scenario: Without a thought you click on "yes" to joining the cause "1 million Facebookers against Obamacare." Or the group "I bet we can get a million people to say no to Glenn Beck." You move on never thinking of it again, until later a potential boss checks in on your page. In the days since you joined, the comment thread has turned threatening and tacky. Do you really want to be associated? Too late. A whole generation of new college graduates and college students searching for internships is desperately trying to scrub their digital record as they head to job interviews. The older you are, the less of a trail you probably have. But young people in particular should be mindful of how they appear. If you enjoy your opinions and want to share them, fine. Then keep your work network off the personal social network sites and reserve Plaxo or LinkedIn for business conversation and networking.

These tools are critical to stay connected, but you have to use them with the assumption that every click of the mouse is forever.

❏ Get out of the house.

Imagine that group of 5½ people competing for every job opening. What are you going to do, how are you going to *think* to put yourself ahead of five of those people in the eyes of a new boss? Often, with a job loss, the family can no longer afford childcare and the out-of-work person is home taking care of the kids. If that's the case, make time every day or at least a few days a week to get out and stay connected to your industry and former colleagues. How?

❏ Network.

Sometimes, just a random connection is what sets you apart from all the other resumes. That person you were painting the neighborhood school gym with on a volunteer program might well hear of a job opening that would suit you. Whether it's the mommy group, the alumni club, where you worship or where you work out, these are all valuable connections when you've lost a job. Staying home and surfing job boards will not, I repeat, will not get you any closer to a job. (I know of no one who has scored a job from a job board or paid job-search web site.) Your best connections are the people you already know, not a random human resource e-mail address.

One loyal *Your $$$$$* viewer, Thomas in East Tennessee, didn't wait one minute to network, and proves that networking isn't just for corner-office-type jobs.

"I was laid off in March by a major electronics retailer," he wrote. "Thank God I was able to call in a few favors and get on with the competition." He checked in with former colleagues who had moved on to new companies. A series of quick phone calls (and his reputation as a good salesman) was all he needed.

Connections work *everywhere*. A manager at a top tech company recently told me there was a job opening in her department. She personally screened 4,000 outside resumes. "Every one of these people was a rock star," she said. In the end, the hiring manager decided to go with someone they already knew, reaching across company divisions to snag someone who had made a previous connection with the boss.

With so many people competing for the same job, how are you going to set yourself apart? Sending out a bunch of resumes and cover letters and posting your material on job web sites is not enough.

Ellen Gordon Reeves is a career advisor and author of *Can I Wear My Nose Ring to the Interview?* She has a simple mantra: "Stop looking for a job and start looking for a person. The right person will lead you to the right job."

Eighty percent of all jobs exist in the hidden job market—they are never posted or advertised—and 80 percent of all jobs are filled by personal referral, she notes. So the most important line in a cover letter is the one that contains the name of the person you and the hiring manager both know. "Dear Mr. X., Susan Smith recommended that I speak with you."

Make the personal connection to set you apart from all the others. "That's what will get your cover letter read and your resume looked at," Reeves says. "Concentrate on lining up as many informational interviews as you can. You've got to get yourself and your resume in front of as many people as possible. Stop wasting your own time by sending your resume hurtling into the black void of cyberspace."

❑ Downplay the gap on the resume.

Focus on the last big win you had for your employer, how you created shareholder value, grew a division, kept costs down, or somehow excelled in your previous career roles. Remember, 44 percent of the unemployed have been out of work for at least six months. That means 44 percent have the same big gap on their resume. Don't lead with it.

"Focus on your strengths and talents," Reeves says. "Who would *you* hire? Someone who comes in and says 'I can't believe they let me go after I gave them the best 20 years of my life. I've been out of work a year, I've got two kids and a mortgage; you've got to give me a job'—or someone who says, 'I have two decades of marketing experience, I have a 99 percent customer satisfaction rate, I raised sales by 20 percent, I think I could do this for you, I love your company, let's talk.' No brainer. You fake it until you make it," Reeves says.

When Brad Karsh was a recruiting director, he received 10,000 resumes, 9,000 cover letters and overall, he says he read fewer than 200. Imagine those odds—only one in every 45 cover letters is read to the end. How are you going to hook the manager in the first five words? How is your letter going to be better, different, more exciting than 44 others?

Karsh is now the founder and president of career coaching service JobBound, a frequent guest on CNN's *Your $$$$$* and the author of *How to Say it on Your Resume*. Most people spend 10 seconds scanning the cover letter and 10 seconds on the resume. "You have to think of the cover letter as a movie trailer," Karsh says. Fast-paced and exciting with a narrative hook to pull you in. He says most job applicants include the same four boring paragraphs: how you heard about the job, why you are interested in it, why you'd be great at this position, and finally how you are going to follow up. "You've written a lot of words and essentially given me no information," Karsh says. Most people just rewrite their resumes. What a hiring manager is thinking, Karsh says, is "Don't waste my time if you aren't going to add value."

A good cover letter has:

- An interesting hook
- Tells a story
- Ties into why you'd be great for the job
- Is personal
- And short

A bad cover letter:

- Is painfully long
- Is too formulaic
- Has no substance
- Is a rewritten resume
- Uses empty buzzwords

Empty buzzwords on a page of dense type is a cardinal sin. Empty words like *facilitate, utilize, transition.* Just say what you mean in clear language. Those words do not make you sound smart. And everyone uses team player and problem solver. It's not creative. Another sin: typos. It's the fastest way to get in the circular file and not the call-back pile. In many cases, the cover letter is even more important than the resume, especially if you are reconnecting with an old colleague or networking to get a shot at this job. If you are already a known quantity, but just trying to reintroduce yourself, then the cover letter is critical. Remember, ideally you are sending a cover letter to someone who knows it is coming, has been alerted by your "network" person in common, and will give your letter a few extra seconds. After that, you've got to hit it out of the park.

For specific examples—the good, the bad, and the ugly—of cover letters, turn to the resources section at the end of this book. Karsh's final advice: Watch out for the fine line between clever and stupid in the cover letter.

Congratulations, you've got the interview and a provisional job offer. Next up:

❑ Be ready for a credit check.

Believe it or not, your prospective employer has every right to run a complete credit history on you. Eighteen states are considering restrictions on just how much financial information hiring managers can see about you, but depending on the position, you can expect scrutiny on this. (Washington and Hawaii already have the most consumer-friendly laws on this.) If you are applying for any position that involves handling money, the vast majority of employers will want to see if there are any court judgments against you, outstanding collections, or any criminal history involving financial crimes. They can scrutinize your job history and will be able to clearly see just how well you manage your own money. A study by the Association of Certified Fraud Examiners[15] found that 7 percent of the typical company's revenue is lost to fraud—and the two red flags for employees who commit this fraud are living beyond their means and trouble paying their bills. The sad fact is, at the very time you desperately need a job, your credit history can become a scarlet letter. The hiring manager can't necessarily see the *score*, but he or she can run a check and see on average seven years of your financial *history*. (There is a difference between the credit score and the credit history. More on this in Chapters 4 and 5.) Employers say it is another valuable tool in assessing a candidate, especially for positions that handle money. But critics say there is no concrete link between how pristine your credit history is and how well you would do the job.

"Not everyone with bad credit has handled their own money badly," railed viewer Bruce. "Some people have yet to establish credit, and others just fell on bad times. It doesn't mean they would be bad at a job."

Privacy and fairness aside, it's a trend any job hunter should be aware of. How widespread? It depends on the job. A hospital job with access to drugs, the elderly, or children will certainly draw a criminal and credit check—it's the law. A job with unsupervised access to the cash register or the bank account will also certainly draw scrutiny. And high-level management jobs with budgets and bank accounts will almost certainly mean a thorough check. How far back are they reaching into your financial history? In general, about six to seven years. The Society for Human Resource Management (see Figure 3.3) surveyed employers and found that almost half of them run credit checks on some of their employees, 13 percent

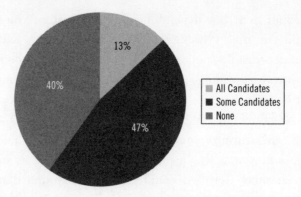

Figure 3.3   Society for Human Resources Management Credit Check Survey

check each and every person who applies for a job, and 40 percent don't bother.

State legislatures may pass laws to restrict some of the employer searches, but until then, the best strategy is to have a good reason at hand (and a nice smile) if the hiring manager asks you why your credit is shot. People from all walks of life have taken a hit over the past couple of years. Good human resource (HR) managers will be able to see that you once handled money well but recession and time out of work have set you back. If you did a deed-in-lieu of foreclosure with the bank so you could move to a new city for another job opportunity—say so. Be up front and tackle it straight on. Remember, just like a record number of people have gaps on their resumes they are trying to fill, a record number of people have messed up credit histories. Focus in your interview and interactions with the potential boss on what you can do to add value to the company you want to work for. More on how to fix your credit history in Chapter 4, but for job-hunting purposes, be aware that your potential boss can see all these details. Of course, if you've kept your financial house in order through the mess of the last few years, this doesn't apply to you at all. And that's exactly where you want to be. There are also federal laws that protect you if you think you have unfairly been denied a job because of your credit history. If this is you, contact the Federal Trade Commission and an employment attorney immediately.

CREDIT SEARCHES: YOUR RIGHTS

Employer must . . .

- Notify you before obtaining report
- Get your consent
- Give pre-adverse action notice

Source: Federal Trade Commission.

YOU HAVE A JOB—PROTECT IT

Networking isn't just for the out-of-work. After all, isn't it a little transparent to start calling up or sending your resume to old colleagues four or five years after you last spoke? Start touching base now even if you have a job. Volunteer a few hours a quarter or once a month to your trade or industry group and make sure that your membership to professional associations is up-to-date.

But the most important advice for anyone with a job—put in valuable face time at work and focus on getting and delivering results in your job. If you've got your job, this is not the time to be taking risks. The first time I said it on CNN, I almost felt bad. I didn't want to crush anyone's dreams or make anyone stay in a lousy employment situation. But it was getting too ugly out there to risk being unemployed. For years, the conventional wisdom had been to take a chance on the start-up, stretch your wings, pick up and leave your current job for new opportunities. But after months of recession and literally hundreds of messages from viewers about their struggles keeping or finding a job, it became clear to me that the smart move was to fiercely protect the job and the benefits you have, no matter what. Even after the recovery clearly began and the economy started growing again, the jobs growth with it was simply anemic.

How do you protect the job you have? Be seen around the water cooler. Be careful on the flextime. You don't want some bean counter at the head office to look at a list of employees and their salaries and cost centers and not know you. Be visible and attach yourself to a critical project or projects. What is your most recent success that saved money or created value at the company? Make sure you know it, and your boss does, too.

All of this means more time and more attention to the job—face time at work, flexibility, taking on extra projects and roles, staying connected and engaged with peers in your industry.

This, after women in particular made incredible gains in recent years with job-shares and flextime and setting up work routines that complement their parenting routines. Many women feel the Great Recession reversed some of the work–life balance gains they have made in recent years.

The cruel reality is that when many women hit their stride in the career, it often coincides exactly with when she is having her babies and raising small children. The United States is the rare industrialized country without federally mandated paid maternity leave, and even many big, profitable companies offer only six or eight weeks paid. The same goes for men—many are just reaching the peak just as the demands from family do as well. Working moms and dads with small children may feel they are operating without a net, at the very time they need to redouble their efforts at work.

Has the Great Recession taken away family-friendly choices? Or made workers feel guilty about trying to balance work and life?

Is it safe to step out of the workforce voluntarily for a few years to raise children, and maintain your position in the workforce?

Economist Sylvia Ann Hewlett studies these trends for the Center for Work Life Policy. She is a font of information about how we live our lives and work our jobs—with all its opportunities and inherent conflicts. She says her research shows increasingly that women are not taking a year or two out. Instead they are going to a three-day week or working flex-time routines—say, telecommuting on Fridays.

"If you step back but don't step out, it's much easier to stay in the game and to resurrect your career and resurrect your earning power," she says, noting that women who leave for a few years to raise children, over the course of their lifetime give up 25 percent of their potential earnings.

"Take advantage of flexibility and step back, step down, but don't step out."

The irony is that the flex programs that helped women do this are at the core of all the job experts' advice for how to survive a tough labor market—be seen at work, be careful of too much telecommuting, and so on.

Further complicating the picture is the fact that this has been called not a recession but a "he-cession." Women have fared much better than men. The unemployment rate for women is roughly 8 percent and for men it is closer to 10 percent.[16] Massive job losses in housing, construction, manufacturing, and financial services have been heavily weighted toward men. On the one hand, women have lost fewer jobs, on the other hand, if their spouse has lost his job, women have lost breathing space and flexibility at home and are more tied to their incomes than ever.

ROMANS'
NUMERAL

8 Out of 10

Number of companies that offer "alternative work arrangements" like flextime, work-from-home, summer hours, and so on.[17]

Never before have more people been working under so-called "Alternative Work Arrangements," and according to data from human resources consultant Hewitt Associates, the policies have largely survived the Great Recession.

"We have not seen organizations dropping these programs," says Carol Sladek, who consults on work–life programs for Hewitt (and works flexhours herself).

In 2005, 59 percent of companies offered flextime, for example. In 2009, that share had grown to 84 percent (see Table 3.12).

Table 3.12   Surviving the Recession—Work–Life Policies at U.S. Companies

	2005	2009
Flextime	59%	84%
Part-time	47	64
Work at home	32	46
Job sharing	26	30
Compressed work schedules	22	31
Summer hours	10	14
Phased return from leave	4	12
Other (e.g., phased retirement)	3%	5%

Source: Hewitt Associates; percentage of large companies offering these work arrangements.

Still, she says companies in general are moving slowly along a spectrum that ranges from a company offering a few job shares here and there, to a company with well-designed flexible policies. Most companies still make these decisions, Sladek says, on a manager-by-manager basis and it can vary by department and division. If your workplace was tentative about flextime, telecommuting, and the like before the recession, chances are they are not evangelists for more such programs today.

"On the one hand we are seeing employers providing more flexibility but on the other, employees have more fears," Sladek says.

"There is still a very strong face-time mentality, and with a recession like this, "there is always this knee jerk reaction that, 'Well, Sally's in the office and Suzy is not.'"

Sladek advises employers and employees to focus on one thing: Results. Ironically, these arrangements could be great profit drivers for companies coming out of the recession. What started out 20 years ago as a "nice thing to do for moms" should be now a business imperative. If they can't offer more money to retain or attract good talent, they can offer flexible schedules to attract workers, instead of more money. Also, job shares and flexible office schedules can save money for the employer. Sladek calls this "the intersection of people, space, and technology."

What started as primarily a benefit for women is changing with new generations of workers.

"We see a lot of twentysomethings who come in and say, 'I am not working in an office—are you nuts?! Gimme a BlackBerry and I am out of here,'" Sladek says with a laugh.

There are workers who prefer 9-to-5 and those who want to work online at midnight. Embracing that is just good business, she says.

With any luck, the mass layoffs are over and companies will need these good workers and their flex policies, and instead of worrying about preserving the jobs we have, we'll soon be in a position to grow your job within your company, take a better job, a promotion, even a move to a new city, as soon as possible. The bottom line for employees is always what they are producing. Always make sure that your contributions are visible—especially if you are making those contributions from your home office.

YOU THINK LAYOFFS ARE COMING

You are doing everything you can to protect your job, but the writing is on the wall: Layoffs are coming. You have seen the numbers for your division and they aren't good. Or you can tell that business is down and managers are huddled in meetings in the conference room. Or worse, there are projects you and your immediate colleagues are not asked to work on. Attorney Robin Bond runs her own employment law firm called Transition Strategies, and has counseled CNN viewers many times to be upfront with your boss. She says that if you know layoffs are coming, approach your boss and share your fears. And then tell him or her how you can help the process. You might be able to negotiate some extra time on the payroll, helping with the downsizing. You might be able to get a transfer to another part of the company before the ax falls. You won't know, Bond says, if you don't ask. And you just might be doing your boss a favor by saying out loud what everyone else knows but won't verbalize. Who knows? You might find out you are safe after all, and there's no more reason to worry. But if it's clear the separation is coming, negotiate your departure with your boss or human resources.

You might be surprised to know that some big companies will keep you on company health benefits for a few months, or give you an extra month in the office—paid—to clear up loose ends. Find out if there are any programs for retraining or employment agency programs to help with the transition and the job search. It might be a long shot but you won't get any of these things if you don't ask.

THE PERMALANCER

Enter the permanent temporary worker, better known as the "permalancer." Unlike past recoveries, temporary jobs are not yet turning into full-time positions and fully 30 percent of the workforce is made up of contract or temporary workers.[18] Sara Horowitz, the founder and executive director of the Freelancers' Union, worries that many of these permalancer positions lack job security, health benefits, days off, sick time, or a retirement plan.

The army of independent workers, freelancers, consultants, temps, and the self-employed grows. The government doesn't specifically count these permalancers, but almost everyone agrees that this will make up an ever bigger part of the workforce.

A few years ago, Horowitz says, there was great debate about whether this trend could keep going—a growing group without health insurance, access to unemployment benefits, no job security. Now there is no debate. It's just a reality.

"I think really what we're talking about is that the way that people are going to work is short term. People are going to go from project to project and job to job. That's what business is going to want, but what I think is really important is that we have to start saying that we need to think about, what does this new workforce need?"

Currently, there is no way for all permalancers or contract workers to buy into unemployment insurance. Health insurance coverage has been available through the Freelancers Union and will now be available after health-care reform. But taxes can be tricky and permalancers have to take special care investing for retirement, because they may not have access to company-sponsored 401(k) plans. Horowitz says permalancers and contract workers have to arrange their finances differently than full-time company workers.

Tig Gilliam, the employment agency CEO, explains the allure for businesses: "Even where they need resources they want a flexible model, whether

INDEPENDENT WORKERS

FINANCIAL PREP

- Set up two accounts
- Deposit 60 percent for taxes and benefits
- Deposit 40 percent to live on
- Hire an accountant
- You must pay taxes four times a year

FUND YOUR OWN

- Life insurance
- Health insurance
- 401(k)
- Disability insurance

that is a temporary worker or a contract worker. It gives them a way to do project-based work or contract work [so] if something does dramatically change later in 2010 they're not in a situation to have to make cuts again."

LONG-TERM UNEMPLOYED

Never in this country has such a big proportion of the unemployed been out of work for so long. It causes grief at home and hurts the labor market overall.

Almost 46 percent of the unemployed have been out of work for six months, at least. "That's an off-the-charts number," says economist Lakshman Achuthan. "The issue is—the real *problem* is—we are having a recovery. It is very real. However, these people are being left behind."

Who are these workers? Construction workers and financial services employees whose jobs evaporated when the housing bubble burst, manufacturing workers who have been losing jobs for more than 10 years now, and a whole host of people displaced because their skills are being outsourced and off-shored.

Steve Udden is one of those people—out of work for 10 months after his job went to China. He is, literally, a trade statistic. A husband and father of two daughters, his job that once was in Foxboro, Massachusetts, is now somewhere in China after the telecom equipment plant where he was a manager moved, lock, stock, and barrel. The United States government classifies him as an outsourced worker through the Trade Adjustment Assistance program—a program that according to the Department of Labor "helps workers who have lost their job as a result of foreign trade." In the past year, the government has seen a surge in applicants.

Says this Red Sox fan, "I feel like a baseball player that got traded from a team that he loved playing for and loved the fans. I loved my customers, my co-workers were like a second family to me."

For 10 months, he has had government-sponsored training, a "trade assistance" cash payment from the U.S. government to compensate him for the job being off-shored, and jobless benefits and COBRA health insurance have helped fill the remaining gaps.

"We are keeping it level and steady and holding the line and right now we are okay," he says. The training in particular has helped him: "It has strengthened my focus on what I want to do and how I can do it to help other organizations and be a better employee to other companies that I may or may not work for."

Steve fits so many of the statistics of the postrecession jobs market: The he-cession, manufacturing collapse, competition from globalization, long-term unemployed.

He never thought he'd lose his good job, let alone specifically to another country. He says the job that replaces his outsourced job could pay less. But he is strangely at peace about the macroeconomics of the situation.

"I'm completely optimistic and believe in the marrow of my bones that I am going to find something that is good for me and my wife and children."

He is optimistic. But it's this segment that worries many economists, even as recovery takes hold elsewhere. "They are being left behind by the recovery," economist Achuthan says. "The only thing that I see that actually starts to address that problem is if you can get a long expansion. It's not about how strong it is, it's how long it lasts."

NO JOB YET? WRITE IT OFF

So here's where we stand: It's harder to get a job, harder to keep a job, and the duration of unemployment is lasting an uncomfortable six months or longer. If this is you, keep every single job-hunting receipt. Your resumes, career coaching, even the babysitter for your job interview may be tax deductible. IRS tax form 529 lists the miscellaneous expenses that you can deduct from your tax filing. There are numerous restrictions. So tread carefully and consult a tax professional if you plan to write off a good chunk of your job-hunting expenses. If you are searching for a job in your current field, have been out of work only recently, and have spent time traveling to cities to research and find jobs, you may be able to write it off.

Writing Off the Job Search

What Can I Deduct?

- Resume and cover letter printing and preparation.
- Travel to another city to research jobs, companies.
- Fees paid to an employment agency.
- Babysitters and travel expenses to job interviews.

What Can't I Deduct?

- Anything related to your first job search—college grads don't qualify.
- Clothes, haircuts, and so on, to look good for an interview.
- Computer to follow job boards and write resume.
- If you have been out of work for a period of years (stay-at-home mom, retired, etc.) you cannot deduct your costs.
- Search costs related to a *new* career.

Keep in mind that even though you cannot deduct your expenses for a job search, if you are searching in a new industry, you may be able to tap into education credits for training in that industry. Check with a tax preparer or the IRS for guidance.

Another frequent question: Is my jobless check taxable income? Congress waived some income taxes on unemployment benefits through the stimulus. The first $2,400 of your jobless check in 2009 was tax-free. There are also new incentives beginning in 2010 for small businesses to hire workers who have been out of work six months or longer. If an employer keeps them for a year or more, the government picks up the tab for social security taxes and gives the employer a $1,000 tax credit.

It's a small consolation after lost income, but it's something.

THE PAYOFF

Everything about the jobs market is a good news/bad news trade-off.

Jobs are coming. But it will take years to re-create what was lost in the recession.

The cream of the crop is already seeing a war for talent. But that doesn't help the record 46 percent of the unemployed who have been out of work for six months or longer. Those workers are in real jeopardy of losing valuable connections and skills in the labor market and missing the recovery.

- If you have your job: focus on results. Know what was your last big win and make sure your boss knows it, too.
- This may be the perfect time to take new projects and new responsibilities at work. The ranks have thinned and companies are looking for new ideas and new talent from within when they can't fill open

positions because of hiring freezes. Maybe you took a pay cut or you felt stuck in place the last few years. Now's the time to move up at work.

- If you are looking for a job, remember the advice to look first for the *person*, not the job. Former colleagues and business associates and friends are the most likely connection for you to help stand out from the sea of resumes. Hiring managers want to go with a known quantity.
- For young people, choose your major wisely. There are 1.65 million graduates of the class of 2010. The kids getting job offers have degrees in business, finance, computer science, engineering, and economics.

4

Debt

13

Americans have, on average, 13 credit obligations on record with the credit bureaus. Nine are credit cards, department store cards, or gas cards, four are car loans and mortgages.[1] This information stays on your record for years, and how you handled each of those 13 accounts can be seen by potential employers.

Chances are, you have a long and detailed relationship with credit and debt and that credit history follows you wherever you go.

For almost a generation now, we've used borrowed money to finance our lifestyles. Debt was marketed as risk-free and essential to achieving the middle class or even living like the upper-middle class.

Our government borrows heavily. Americans borrow heavily. And much of the American Dream, is, in fact, built on borrowed money.

We borrow to send a kid to college. We borrow to buy a car. Or two or three. The U.S. Treasury borrows money from investors and other countries like China and Japan to run the government. Small businesses borrow money based on what they think they will sell or their projected revenues for the month ahead. U.S. families borrow money every time they use a credit card. Big banks borrow from each other overnight. And they borrow from the Federal Reserve for short-term obligations.

Borrowed money is the oxygen of the modern economy. Students can buy an education that will help them earn more money in their careers, and young couples just starting out can buy a home to raise their families in. A credit card buys you the convenience to make purchases without cash, and pay all of those purchases off at the same time when you get the bill.

Or at least that's the way it is supposed to work. Somewhere along the way, this country went a little crazy with the borrowing, bypassing saving altogether. Ben Franklin coined the phrase, "A penny saved is a penny earned." Our grandparents were afraid of debt—they scrimped and saved and paid cash.

But for the past 30 years, America said instead, "Charge it!" and the average card-carrying adult (or teen, in many cases) holds on average 3.5 credit cards each.[2] Half of all college undergraduates have at least four cards. An estimated 64 million adults admit to not paying their bills on time (that means interest and fees!),[3] and according to an oft-quoted *New York Times* analysis, if you stacked up all the credit cards and store cards in use in the United States they would extend 70 miles into space.

It was Shakespeare who famously said: "Neither a borrower or lender be." We are loaded up with credit cards, car loans, and home mortgages: It's safe to say that Shakespeare's sage advice is a little outdated for the modern United States. And that's okay so long as you know where you stand with your debt and what role it plays in your financial strategy.

The average consumer with an open account has:

- $7,701 in credit card debt.
- $177,186 in home mortgage loans.
- $50,889 in home equity.
- $14,873 in auto loans.
- $27,777 in student loans.[4]

The statistics are exhausting.

This chapter examines the difference between the smart use of debt to grow your circumstances and invest in your future and the accumulation of debt that simply cuts down your options and weighs you down financially. We revisit some important lessons on smart credit use, old-fashioned rules of thumb that are timelier than ever today. We take a little walk together through time to see how our perspectives changed over the past generation that made us somehow think our emergency fund was not cash in the bank but a credit card or a home equity line of credit. (Hint: Nothing ever substitutes for cash in the bank.) And we meet real people as they struggle and triumph over their piles of debt: a young couple whose home equity line of credit (HELOC) was closed without warning; a mother of two who is helping put her husband through medical school on credit cards and loans; and a law-school dropout who is adjusting to massive student loan obligations and the realization that he won't be a lawyer to help pay it off. We explore how much student debt is an investment and how much is too much. And we walk through the new landscape for student loans. Did you know that when Congress overhauled health care, it completely remade the federal student loan program? We explore new rules and new protections for you in the pages ahead.

MIRACLE OR MIRAGE?

Until the crash of 2008, it had never been easier to borrow money and use it for just about whatever you wanted. Often we used it to buy things we couldn't otherwise afford. And rising home values helped mask the difference between what we made or could make in the future and how we spent it right now.

When my mother went to college in the late 1960s, she had two new pairs of shoes and five handmade dresses. If she really wanted something but didn't have the money for it, she would put it on layaway, returning to the store to admire it each time she paid an installment. Flash forward to the 1980s, when widespread use of the credit card meant you could take that coveted item home and enjoy it while you paid it off. What a revolution! Americans could take from their future earnings to enjoy today what they otherwise couldn't afford. Wages and household income were steadily rising and the postwar economic machine was humming. Technology was spawning new industries and innovations and there were more opportunities in the U.S. workplace than ever before. Borrowing from the future, when the future was certainly bright, just made good sense. And that free flow of credit made the economy grow even *more* briskly. Our living standards rose, and millions of people inched their way into the middle class. By the turn of the new century, a record number of Americans became homeowners and we bought more than 16 million new cars a year.

Along the way Americans began buying and enjoying more than they could ever dream of paying back. Imported consumer goods got cheaper and cheaper, so we could buy more and more and we did. And the cash-based days of five beautiful dresses and two well-made pairs of shoes morphed into middle-class expectations of big houses full of imported consumer goods— all paid for with credit.

Imagine a $20 Barbie doll, plucked on impulse from the Walmart shelves and given for little Janie to love. A year later, that $20 is still on the credit card, Barbie's hair has been cut off and her dismembered trunk is in the toy chest, and Mommy now owes more than she ever paid for Barbie because her interest rate is 24 percent and she was late with a payment, which threw another $35 on the bill. By the time Barbie is paid off, Janie will be taking on student loan debt.

Would you borrow money at 3,520 percent interest to buy that Barbie? If you bought Barbie and overdrew on your debit card, you did. The Federal Deposit Insurance Corporation (FDIC) studied overdraft fees and found that overdrawing your debit card by $20, then adding on a $27 overdraft penalty, and then paying it off in two weeks translates into an annualized interest rate of 3,520 percent. It sounds crazy. What smart consumer would ever pay 3,520 percent interest? Take one impulse purchase, add disrespect for credit and a dose of living beyond our means, and it happened every single day. New rules from the Federal Reserve will protect Janie's mother, to a degree. From now on, the overdraft charge can't exceed the cost of the overdraft. (Chapter 5 explores these new rules—and new traps.)

The 1980s and 1990s and early 2000s were great for the middle class, but how much of that was a mirage? Stuff worth $200—from a trip to the mall made us feel rich. Our kids had more creature comforts than our grandparents could have ever imagined. But at what price? Almost half the country is carrying substantial debt of all kinds at the same time our ability to pay it back is shakier than ever. Nearly 37 percent of Americans carry more than $10,000 in nonmortgage debt.[5]

The country and its citizens spent vast amounts of money that they didn't have. It could not go on forever and now that bubble has popped. You've probably heard it put this way: There is global deleveraging. From companies to banks to consumers, we are putting money in savings and paying down debt. It sounds so reasonable and rational, but when an economy like ours relies on consumer spending to drive 70 percent of the economic activity, it means as we "delever" and get our financial houses in order, it slows the economic recovery.

$626 Billion

ROMANS'
NUMERAL

How much consumer debt Americans have shed since October 2008.[6]

People are shocked and scared and paying down their debts. According to Equifax, credit card and bank card debt is down 12 percent since October 2008.

"Make no mistake, whether willingly or not, the U.S. consumer has been on a debt purge for the past year and a half," says Equifax's Tom Madison.

It's happening everywhere.

Consider Maria, who finds power in her newfound restraint with spending on credit. "I'm a good shopper. I'm an educated consumer. I don't have to have the best of everything," she says.

Then there is twentysomething Sarah, who for the first time in her life confesses, "I am more cautious in terms of, like, getting what I really need instead of kind of just splurging."

And Steve has gone all the way: "I think we've been cutting down on just about everything!"

It's happening in all ages and all demographics. Trend watchers and retail analysts say the pendulum has swung away from debt-fueled conspicuous consumption.

"For many of us particularly in the Baby Boomer generation, we could live the rest of our lives on fruit, vegetables, pasta, wine, olive oil, and yearly doses of socks and underwear. And maybe a little chocolate," says retail tracker Paco Underhill, CEO of Envirosell. "What do we really need?"

That pretty much covers it, doesn't it? What do you need? What can you afford, how will you pay for it, and how long will it take you to pay for it? These are the fundamental "new" questions when considering how to use credit for a trip to the mall, a new car, a college education, or a condo.

Bottom line, Americans have to cut down the debt and save more. Are you? It's a priority for smart families everywhere, and the first step to feel confident again about your financial circumstances.

SIT ON AN APPLE BOX

At the beginning of 2010, economists began to worry about the statistics showing consumers were borrowing less money. The outstanding loans as reported by the Federal Reserve Bank showed that consumers were paying down their debts and lenders were being stingier with lending money. Because credit is the oxygen of this modern economy, the economic brainiacs were watching these numbers very carefully. If we don't borrow and we don't spend, it constrains the economy.

That's the macroeconomic impact of less borrowing. On the microeconomic level—you and your family budget—less borrowing more likely means security and future prosperity.

In my reporting of the financial crisis over the past few years, the message has been consistent from all corners:

From Bankrate.com senior financial analyst Greg McBride: "Get down your debt," he says.

From former Treasury Secretary Henry Paulson, the former Goldman Sachs CEO, free-market advocate, and architect of the biggest bailouts in U.S. history: "We have to save more and spend less as a country."

I even asked Joel Osteen, the megachurch preacher and best-selling author if he thought that Americans had an ethical obligation to live within their means and stay out of deep debt.

He is, after all, what many call a "prosperity" preacher who has made millions telling his flock to remain positive in their attitudes and they will "thrive" spiritually and financially.

He told me Americans should expect God's blessings and abundance, but must also have realistic goals about what they can afford, how much they borrow, and how they can pay it back.

"The ideal thing is to not have debt; the scripture says way back in the Old Testament, God says you will lend and not borrow, that's part of the blessing," Osteen said. "Now I think that practicality is, you know, most people we have debt on our home, but . . . don't just say okay, I'm going to have this home debt for 30 to 60 years."

He's keenly aware of how debt can be a valuable investment for growth when used properly, and Osteen himself borrowed $100 million to renovate the old Houston Rockets arena to become a church building that can house 25,000 people on a Sunday morning.

He saw this as good debt, to grow his flock. But at his core, he says he is financially conservative and urges the same for his followers.

"See, my dad came out of the Depression, he would never buy anything on credit, everything was paid for, he taught us to, you know, you fill up the barrel once, you get some savings and then you live off the top of the barrel. Where I differentiate a little bit with my dad is when we came over to this facility, it was going to cost $100 million." If he waited to raise the money from his parishioners, it would take years to save it up. If he borrowed the money, he could start building immediately and attract new parishioners to help pay the debt off. He took the leap of faith and borrowed the money. In just a few years, he has paid off $60 million of that debt. And the church is growing.

Isn't that a contradiction, I asked him? More like an ethical balance, Osteen says. In our modern economy, there is the "ideal" situation, which is being completely debt-free, alongside a more practical attitude, using debt to advance your situation with the ultimate goal, as Osteen explained it: "I don't want to be in debt the whole time."

Will you be in debt the whole time? Ask yourself a few simple questions: Can I pay this money back, and when? What is this debt for? Is it an investment or a burden? Does borrowing this money increase my chances of making more money or advancing my situation?

Osteen told me an anecdote that reminded me so much of the Depression mentality of my own grandparents. He said, "My dad always said sit on an apple box until you can afford a chair, and that's kind of the mentality we have."

Over the past 30 years too many people somehow thought they were too good for the apple box and *deserved* the chair, no matter what. For some, they thought the unrealized value in their homes or stock plans justified borrowing to buy the chair. For others, it simply didn't occur to anyone they had to earn it.

GENERATION DEBT

> "I don't have a job or any savings and my unemployment benefits run out soon. I really need a car and dealer after dealer won't give me a loan. If we bailed out these car companies with taxpayer money, why won't they give me a loan?"
>
> *—Manny in New Jersey*

Manny has a bubble view of credit—that it is free and easy. The bubble popped and Manny is taking the bus. He was a caller to a CNN radio program I hosted, and he was thoroughly miffed that he couldn't borrow money. He had done it before without any savings or employment, and he was furious that the bailed-out banks and car companies were being so stingy.

The fools' gold days of "No income, no job, no savings? *No problem!*" are over, Manny. As recently as 2005, Manny may have been able to get a car loan, a house loan, and a half-dozen low-interest credit cards. During the bubble, we thought of credit as the equivalent of water or oxygen—there for the taking and essential to live. Today we have to go back to the original purpose of credit—as an investment in the future. Manny is not going to get his car loan. Yes, the government bailed out the car companies and the banks. But don't sit around and wait for a bail out because except for a few tax credits (that have now expired) we can only count on ourselves.

We must treat credit—and the debt it creates—with the utmost respect. If we do, it is an invaluable tool to our finances. If not, the result is ruinous.

The first thing to understand is the difference between good debt and bad debt. Joel Osteen—who believes everyone should strive to be debt free—explained the good debt/bad debt balance in his choice of expanding his megachurch. Since you probably are not going to borrow $100 million like he did (or sell millions of self-help books), here are two examples a little closer to most personal situations.

Marc Newman is a 28-year-old schoolteacher in the Bronx. He studied philosophy and political science as an undergraduate, then enrolled in law school. He took out federal student loans (now at 4.75 percent interest) and private student loans (at 14.75 percent interest) and lived mostly on credit cards. He budgeted scrupulously, and was careful to find low introductory rate credit cards (some as low as 3.99 percent for one full year) knowing that he was piling up education-related debt and he needed to keep his interest rates as low as possible.

Along the way, he decided he did not like law school and quit.

He enrolled in a free government program to train him to become a teacher (thereby not adding any more education debt to his tab) and now works for just shy of $40,000 a year as a special education teacher. He lived with his parents for a time after his father lost his job, so that everyone could cut down on living expenses. He pays one-third of his income on servicing his debt (including $10,000 in credit card bills).

Now meet Mary McKinley, a stay-at-home 40-year-old mother of two. She manages the family money and lives in an apartment complex subsidized for middle-class earners. Her husband is in his last year of his medical residency, and the family has used loans and credit cards to finance their life during his medical school and as they have grown their family. As she budgets out three and five years into the future, she can clearly see where the debt curve turns and her husband's income will grow faster than her debt burden.

Mary and Marc are each diligent with their budgets. They are not late with their payments and they pay more than the minimum. Both are brilliant at managing their burdens and both are eager to invest and grow their money as soon as they are able.

But one has good debt, the other bad debt.

Mary's family is using credit to invest in their future—accumulating "good" debt. But the moment Marc dropped out of law school, his debt immediately transformed into "bad" debt and for him, it will be much more difficult to improve his circumstances and grow his money.

At the heart of so many stories of financial distress, there is either a misunderstanding of the difference between good and bad debt, or a moment where the good debt went bad.

It's one reason why taking on any debt must be a carefully considered decision—with the knowledge that taking on debt is always a risk.

That can happen with a student loan, a home mortgage, a home equity line of credit. For years, personal finance experts said the path to wealth was using credit to create leverage and grow your living standards (piggybacking on rising housing prices). But remove the housing bubble from the equation. The typical U.S. family simply must view big debts more cautiously.

RESPECT CREDIT, PAY OFF DEBT

Here is where it all began: the misuse and disrespect of a powerful tool for wealth and progress—credit. When used properly, credit fuels prosperity. When misused, it can fuel personal financial disaster.

Certainly some consumers lived the high life with no thought to how they would pay the piper. Yes, it's hard to have much sympathy for them, and we all know someone who lived in a house that was too big for them and drove cars they couldn't afford at the same time you were shoveling 15 percent of your paycheck into the 401(k), only to see the financial crisis knock 25 percent off your investments.

But millions of people were not living large, and accumulated debt because the U.S. economy wasn't working for them: wages weren't rising but their costs were. Home prices were on fire. For every person who made a killing selling a house in the bubble, there is a buyer who got in to a home that today is worth far less and he or she still owes a very big debt.

By no means am I blaming the victim here. At the same time, the banks were in the midst of an epic consumer binge. Lenders, too, misused and disrespected the powerful tool of credit. In fact, if they weren't pushing it like a cheap drug and getting the masses addicted to it, millions of people wouldn't be struggling like they are right now. (You know what I am talking about—the dozens of preapproved credit card offers in your mailbox every month, the super-easy home equity line of credit, the mortgage with little or no money down and barely a check on your income.)

This is how wild the lending craze became. According to Tom Madison at Equifax, in May 2006, Americans opened up 330,000 HELOCs.

He says roughly one out of every 750 people in the U.S. opened a home equity line of credit in just one month.

"Holy Cow. We were pretty caught up in the home price appreciation fever," Madison says. "Suddenly our homes could fund all sorts of things we couldn't otherwise afford and we used them like credit cards. We used HELOCs to buy cars, furniture, electronics, home improvements, more property, you name it."

(According to Madison at Equifax, lenders opened just 50,000 HELOCs in January 2010.)

Now those banks and lenders are reeling in the excesses they helped create and profited from.

Even if you weren't a profligate spender of borrowed money, the New Normal will look different to you. Even if you pay on time, and have made no mistakes with your credit cards, don't be surprised to get a new annual fee tacked on the bill. Your unused credit lines may be lowered and your home equity line of credit may be shut down, for no reason other than the zip code you live in.

That's what happened to Matthew and Barbara Moskowitz. Citibank sent them a letter thanking them for always handling their credit "responsibly," but told them in the letter because home values are falling, "We are suspending your home equity line of credit." The couple was furious. Citibank had wooed *them* to open the credit line, they had spent only $3,000 of it and left $52,000 open. (Citibank would not comment on individual customer accounts.) Now suddenly, Citi, reeling from its own bad business mistakes and essentially a ward of the government, was closing the Moskowitz's HELOC. Even worse, the letter told the Moskowitzs that they could ask for a property assessment to get the credit line reinstated, but they'd have to pay $650 for it and they were not guaranteed to get the line of credit reinstated.

The Moskowitzs had no plans to tap the open credit, but liked the idea of having that money there as a safety net. Worse yet, Matthew and Barbara wondered if their credit score would drop because the amount of credit available is a key element in determining the credit score. This is a couple that pays the bills on time and takes pride in a solid credit score. Matthew shakes his head in astonishment as he rifles through his paperwork. And he says what I hear more than anything else: "Didn't we bail these guys out?"

Yes, we did. But the bottom line: That sentiment and a dime won't even get you a cup of coffee. Or a line of credit.

THE DREADED SCORE

Matthew and Barbara were making all the right moves, and still the banks were reeling in their credit line, simply because of their zip code. Fortunately, credit guru John Ulzheimer says a big hit to their credit score is unlikely. The credit score formula knows the difference between a HELOC and a credit card, he says, and will not count the HELOC against the couple when the "credit-utilization ratio" is determined.

Still, furious viewers frequently e-mail and call with their stories of closing out unused credit cards, thinking they were doing the right thing getting their "house of cards" under control, only to find out it hit their score. And how many times have I heard the complaint that the credit score has fallen because of mysterious factors outside of a borrower's control? The banks and the credit agencies seem to have all the power in this equation, and the number—that all-important number—seems like a scarlet letter or a gold star. Only you don't know what the rules are for earning one or the other!

Unless you are about to buy a car or a house, *don't worry about the credit score*.

What kind of crazy advice is that? Simple. If you follow smart rules with your money every day and month, and take special care in the six months before you need to borrow money from a bank or buy a car, the credit score will fix itself. Agonizing over the ups and downs of a number you can't control will drive you nuts. And if you are simply going along with your life, paying your bills on time, a dip in the score because of something outside your control shouldn't concern you. Really.

In a way, we obsess over it because we are overachievers. It's usually the people who have the least to worry about who get the most irritated when their score is cut for some reason they have no control over. *Don't waste your mental energy* on it.

Unless you are about to purchase a car or a house, forget about it and focus on paying down your debt and building up your savings and excelling in your job. If your financial house is in order, the credit score will follow. Too often, we are triaging credit card bills, paying hundreds of dollars for property assessments to try to salvage a home equity line of credit, and juggling store credit cards that we don't need or want in a lame attempt to "keep the score up." Who cares? Don't let yourself play that game.

Some borrowers need to cut up and close their credit cards, even though it will hit their score, because it is the right thing to do if they have been tempted by those cards and overspent on them in the past. To end this vicious cycle of overspending and overborrowing, they need to close the accounts and hurt their scores. Another borrower may be thinking of a first home purchase in six months. She should keep all the cards open, and pay them off every month. It depends on your track record and your diligence. (Chapter 5 explores credit card strategies for credit scores.)

It may seem mysterious, but the credit score is really a measure of how much debt you have available, how much you are using, and your track record with it.

Let me be clear, I said *don't worry about the credit score*. I didn't say *forget about it*. There is a difference. There are mistakes and omissions in your credit history, and often you don't find out until something goes wrong. And most of us aren't even looking until we are borrowing money for a house or a car, and by then, it might be too late to fix it in time.

But you must fix any errors, because if you need to borrow money, the sketchier the score, the more money it will cost you. If you are in the market for a house or a car, the lower the credit score, the stricter the terms of the loans. According to the folks at FICO, a 100-point difference on your credit score can mean $40,000 extra in interest in the cost of a 30-year, $300,000 home loan. Ouch.

The government mandates that the credit agencies make available to you a free report every year, available by calling 1-877-322-8228 or visiting online www.annualcreditreport.com. It is free, made available by the credit bureaus that keep this information and make it available to lenders. It's your right to have a copy, too, and you should check it once a year to make sure there are no mistakes.

According to a recent survey by the National Foundation for Credit Counseling, 65 percent of Americans have not ordered their free report and 31 percent of Americans have no idea what their credit score is.[7]

There is a difference between a credit report and a credit score. Your "credit report" can go back several years, and it is your financial scorecard.

Your credit history lists the debts you have outstanding and chronicles how responsibly you have managed your debt. It also includes the "credit score." That score is a proprietary model determined by FICO and reported by the three credit agencies Experian, TransUnion, and Equifax. VantageScore is a more intuitive letter grade system, but it is less widely used.

Basically, you can think of the credit score like this—a range of numbers between 300 and 850. The higher the score, the better.

People with a FICO credit score of 760 or higher get the lowest interest rates on a 30-year fixed-rate mortgage. Above 740 gets the best rate on a 15-year home equity loan, and above 720 score the best car loan interest rates.[8]

Bankrate.com senior financial analyst Greg McBride puts it on a scale like this:

- Anything above 700 and you are in pretty good shape to borrow money.
- Around 740 and higher you can borrow at the lowest interest rates.
- Below 680 not only will it be more expensive to borrow, but you may have trouble borrowing.

Ryan Mack, president of Optimum Capital Management, says everyone should be budgeting, planning, and using debt wisely and they will move themselves toward 750.

There are five main factors:

1. Your payment history. Do you pay your bills on time? This accounts for more than a third of your total credit score and it is the single most important factor.
2. The amount of money you owe and how much credit you have available. Are you maxed out?
3. The length of your credit history.

4. New credit.

5. Types of credit you are using.

How do all these things stack up together? Mortgage giant Wells Fargo's own mortgage application material is clear for borrowers looking to get a loan from the bank. "If you have had any history of nonpayment or late payments on any loans or debt, this may lower your credit score and increase your interest rate and costs. People with high credit scores consistently: pay their debts on time: keep balances low on credit cards and other revolving loans: and apply for and open new credit accounts as needed."

FICO won't exactly say how it determines this all-important score— it's kind of like Coke's secret recipe or the Colonels' blend of herbs and spices. But we know quite a bit about the factors that move it one way or the other.

7 Years

ROMANS'
NUMERAL

How long a missed debt payment (even one credit card late payment!) will stay on your credit report.

The best defense with your credit score is to pay your bills on time, every time. Even one missed payment can knock a score down as many as 110 points.[9] A default on mortgage payments is particularly devastating. A foreclosure is disastrous. Keep your balances low. Even if you pay your credit card in full every month but you rack up huge purchases that eat up almost all of your credit line, it can knock your score down and look risky to a loan officer evaluating you. (In the eyes of the credit score magicians, it makes you look like you are maxed out.) Aim to keep your credit utilization ratio routinely below 30 percent, and ideally below 10 percent in the months before you apply for a car loan or a home mortgage. That means that if you have a $30,000 credit limit on your cards, you shouldn't charge more than $3,000 a month as you get ready to borrow money.

What's particularly maddening is that a misstep costs you more points on the credit score if you start from a higher score to begin with.

"People obsess about the credit score but they really need to get their financial house in order," says Bankrate.com's Greg McBride. "Paying your bills on time, every time, will get you where you need to be."

This score—and your entire credit history—is viewed as how well you have managed your debt and your bills. Obsess less about the score itself and more about the habits it takes to keep the score solid, and you'll win in the long run.

Free Credit Reports

Have you checked www.annualcreditreport.com for any mistakes and errors on your credit history? (This is free, and mandated by the government for you to access at no cost once a year. Don't confuse it with the free reports advertised in those catchy ads.)

- Clean up any mistakes.
- If you will be borrowing money in the next 6 to 12 months, do not keep high balances, close out old cards, or apply for several new lines of credit in rapid succession.
- Remember, you want your history to look stable and predictable.
- Boring is better.

FICO's Craig Watts says that there are two quick ways to raise your score: Pay down high balances on your credit cards and clean up mistakes on your credit history. Another rule of thumb: "Time heals all wounds," he says, meaning the longer you pay your bills consistently on time the more the score will inch up.

Chapter 5 has strategies for managing your credit card bills and your debts to keep the score up if you are in the market to borrow money. If you are not, then remember to pay your minimum payment every month on time and don't charge more than 10 percent of your available credit each month.

STUDENT LOANS

$22,375

ROMANS' NUMERAL

Median student debt for graduates of four-year private university (up 5 percent over the past five years).[10]

As a country we are paying down debt on everything but student loans. Equifax's Tom Madison says the number and size of student loans are up 50 percent since 2007.

"Not a surprise due to financial pressure, stagnant income levels, and unemployment," Madison says.

Two-thirds of students take on debt to pay for their college educations. Graduate from a private university after four years, and you can expect almost $23,000 of debt to pay off.

Most students use a combination of their parents' savings, loans, grants, university financial aid, summer job earnings, and more loans to pay for school. It's a delicate ballet of financing to figure it out.

- 66 percent of students need financial aid—average financial aid total is $9,100.
- 52 percent receive grants averaging $4,900.
- 38 percent take out an average $7,100 in student loans.
- 27 percent receive Pell grants, on average, of $2,600.
- 34 percent of all students take out Stafford loans, averaging a total of $5,000.
- 4 percent of students' parents take out an average $10,800 in parent PLUS loans.[11]

There are dramatic new changes to the way you borrow for college and pay for it. As part of health-care reform, the Obama Administration and Congress overhauled the federal student loan program, cutting out the banks that once provided government-backed loans. Here's how it will now work.

The president says no American should have to go broke to pay for college. Supporters in Congress say this overhaul ends 45 years of corporate welfare to lenders who received government subsidies to lend to students, and the federal government guaranteed those loans anyway.

They say this federal takeover of the government-backed student loan business will save more than $60 billion over the next 10 years, money that can be plowed into more Pell grants and more low-interest loans for struggling and middle-class students and to community colleges and historically black colleges.

Of course, not everyone thinks it's a great idea for the government to run the student loan business. Senate Republican Leader Mitch McConnell isn't convinced that government bureaucrats can do better than private industry. His staff emailed me as I was reporting this story to say it's nothing more than another attempt by "the government to expand its tentacles further into [Americans'] lives and the economy."

Regardless of the politics, it is now the law of the land. And CNN's polling found that a majority of Americans like it. A CNN/Opinion Research Corp poll of 1,030 adults found that 64 percent approved of the new law, and 34 percent opposed it. Eighty-two percent of Democrats polled approve the plan, and 52 percent of Republicans approve, showing a rare issue where a majority of both parties agree.

The benefits are most pronounced for kids whose parents have low incomes, and for graduates who enter public service. An expansion of the Pell grant program will raise the size of Pell grants to $5,975, and fund more than 800,000 more such grants over the next 10 years.

The president hails this as the most significant reform in student lending since the GI Bill. So how will it work for students?

First things first: There are few changes students will see and touch before 2014. Graduates of the class of 2009 or 2010 with a boatload of loans will see no changes in their repayment expectations.

The big change comes almost immediately to the middlemen who used to make these loans—they are cut out of the process. Students won't have to shop around for private lenders of federally backed loans; instead, they can head straight to the school's financial aid office for help. Their loans won't change much—same amounts, interest rates, and fees.

STUDENT LOAN REFORM: WHAT'S IN IT?

- Improved repayment options.
- A streamlined federal-loan system.
- Competitive loan pricing.
- Support to stay in school and manage debt.
- Increased funding for Pell grants.
- Community college funding.

REPAYING STUDENT LOANS: NEW CHOICES

Enrolling in 2014 or later:

- Limit payments to 10 percent of income.
- Forgive remaining debt after 20 years.
- Forgive debt in 10 years if in public service.

Later on, students with federally backed loans could see better repayment terms. Basically, paying off those loans will get easier—it's called income-based repayment—especially if you are in a low-paying field or you go into a public service industry like nursing, teaching, or become a public defender.

The new income-based repayment rules are a safety net for borrowers who graduate and work in low-paid fields and can't afford their debt burden. It limits their monthly federal student loan payments to 10 percent of their income, and after 20 years, whatever is left is forgiven. Enter public service, and the debt is forgiven in 10 years. It's a way to keep smart students entering fields that traditionally don't pay well, that they otherwise might avoid if they have to borrow for college. Most graduates will pay a hefty portion of their tab, and the more they succeed, the more they will end up paying.

Student loan reform is meant to help future students like Connecticut college student Nicole, an aspiring lawyer with a 3.73 GPA when we first met, and a university balance due of $5,000.

"It's become so expensive and it feels like it's so out of reach," she said.

She would know: Despite a complicated spreadsheet of subsidized loans, grants, scholarships, and work-study she almost didn't make it to her sophomore year at a private four-year college.

"If I can't stay next year, I am pretty much in the water. I'm done," she told me.

Like many bright, low-income kids, she is paying her own way through college. After her father abandoned them, she and her mother struggled for cash, and for a time were on welfare and even homeless. An academic overachiever, she was determined to change those circumstances.

A first-class education is how she'll do it. But grants, loans, and a part-time job aren't enough.

She's one of an estimated 600,000 qualified students every year who don't get their degree within eight years—because of money.[12]

Nicole's friend Gary—an aspiring engineer—is one of those. His family did not have good enough credit to get private loans to put him over the top to pay for school.

"I don't want to suffer like my family has through the years," Gary says. "I don't want to live from paycheck to paycheck, you know, working fast food or some other job that won't let me provide."

He's taking a year off now, saving money and working. But college is still his goal—a goal that gets more expensive by the day.

Although many people applaud the overhaul of the student loan system, they also note that the reform will not keep tuition costs from rising.

ROMANS' NUMERAL

439 Percent

Growth in the cost of attending college from 1982 to 2006.[13]

Like health-care costs, tuition has only gone higher, far outstripping inflation, growth in the economy, or growth in wages. (Colleges argue that they also have record large financial aid packages to blunt the impact, but there is no question that college costs are rising faster than just about anything else.) Families have to dig deeper than ever to pay for an education at a time when an education has never been more critical to success in the economy.

Unfortunately, the student loan overhaul does not address directly the rising cost of college. It does give funding to community colleges, and some community colleges and universities have developed closer ties so that students can attend a lower-cost campus for the first two years and then transfer into a degree program at an accredited four-year university. As the student loan reform rolls out, it's an option to consider if you are juggling retirement planning for yourself and an education for junior.

A word here about advanced degrees. This is where the really epic borrowing and debt kick in, but these degrees also tend to pay much better and offer better earnings to pay off the debt. Plan carefully.

Nicole at the University of Hartford—if she really wants to be a lawyer—will have to scramble for tens of thousands of dollars more to complete her education. Yet she bristled when I suggested maybe she just didn't have the money for a fancy private school and it would be smarter to attend a community college or a state school.

"Why should I have to? All the kids who can afford it don't have to and their grades aren't as good. That's not fair."

Besides, her transcripts were frozen because she had an unpaid bill at the bursar's office—she couldn't transfer if she wanted to.

How did she close the gap? After our CNN story aired about how the recession was making it even more difficult for students on the margin to survive, Nicole was inundated with scholarship offers and cash grant offers—one even from a soldier in Iraq. Her story resonated with a partner at a Tennessee law firm, who offered her a scholarship and a paid summer internship to gain work experience before law school. Nicole's case was unique—her story touched people in the midst of a crushing recession, people who found themselves in better circumstances than others, or who wanted to make it easier for a bright young woman to get a degree than it had been for them.

With their help, she paid the $5,000 bill. That takes her out of the statistic that 600,000 young people don't finish their degree within eight years because of money. But it doesn't change the circumstances today for the 599,999 others.

New income-based repayment scenarios will help future Nicoles pay off their loans once they graduate. If Nicole, for example, were to become a public defender with her law degree, her monthly student loan payments would be capped at 10 percent of her income and eventually her remaining student debt would be forgiven. Sounds good, right? But Nicole and students like her will still have to scramble to get enough in loans upfront.

FinAid.org has excellent calculators for income-based repayment. See http://www.finaid.org/calculators/ibr10.phtml for a calculator using the new version of income-based repayment. The calculator for the original income-based repayment plan can be found at http://www.finaid.org/calculators/ibr .phtml.

Viewers immediately began asking, "Why should I save for college if it will be easier for my kid to get loans and pay for it." Call it bailout skepticism: Lots of folks have been playing by the rules and fear that people who don't save are getting a better deal.

Student loan expert Mark Kantrowitz is the publisher of the FinAid and FastWeb web sites and scoffs at that line of thinking.

"The income-based repayment plan should be viewed as a safety net for borrowers who are unable to afford their monthly loan payments," he says, "not as an opportunity to borrow excessively instead of saving for college."

$200 SAVED NOW OR PAY $396 LATER

Bottom line: Keep saving for college.

"It's cheaper to save than to borrow," Kantrowitz says and offers this math. Saving $200 a month at 6.8 percent interest for 10 years yields about $34,400. If instead of saving, you were to borrow this amount and repay it at 6.8 percent interest over 10 years, the monthly loan payment would be $396.

"The difference is that when you save, you earn the interest, while when you borrow, you pay the interest," he says.

See http://www.finaid.org/calculators/save-or-borrow.phtml for a calculator to explore the scenarios under different interest rates. If you think saving and investing now will return less than 6.8 percent, you can run the numbers yourself. Kantrowitz chose 6.8 percent because that's the interest rate on the unsubsidized Stafford loan and because it is about what you could expect to earn, on average, using an age-based asset allocation in a typical 529 college savings plan. "Barring," he says, "unusual events like the unprecedented drop in the stock market in 2008."

The big lenders have been shut out of the government-backed loan business, but the market for private student loans is not disappearing. On the contrary, the lenders that are shut out of the federally backed student loan programs may actually compete more in the alternative market for student loans. Some financial aid experts say their rates and fees could creep higher. They may well demand higher credit scores and even a cosigner. Remember: The government does not guarantee these private loans so they will have tougher terms for the students.

But faced with billions of dollars in losses from being excluded from federally backed programs, some lenders may get aggressive on student lending. The largest private student lender, Sallie Mae, announced rates as low as 2.87 percent on its Smart Option Student Loan.

It's an $11 billion market, mainly used to cover the expenses not paid for by federal loans, financial aid packages, grants, and family savings.

After a credit crunch in the heat of the crisis crippled new private loans, the situation is easing. But many of these loans are variable, meaning that private loans will get more expensive if interest rates rise. Fees can rise, too.

In general, the rule is: "Always borrow federal first," Kantrowitz says. The rates and the repayment schedules are better.

So how much can you borrow? Students can borrow from $5,500 to $7,500 a year in federal Stafford loans. Their parents can borrow more with PLUS loans.

Kantrowitz for years has used this rule of thumb: Don't borrow more than you expect to make in your first year of working.

How much is that?

ROMANS'
NUMERAL

$47,673

Average salary offers for the Class of 2010 bachelor's degree candidates, down 1.7 percent from the Class of 2009.[14]

That's the average salary offer for everyone. It varies by degree. Liberal arts candidates will face a much tougher start than others. Not only is demand for liberal arts graduates down, so is the starting salary—down 8.9 percent to $33,540, according to a survey of students earning bachelor's degrees across 70 disciplines.

Assuming you get a job offer, paying back student loans will be uncomfortable, but doable. You want the right blend of savings and scholarships to ease the burden. There are also grants (meaning you do not have to pay them back) and scholarships. In my view, every high school senior, no matter what their academic background, should be shaking the trees for college money.

There are small scholarships to fit just about every talent and interest out there—even Happy Joes, the pizza place I worked for in high school had a grant—so look high and low for even a few hundred dollars to help you pay for books or board. If it means that Saturdays in senior year spent writing essays, so be it. Consider it good training for college anyway. The smart kids are hustle, hustle, hustling for scholarships and grants. You want to amass as much free money as you can before tapping loans. It's an incredibly important lesson in debt and consequences for young people.

Applying for a handful of scholarships is not enough. Check www .fastweb.com and www.scholarships.com. Check with the parents' employers to see if they offer grants or scholarships for the kids of their employees, contact local civic groups, religious groups, anything to see about local grants.

After you've raised some money you won't have to pay back, then you have to figure out how to borrow money you will pay back with interest.

Bring your best bargaining power to the table. Let's assume you are accepted to three universities and all three are working on financial aid packages for you. If one school has a better deal than the others, get the other two to match it.

Students also need to understand that the cost of borrowing that money doesn't track dollar for dollar. Think of this: Borrow $25,000 to pay for college and you'll probably pay back more like $35,000. Here's the math: Assume you end up borrowing $25,000 for a four-year degree at a private university. The interest rate is 6.8 percent and the loan fees are 4 percent. For 10 years you'd pay $299 a month to pay off a total of $35,962. That's almost $11,000 in interest.

Borrowed money isn't free.

I'm not sure that most kids think like this—they are just frantic to raise all the money they need to get to college. I can't tell you the number of frustrated parents who feel like they've been penalized for all their savings when they go to the financial aid office at the university and find that their savings might actually lower the amount of total financial aid their kid gets. But do you really want to risk not saving the money and not getting the education the kid needs? Recapping the advice from financial aid expert Mark Kantrowitz:

- It's better to save for than borrow for college.
- Always borrow federal first.
- Your total loans should not exceed what you expect to earn in your first year out of school.

A quick reminder here: Do not sacrifice your retirement savings for college spending. You can borrow (or better, your kids can borrow) for college. You cannot borrow to fund your retirement. In a perfect world, you have a steady income and a stable family budget that allows you to put away for both. If you must make a choice between saving for college and saving for retirement: Retirement should always win.

A little tip for new parents—you cannot start saving too early. How about this for a goal: When the baby graduates out of diapers, use the money you would have spent on Pampers and instead put it automatically in a college savings plan. You can do the same with formula. By the time the baby is two or three years old, you could be easily diverting $100 to $150 a month you once spent on infant supplies into a college fund. But remember, this is only if you are already saving for retirement. If you aren't, then the diaper money needs to go into the 401(k).

Student loan guru Kantrowitz says that if your employer has a match for your 401(k), max that out first, before saving for college. If you are investing in a 529 plan, be aware that 32 states and the District of Columbia offer tax credits or tax breaks for those investments. Line up your investments against your liabilities and carefully choose how best to arrange your bills against your investments to cover everything.

More on how to balance investments and savings in Chapter 7.

KEEPING DOWN COLLEGE COSTS

ROMANS'
NUMERAL

1 in 5

Smart students who arrive to college with AP credits equal to one semester.

Some competitive (and expensive) universities have made pledges in recent years to hold down tuition and debt for middle-class students. For a list of the 50-some schools offering financial aid packages with no loans or limited loans, go to www.projectonstudentdebt.org. (It's a diverse list, including for example, Arizona State University, Emory University, Oberlin College, University of California, Yale University.)

Others have three-year undergraduate degree programs, geared either to bright students who may have graduate degrees ahead of them and, therefore, much more education debt, or middle-class students who couldn't otherwise afford the four-year degree and don't qualify for as many loans and grants.

Senator Lamar Alexander is a former education secretary and university president who is a proponent of three-year degrees. He says a three-year degree isn't for everyone, but for those who can swing it, it saves much more than just a year of tuition.

"It is feasible," he says,[15] noting that 5 percent of students already graduate in three years, and that's without widespread three-year programs.

"You have to be well prepared and you have to take more courses during the three years but you can save about $43,000, which is the cost of the fourth year plus whatever you earn in the workforce that year," says Senator Alexander.

It means, of course, less time to mature, less time to pursue extra-curricular activities that make a student well rounded, less time for a study-abroad program. But it also means substantially less debt.

And many students may well use this as a stepping-stone to even more education.

"Students looking at years of graduate school or medical school are well prepared enough when they arrive at undergrad to finish in three years and get on to medical school. That was even true when I was in college," he says.

He calls three-year degree programs the higher education equivalent of a fuel-efficient car.

It's especially helpful because those students with advanced degrees face a mountain of student loans.

The vast majority of students who attend graduate school, medical school, law school, and the like, rack up huge amounts of debt. But if you plan carefully and choose the right major (and finish!) the earnings potential and differences in job security is stunning. The more education, the more earnings potential, and the lower the jobless rate (see Table 4.1).

If there is even a remote chance that you are looking at several years in school beyond the undergraduate degree, check to see if there is a three-year option. If not, try to get to college with some college-level knowledge under your belt. A relatively small number of students work on their own

Table 4.1   How the Degrees Stack Up

Degree	Median Cumulative Debt ($)	Weekly Earnings ($)	Jobless Rate (%)
High School	N/A	626	9.7
Associate	N/A	761	6.8
Bachelor's	19,999	1,025	5.2
Master's	43,210	1,257	3.9
Professional	81,170	1,529	2.3
Doctoral	54,420	1,532	2.5

Source: U.S. Department of Education Institute for Education Studies and Bureau of Labor Statistics 2009 annual averages for ages 25 and higher.

to finish college in less than the traditional four (or in some cases, five) years. Typically they do it with bigger class loads each semester and summer semesters. Or, they do it by trying to test out of introductory classes and get started freshman year a semester or even two ahead of their peers. In most cases, this will help you graduate in four years and not have to go through another expensive semester. But for the 5 percent who have the smarts, maturity, and dedication, it could save tens of thousands of dollars.

1.7 Million

Number of students who took AP exams in 2009.[16]

More than 3,000 universities and colleges accept AP (Advanced Placement) scores from students to give them credit or move them ahead. Generally, students earning a 3 or higher are considered for course credit after the relevant department reviews the exam. Some courses of study only accept AP scores of 4.

The College Board has a helpful tool to check university policies on AP exams. But always check with your admissions office to be sure: http://collegesearch.collegeboard.com/apcreditpolicy/index.jsp.

The AP exam fee is $86, less for qualifying low-income students.

Depending on which university you choose, many accept college credits earned through CLEP (College Level Examination Program) testing. It can move you a class or semester ahead in math, English, or foreign language (there are 33 to choose from) and help you skip some introductory courses. The cost to take the CLEP test is $77, and if you pass, it could save you literally hundreds of dollars on tuition, to say nothing of the time spent in the classroom. (There is something quite confidence-building about entering your first year in college with two or three class credits under your belt. I did this with foreign language and was able to build a double major with no extra effort and no extra time.) Check out http://www.collegeboard.com/student/testing/clep/about.html for more details and check with the prospective university admissions office for their policies accepting these credits. There are 2,900 colleges and universities that accept CLEP testing for credits, and about half of the schools conduct the testing on their own campuses at the start of the semester.

Ask the admissions office if there is an unofficial path to an undergraduate degree that cuts a semester or a year off tuition. And carefully compare the

COLLEGES WITH ESTABLISHED THREE-YEAR DEGREE PROGRAMS

- Hartwick College, New York: "No strings attached, no online courses," the college promises, just three rigorous years of class load for a liberal arts education.
- Judson College, Alabama: The nation's fifth-largest all women's college has offered a three-year option for more than 40 years. Students can take what is called a "short term" in May and June to lighten their class load during the school year.[17]
- Bates College, Maine: The Bates Three Year Option, as it is known, requires five classes per semester instead of four. There is less flexibility and a more demanding pace.[18]
- Ball State University, Indiana: Since 2005 BSU has offered three-year programs in 30 majors, including accounting, criminal justice, communication studies, economics, entrepreneurship, finance, history, human resources, marketing, nursing, premed, social work, and women's studies.[19]
- Lipscomb University, Nashville: More than 50 majors qualify for a three-year degree. Academic advisers work closely with students on scheduling to make sure that all the required classes are taken in the proper sequence to avoid scheduling glitches. Also, the university offers a $1,000 voucher for qualifying students who pursue a three-year degree.

cost of private versus public colleges for the undergrad degree, particularly if the student is going to be pursuing advanced degrees.

Students heavy on smarts and light on money can also consider a tuition-free (but quite competitive) college—like College of the Ozarks, the U.S. Naval Academy, or Cooper Union in New York city.

STUDENT LOAN DEFAULTS

So you've got the degree and the debt to go with it.

Ignore your student debt at your own peril.

The IRS can garnish your wages or hold back an income tax refund to recoup losses on a loan it has guaranteed. Student loan defaults are on your credit history. Even if you file bankruptcy, only a small percentage of filers are able to wipe away their student loan obligations.

According to the American Bar Association,[20] the court won't throw out your student loan debt unless you can prove "undue hardship." Undue hardship requires filing a separate motion in the bankruptcy process and personally explaining to the judge why paying those loans will prevent you from having even a minimal standard of living. You must also prove that you have made an effort to pay this debt, making loan payments in the past and/or arranging forebearances. If you have ignored these student loan bills for years and end up in bankruptcy court, you basically have no recourse.

In short, these are not loans you can just forget about. They will follow you.

MORTGAGE DEBT

ROMANS'
NUMERAL

$573 Billion

The beloved mortgage interest deduction for American homeowners.[21]

Just as higher education is seen as critical to achieving and staying in the middle class, homeownership is the physical symbol of the American dream. Both are big debts that can pay big benefits.

With the mortgage, you can write off your mortgage interest and get money back on your taxes. That's why the mortgage is the most beloved tax break in history. It is big, and politically protected, and helps lower your tax burden while you live in an asset that—until recently—has never failed to appreciate in value.

It is essentially the government giving Americans their very own economic stimulus every year, just for being homeowners. The long-held theory is that homeownership brings stability to a neighborhood, to the schools and the tax base, and is good for the United States. Public policies, regardless of the party in power, have pushed homeownership and rewarded it in the tax code.

A big tax break on your mortgage interest aside, Americans are turning more cautious on their mortgage debt.

Two years after a home price collapse that has devastated the state of home-ownership in this country, a survey by Fannie Mae[22] shows that Americans still want to own a home, but think homeownership is harder for them to attain than their parents, and it will likely be harder still for their children.

A majority of renters say that if they move, it will be into another rental, not their first home. And one in five Americans says their credit simply is not good enough to qualify for a home.

Heartbreaking pessimism, with a dose of smart reality, might just be exactly what the housing market needs. The same survey found that more Americans are thinking about their home in a way that goes much deeper than financial gain. Most people are likely to buy a home for nonfinancial reasons—like it's the right house in a safe neighborhood with good schools. And Americans with traditional, fixed-rate mortgages were far more satisfied with their home than those with other types of mortgages.

After how terribly we've been shaken, smart homeowners are adjusting their expectations. It's an important first step to restoring a sane view on what housing can do for our lives and our money.

It can't be said enough: A home can be a valuable wealth-building tool if you respect the debt it creates.

5 Hours

ROMANS'
NUMERAL

How long on average prospective homebuyers research their loans.[23]

For something that is likely the biggest single purchase people will ever make and the single biggest debt they will ever take on, most people spend less time researching their home loan than they do a vacation. That's even *after* all they know about the inappropriate home loans at the heart of the housing crisis.

If you are the lucky one in a position to take on this massive debt, read every word of every document. Some of these documents sound as if they have been written by old men in powdered wigs—complete with legalese and arcane clauses. The mortgage document itself can run 8- to 30-pages long, single-spaced with small dense type. You are literally signing your life away so ask questions of the real estate lawyer and mortgage banker and don't sign anything that they have explained to you unsatisfactorily. You are the customer and you're likely paying a juicy lawyer fee, so get the most out of it.

If the situation is right for you and you do your research and understand your debt burden, the time has never been better to buy a home. Home prices are down, there is a lot of supply on the housing market, and there are 5.3 million "sidelined sellers" waiting to put their homes on the market in the next 12 months if they see signs that the housing market is improving.[24] That means even more options for buyers. Interest rates are historically low. But that won't last forever.

WILL BORROWING COSTS RISE?

The cost of debt is likely to go higher. We have emerged from a period of unbelievably low interest rates. As the economy stabilizes, borrowing money will get more expensive. Mortgage money, auto loans, credit cards—basically all borrowed money will carry higher interest rates certainly in the next few years. After the crash, the Federal Reserve was buying up debt to keep interest rates low and help the economy. But as the crisis fades, these emergency measures will be unwound and interest rates will be allowed to creep higher. Not only has the Fed been buying Treasuries, but it has kept the so-called Fed funds target rate at a record low just above zero percent. That can't go on forever.

On auto loans, some experts say they could remain competitive well into 2011. Demand for cars has been weak, because the consumer is strapped.

That means there is still more financing available than people willing to buy cars. Shop around for incentives and zero percent financing. Auto loans average 4.4 percent in March 2010, according to research by auto web site Edmunds.com. That is much lower than the 7.3 percent average auto loan rates back in March 2007, before the worst of the economic crisis.

And as you see in the next chapter, credit card interest rates could rise, even for the best borrowers. Already the average credit card interest rate in just six months rose to just above 14 percent from 12.7 percent.[25]

Of course, what you pay to borrow money will depend on market interest rates, how much you are borrowing, and your credit score.

For an interactive guide to interest rate averages for car loans and home loans in your state depending on your credit score, visit www.myfico.com/HelpCenter/FICOScores/.

THE PAYOFF

Credit is a powerful wealth-building tool. Mortgages and student loans are "good" debt so long as you are aware of the risks and manage the debt so it advances your financial future.

They are also the largest debts you will likely ever take on. So for college debt, always save for retirement first. Then, raise as much money through savings and scholarships and grants as possible before turning to debt. Take as many AP and CLEP exams as possible to start college a few courses ahead. Choose a career that will allow you to pay off the burden. And don't ignore student loans, they can follow you forever and are difficult to shed even in bankruptcy.

As for that other "good" debt, borrowing to buy a home has never been cheaper but with a whole set of new perils. (Weak jobs market, stingy bankers, higher lending standards.)

Chapter 6 offers valuable tables to determine which is most important to you—the home's price, or the interest rate. Because as interest rates rise, it will mean you can afford less house for the same monthly payment.

But first, the debt more of you complain and worry about than any other: Credit cards.

5

Credit Cards

46 Years

The time it would take to pay off $10,000 in credit card debt at 18 percent APR if you pay only the minimum payment and make no new charges.[1]

A new world arrived in the mail. For the first time in your life, the credit card bill shows you how long it will take to pay off your debt if you make only the minimum payments and make no new purchases. It details just how much you'll have to fork over to become debt free in three years, and it now quite clearly in black and white spells out the gobs of interest and fees you are paying if you don't pay your credit card bill in full every month.

For many Americans it will be a horrible shock.

No longer will the truth hide behind dense black-and-white type and boxes with APRs and asterisks.

These are valuable protections that might very well serve to shield some from unfair fees, prod others into becoming debt free, and for still others, open their eyes to the fact they have been living beyond their means.

Even if you aren't a prolific spender on plastic, these rules affect you: Credit card lenders are ditching unprofitable customers, slashing credit lines, and trying to find new ways to make up for the lost revenue of the hundreds of thousands of people who have simply stopped paying their credit card bills.

There is not a person with plastic in his wallet or her pocketbook who won't notice these changes—either in credit scores, rewards programs, interest rates, or credit limits.

In this chapter we explore the new safeguards to prevent the credit card companies from charging you too many fees and jacking up interest rates on existing balances. We explore innovative ways to pay off the cards, and smart tricks to pay down debt without sacrificing your credit score or too much of your lifestyle. And you see how smart consumers who always manage their credit wisely can also be in for some nasty surprises and how to fight back.

CREDIT CARD "RICH"

But first, credit card debt is the dumbest and most expensive debt there is. It is also the most common and the most rationalized by people who are drowning in it. In few cases it is "good" debt.

One viewer, John in Massachusetts, found me on Facebook to tell me his tale of evil credit card lenders preying on the middle class. "The credit card company first hooks you in with a low rate, or even with a reasonable interest rate, then they change the ground rules and rate-hike it up," he lamented.

John's paying the minimum, but barely, on $10,000 in credit card debt. He and his wife earn more than $100,000 a year. So why the big balance?

"Life throws you curve balls," he explained. In 2008, one of his cats had skin cancer and required $2,000 in surgery. Then another cat had a stroke and $3,500 more went on the card. Then his wife's Cadillac needed $2,200 in repairs and he found himself saying to the guy in the shop, "Gee, do you take Visa?"

Then he notices a leak on the driveway. A rusting gas tank and fuel pump on his Suburban means another $1,500 in repairs.

The list goes on and on.

"Everything here was totally unexpected and had to be dealt with. This wasn't 'drunken sailor' spending!"

John blasts the lenders for their fees and rising interest rates.

He's got a 29 percent interest rate, something he says is un-American and usurious, especially after taxpayers bailed these guys out.

With great passion and a command of a wide variety of details about the Treasury Department's bailout of banks, he railed against a corrupt system hell-bent on keeping the middle class up to its eyeballs in expensive debt. How was he ever going to get ahead? Groceries, mortgage, gas, and repairs each month ate up his disposable income, meaning, technically, he would never dig his way out of the debt on the cards unless he won the lottery or received an inheritance.

His rage is widespread among people truly struggling to pay their bills at the same time the credit card companies are reeling in the credit and getting tough on late borrowers. What he failed to realize is that well before the banks got stingy, he was living beyond his income with no savings cushion, so that one, two, three financial setbacks did him in for good.

Here is what John and millions of Americans forgot in the last 15 years—it's not your money and never was. Credit cards don't take the place of savings. No, it's not fair that the banks got a break in their hour of need and you don't. But that won't change a doggone thing when you go to write that check (and pay all that interest) every month. Credit card lenders are not there to do you a public service (as much as we'd like them to after those fat handouts from the Feds). They are out to make money off you. Their business model is simple—lend money to people who need it for short terms and make money off them when they don't pay it all back at once or they pay late. To boot, they get rich transaction fees from the merchants who accept their cards. End of story.

Even after important new reforms are enacted to protect you, you've got to think of credit cards as the old company store at the coal mine, like the old country song "Sixteen Tons":

> Saint Peter don't you call me 'cause I can't go.
> I owe my soul to the company store.

If you are making only minimum payments on your debts, you might as well owe your soul to the banks.

There has been so much outrage against lenders in recent years, you may be surprised to learn a majority of Americans pay their credit card bills on time and use their credit cards exactly as they should: as a revolving line of credit that is paid off in full each month and is a convenience. But millions of others are drowning in unpaid credit card balances, unsuccessfully closing the gap between what the economy provides them in terms of opportunity and what it costs to live. Millions are blissfully living beyond their means. But that's not the whole story. Not even close. For low-income and middle-income Americans, a surprisingly high percentage (52 percent) says medical expenses are the driver of their credit card debt.[2] That is not living beyond their means—it's using credit cards to *live*. Whatever the reason, anyone carrying balances or missing payments are nailed daily with high interest rates and penalty fees.

After taxpayers rescued the big banks, many people want to know where Main Street's bailout is and why they are stuck with a menu of fees and high interest payments. The populist rage may be justified. But it won't get you very far.

Adam Levin, the founder of personal-finance site Credit.com, says you can't just blame greedy banks. "The consumer has the ultimate responsibility for this. If you don't have the money, don't spend it."

Ironically, it was the financial services industry that peddled the cheap money for years making it just so easy to borrow. A wallet-full of credit cards was a national pastime—as purely American as mom, apple pie, and baseball. And too many families had no real sense of just how expensive it is to use other people's money. When housing prices were rising, the credit card offers were filling your mailbox and the *feeling* of wealth was there—it was easy to overlook that credit cards were allowing anyone to live far beyond their means.

According to a 2008 Demos report, "The Plastic Safety Net":

> During the height of the housing bubble, from 2001 to 2006, homeowners cashed out $1.2 trillion (2006 dollars) in home equity and households accumulated nearly $900 billion in credit card debt. As households tapped their savings and spent nearly all of their incomes, the nation's personal saving rate dropped to 0.4 percent of disposal income by 2006.

Awash in easy credit and spending the money saved in our houses, the cracks began showing long before the bubble burst. In 2006—near the peak of the bubble—nearly half of all credit card holders had missed a payment that year.[3]

Three years later, the housing crisis was so deep and Americans' cash flow so wrecked that an alarming number of Americans were paying their credit card minimums before paying their mortgages. They simply could not live without borrowed money to tide them over each month.[4] Against all the established money rules, it was more important to keep their charge cards greased up than pay the mortgage on their home. It's like an alternate universe of personal finance!

What started as a charge card and an important convenience for travel and business expenses in the 1970s and 1980s turned into a staple of middle-class life—allowing everyone to buy now and pay at the end of the month when the paycheck arrived. From there, it turned into the safety net for millions of families without savings and without a cushion in case of an expensive emergency. And then the jobs crisis meant for many the credit card was filling the car with gas and putting food on the table.

Now Americans are paying off those cards, realizing as a nation that there is a downside to that flexibility—the downside is onerous terms from the banker and uncomfortable debt that has to be paid back. Americans have already been paying off or carrying less of a balance on their cards. Credit card debt is down 8.7 percent since early 2008, to $847 billion.[5] That's because of the recession. Now that the ugly truth will be so easy to read on the credit card statements, there is no question that behavior will likely start to change.

Everyone, by law, will now see the true cost of borrowing money with credit cards.

Think of that $10,000 sitting on a credit card—that same chunk of money I just told you could take 46 years to pay off if you only pay the minimum. You are really paying far more than $10,000 for whatever it is you charged on the card. Pay only the minimum and that $10,000 will cost an amazing $27,863 in interest.

That's right. Put $10,000 on a credit card, pay only the minimum, and by the time you pay it off you will have paid almost $40,000 to the credit card company.

BEST CALCULATORS

The following sites will help you to learn more about how much your credit card purchases *really* cost:

- http://www.federalreserve.gov/creditcardcalculator/Default.aspx
- http://www.bankrate.com/calculators/managing-debt/minimum-payment-calculator.aspx

The question to ask yourself in this chapter is whether your relationship with your credit cards is making your life better or worse. As you think about that, here are the new rules that are now the law of the land to help protect you from unfair fees and punishment from your credit card lender. With them come unintended consequences for smart consumers who may have fewer choices.

NEW RULES, RIGHTS, AND TRAPS

Congress has passed the most exhaustive protection for credit card consumers ever. After a year-and-a-half phase-in to let the banks adapt, finally all the rules are in place.

These new laws are meant to bring into the light all the dark secrets of credit card rules and fine print and help you truly understand the cost of borrowing money on credit cards. It regulates everything from the font size of your credit card statement, to the advance warning you get before your bill is due, to how old you must be to get credit.

Your new rights:

- The monthly statement must clearly show how long it will take to pay off the balance.
- Total interest and fees paid so far this year must be clearly tallied.
- How much do I need to pay each month to be debt free in three years?
- The card issuer must give you 45 days' notice before raising interest rates.
- They must give you 45 days' notice before changing an annual fee, a new cash advance fee, and late fees on your account. You can reject

these new terms. The card can be closed by the issuer and you have five years to pay it off in full.

- Interest rates cannot rise on existing balances in most instances. If interest rates rise after the first year it only applies to new purchases, not the balance on the card.
- Credit card payments above the minimum must go to debt with the highest interest rate first.
- Limits the "overdraft" fees a bank can slap on cardholders.
- No more cards for people younger than 21, unless they have a cosigner or proof they have sufficient income.
- Limits credit card companies' marketing on college campuses.

In most cases, the company must give you the option to close out the card rather than accept any new interest rate, charges, or change in terms before they take effect. The credit card can be closed and your minimum monthly payment can be raised in certain situations if you reject their terms.

Interest rates can still rise on cards with special introductory terms. Keep a close eye on the phrase "go-to" rate. This is what the interest rate will rise to once the introductory period expires.

CREDIT CARD GOTCHAS

$24 Billion

Amount in overdraft fees collected from consumers in 2008.[6]

Americans spent more money on bank overdraft fees in 2008 than they did on fresh vegetables, postage, cereal, or books. We nearly spent more money on bank fees than we did on major appliances. (At least when you buy a washer and dryer you get clean clothes! You get nothing in return for bank fees.) One of the most important new benefits of the new laws means that your credit card must get your permission first, before you will even be allowed to overdraw the account.

Hint: Smart consumers do not sign up for overdraft protection. If you do not have the money in the account, you should not be spending it, and you certainly don't want to pay fees to use money you don't have in the first place. Banks long played this as a "convenience" to their customers, who would be embarrassed to have their debit card rejected because they didn't have the money in the account or their credit card turned down because they were over the limit.

Analysis by Bankrate.com shows bounced check fees draw an average charge of $29.58. Before Congress shut down the overdraft fee machine, those fees could reach $36 a pop. And many banks could shuffle the order of your purchases, so you could get the overdraft charge again and again on the same day. Across the country, the same person could buy a latte, then milk and bread at the grocery store, and then fill up the gas tank, and pay an overdraft charge on each.

Those days thankfully are over. There is a limit to how many times you can be hit with overdraft charges, and some banks—led first by Bank of America—don't allow overdrafts any longer.

Starting in the fall of 2010, the debit card overdraft charge cannot exceed the size of the overdraft. That means no more $35 overdraft charges for a $4 latte. And the Federal Reserve is shutting down the awful "inactivity fees" that were cropping up after credit card reform. No longer will the bank be able to charge you $19 a month for *not* using your credit card.

But even as lawmakers and the Federal Reserve work to shut down the fee machine, you can count on the lenders to try to find new ways to generate that money.

- No good businessperson wants to give up $24 billion in revenue easily. That's why some ingenious new charges popped up even before consumer protection laws to prevent credit card shenanigans went into effect. **No more free checking**. The days of plunking $500, $1,000 or $1,500 in a bank account and keeping it there for free may be over. The major banks are already planning to add basic fees to many of their formerly free checking accounts. Credit card reform shuts off the fee spigot for them, a flow of cash that had subsidized the administrative costs of checking accounts up until now. Unless you keep a high balance in the account (more than, say $5,000) or you have multiple relationships with them (mortgage, auto loan, savings account, and so on) you can expect a monthly maintenance charge. Shop around. Consolidate your financial accounts and ask for free checking if you are keeping all your relationships under one roof. Also check credit unions. They offer free checking.

- **Denied!** Card issuers can still close your account without notifying you, and can cut your credit limit without notice and warn the analysts at Credit.com. If you have a good history with the credit card company, you can try to call and restore the credit limit, but in many cases, you're out of luck, especially if they dump you as a customer.

- **Fees for a rewards card**. Even good customers may find the rewards programs they have used for years might come with more fees attached to redeem awards, or even new annual fees. Even if you are a prime customer who pays on time and rarely carries a balance, you will find new fees as well. Your rewards program may be cut: Some 5 percent cash-back programs have already switched to cash back for only certain categories.

- **Students must have a cosigner**. It will be harder for young people to pile up the credit card bills, an important first step to learning some financial responsibility, but it also means that college kids who have parents without good credit histories may find it harder to get a card of their own. The under-21 crowd will need a job with good income or a cosigner to get a card in their own name. Gone are the days of the prescreened and preapproved credit card offers stuffed into the textbooks you buy. Bankrate.com lists four options for anyone under 21 years old who needs a credit card: (1) Get a cosigner; (2) become an authorized user on your parents' or grandparents' card; (3) use a prepaid card; or (4) a debit card.

- **No mercy if you are late**. If you miss payments and carry huge balances these new protections don't help much. Pay the minimum on time. Use automatic bill pay to pay the minimum if you are prone to cutting it close each month and then pay the full balance online if you can swing it. But remember, your goal is to pay these cards in full each month. Then your interest rate is zero. There are no late fees or penalties and you can begin to build wealth elsewhere. Remember, you want to build *your* wealth, not the credit card company's.

- **Foreign currency fees**. There are no restrictions on the fees credit card companies charge you to use your credit card overseas and convert your borrowed dollar into a borrowed Euro, pound, or yen. Already those fees have risen for travelers overseas.

- **Charging for paper statements**. Get ready for this. If you are juggling numerous credit cards and trying to manage them all, you should be following them closely online anyway. Ditch the paper and make a habit of checking your credit card statement online every week or two.

- **Higher base interest rates**. You must have 45 days' notice that your interest rates are rising. The average interest rate for borrowers was 14.67 percent in February,[7] but experts warn that even for good borrowers, interest rates could reach 18 percent as the new rules go into place. Anyone with a poor credit history can expect higher interest rates than that. Remember, if you pay your card off in full each month, your effective interest rate is zero. This should be your goal every month.

- **Out of luck**. Credit counselors say that already people with low income and sketchy credit histories are having their credit lines cut or are even losing access to cards. Banking analyst Meredith Whitney warns that credit card reform will make it "more expensive to be poor."[8] We are in the midst of a huge consumer deleveraging that has just begun: Too much credit is available to too many people, and that bubble is still bursting. It means banks, to protect their profits, may well cut out risky borrowers. New laws mean that banks cannot raise interest rates right away on borrowers who have become late or missed payments, so they may well simply stop lending to customers like this. That forces consumers with low incomes to borrow money from payday lenders and check-cashing storefronts at high interest rates and with high fees.

79.99 Percent APR

A high-interest credit card rolled out on a trial basis by Premier Bankcard in late 2009.

There is nothing in the new consumer protection laws to prevent credit card issuers from charging unbelievably high interest rates. One credit card issuer in late 2009 rolled out a trial card for people with bad credit or no credit with an APR that could reach 79.9 percent! Certainly anyone with a credit card balance gasped at the possibility of paying such high interest. There's an interesting twist in this seemingly outrageous story, however. Customers were lining up to get their hands on this card. Why? Because people with rotten credit histories were being shut out of owning a credit card. Big lenders simply would not take a risk and loan money to someone who has filed for personal bankruptcy or has $50,000 on 10 cards they are not making payments on.

This trial card was a limited test to see if there was a market for people with bad credit or no credit, who would pay their fees upfront for the chance to rebuild their credit history. To most people, it sounds like highway robbery, but for thousands of people, it's the only way they will ever get a credit card.

Here's how these high-interest cards work.

The credit limit is very low—only $300. The idea is for the cardholder to make modest purchases each month and slowly prove that they are credit-worthy. They begin to build a history with the credit bureaus of paying their bills on time. As the company pointed out, this card was meant for people to pay off each month in full. Then there is zero percent interest. But since this is a high-risk group of card users—the highest group out there with long histories of not paying their bills—79 percent was the cost of doing business to provide credit to this risky group.

Viewers called it an outrage, usurious, unfair, and criminal.

To the people lined up to get these cards, there was no other choice. If you have no credit history or a low credit score and you can score one of these cards, only use it properly as a valuable tool to rebuild your credit profile. You must pay on time, religiously, and the 79.99 percent APR is irrelevant—your actual interest rate is zero and each month you are adding a new positive piece of data to your credit report.

DEBT FREE IN THREE

$19,000

How much the typical consumer has access to on all their credit cards combined.[9]

The majority of Americans pays off their credit cards every month and do not carry a balance. If this is you, congratulations. If it is not, it's time to set the goal to be credit card debt free in three years.

Getting a grip on just how much this borrowed money costs is an important first step to becoming smart, not just credit card bubble "rich."

Finally, credit card issuers now have to spell it out, telling you exactly what you must pay each month—to the penny—to get rid of that credit card debt in three years.

Also at the top of your new credit card statement will be a prominent alert and a toll-free number to call for credit counseling if your debt is out of control.

It will mean spending only what you absolutely must, freezing all extraneous spending, and ruthlessly assessing what it is you are buying and why. Paying well over the minimum each month—and trying to achieve two payments each month if possible will eliminate any late fees and loads of interest, helping get you to that goal.

Of course, that takes discipline and attention to the bills. Something a recent financial literacy survey by the National Foundation for Credit Counseling found millions of Americans are not practicing.

RISKY BEHAVIOR

- 67 percent pay for most purchases with a credit or debit card.
- 56 percent do not have a budget.
- 28 percent admit to not paying their bills on time.
- 30 percent have no savings at all.

Source: National Foundation for Credit Counseling, Financial Literacy Survey.

That combination of lots of plastic and lack of planning is a recipe for debt. That same survey found young adults and minorities were at even greater risk for not paying bills on time and not having a budget or any kind of plan at all for making sure that the money lasts as long as the month.

Credit counselor Gail Cunningham, a 24-year veteran of helping people pay off their bills, watched a Wisconsin couple—the Hildebrandts—pay off $100,000 in credit card debt over four years by slashing household expenses and working virtually round the clock to earn more money. (The husband took on another job and even slept in his car between jobs to save gas money!) They paid down debt so aggressively, that they dramatically raised their credit score, and were eventually able to become homeowners.

The Hildebrandts did what most families can't imagine—their entire family life was geared around paying off debt that had taken them more than a decade to accumulate. They overspent for years and decided it was time to pay the piper and treat debt and credit with the respect it deserved. (For them it was a question of morality. Devout Christians, they said bankruptcy was not ethical because they had run up the debts themselves out of foolishness, not out of any kind of tragedy or hardship.) It took them four years. Most people don't have six-figure credit card debt, so for them, they should strive to be debt free in three years and they won't have to go as far as sleeping in the car. A few simple, smart rules to get started:

- **Figure out how much you need to pay each month**. There are numerous online calculators to help you do this. For example, to pay off one credit card's $5,000 balance at a modest 12 percent interest would take $166.07 a month for 36 months. (Try http://www.bankrate.com/calculators/credit-cards/credit-card-payoff-calculator.aspx.) That same $5,000 on a higher interest card charging 18 percent interest would cost $180.76 each month to pay off in three years. In most cases, make minimum payments on the low-rate cards and pay as much as you can on the higher interest rate cards. It won't feel like it now but it will save you money in the end.
- **Pay your bills on time**. Your debt load only grows with interest. And if you already have a few missed payments and a big balance, chances are your interest rate is as high as they come. Use credit card

payment calculators listed in this chapter to find out how much you need to pay each month to dig out of the debt.

- **If you can't afford it, put it _down_. Don't put it on a credit card**. Before you can begin to pay for the debt you have racked up, you have to cut how much you are adding to the pile. No one has successfully become credit card debt free by keeping the spending standards that got them there in the first place.

- **If you must, switch to cash, a prepaid credit card, or a debit card**. (And make sure that the debit card does not have overdraft protection. You do not want to get slammed by fees.) Owning and responsibly using a credit card is frankly a necessity in American. life. But try, even for one month, to get a sense of what your discretionary spending is, and whether actually handing over cold hard currency makes you think twice about the purchase. It was so easy to overspend on plastic for so many years that people forget what the real value of what they are charging is. If you want to keep track of what you are consuming by using a credit card, fine. Use one credit card for one to three months and closely track online what you are spending your money on. If making a budget is not helping you by now, then cut up the plastic and try going it alone with cash or debit cards until you can control the spending. Link your cards to a money management web site like mint.com to help you keep track of everything.

- **Calculate the cost of your debt**. Pay off a $5,000 credit card balance in three years and you really pay anywhere from $7,000 to $9,000, including interest. Miss some payments and it's worse. Be brutally honest with yourself: When you pay off the balance, you will have paid far more than the value of the goods and services you bought. Was it worth it? Remember that when you go to buy anything on credit.

- **Wake up every morning and pledge to yourself to be "debt free in three."** There are several strategies for paying down credit card debt. The old-school advice was this: Put the cards in a Tupperware bowl of water and put them in the freezer. You will see them there in a block of ice and know that you are chipping away at them, but that it will be a cold day in hell (or the icebox) before you can use them again. That's still helpful advice, but you can't just freeze them up and forget about them anymore. Obviously you have to pay the minimum each month to avoid late fees, but now you could also get the dreaded "inactivity" fee for not using them. Until they are paid off, you might have to actually make a purchase every month on each card or rack up $19 fees. For those of you with multiple cards at multiple interest rates, it means that you can't just forget about these cards. You need a strategy and discipline.

Everyone should keep the lowest-interest rate card available for emergencies. Delete the saved credit card information from Amazon, Target.com, and any of your online profiles. You cannot be tempted to spend $50 here and $75 there in online shopping. Another "three" rule: To be debt free in three years, you need to wait three days before you make your purchases. If you want a consumer good badly enough, wait three days and then go back and buy it. You'd be surprised how a time lag cools your enthusiasm and helps you recognize an impulse purchase versus something that is an investment for your family.

- **Earn rate versus burn rate**: You have to make more money than you spend. It is as simple as that. It's your earn rate (how much you make) versus your burn rate (how much cash you burn). Much like counting calories, it is easier in principle than in practice. You can also think of it as a debt diet. To lose weight, you must exercise more or eat less. To melt away the dollars that have piled up on your financial waistline, you must either eat less (spend less money) or exercise more (find more income). Losing weight and cutting debt really have much in common. The solution to both seems simple, but is harder than it sounds. Both require willpower. And different debt diets work differently for different people.

- **Aim for zero**. When you pay off the balance in full, each month, your interest rate is zero, no matter what the listed APR. That's right. Zero. There is no reason to pay interest rates for the convenience of using plastic. That's the ultimate goal of being debt free in three years on your credit cards.

- **Watch for the danger signs that you are living beyond your means**. When you're digging out of the debt—and especially after— be especially watchful for the behavior that led to the debt in the first place. Again, the diet metaphor: Once you've lost the weight it is easy to have the pounds creep back on. The same is true with your money. It's one of the perils of the wave of debt consolidation in the 1990s and early 2000s. When housing prices were rising, Americans rolled all their debts into one and paid them off with home equity. The underlying behavior that led them to accrue all that debt was never addressed. We "fixed" our credit card problems by borrowing money from somewhere else. It wasn't a true fix. If the money consistently does not last as long as the month, if you are carrying growing credit card balances each month, and if you find that you are juggling bills to make sure that you have enough money in the account, you are living beyond your means.

- **Set up automatic payments online to avoid late fees**.

Once you are living within your means, then paying down debt comes next. And once that debt is paid off, it gives you incredible breathing room to build savings and begin investing, things that can raise your standard of living again.

CARD PAYMENT STRATEGIES

Becoming debt free will take a strategy and discipline in following that strategy. Clinical psychologist Jeff Gardere says that the whole family needs to be involved. "It's not a secret, it's not dirty laundry. You need to know what it feels like to be in debt, how it can hurt you, and how it is not financial freedom," Gardere says. "There are better things to do with your money."

Before you can do something else productive with your money—you've got to pay off the credit card debt. Here's how.

> **Strategy 1—Pay the highest interest rate card first**. You will spend less money in interest payments this way. The difference over three years of paying off credit card debt at 12 percent versus 20 percent is dramatic and can reach into the thousands of dollars. Remember to pay minimum monthly payments on all your other cards and if you have tucked them away, make sure you are not getting any monthly fees.
>
> **Strategy 2—Pay off the card with the lowest balance first**. If you need the psychological boost of cutting back on the number of cards,

this is the way to keep going. For some personality types, I've found it just gives the whole process of digging out of debt at least a small sense of accomplishment. You will pay more in interest if you triage your bills this way and pay the lowest balance card first. But if you need to knock a card off the list for inspiration, by all means, do it.

Strategy 3—Pay off the highest balance credit card first. Here's why. A credit card company may look at a card with a huge credit line and a huge balance and decide you are maxed out and cut the credit line. Now you have lost the availability of credit, and it could hurt your credit score. Work hard to pay that high balance card down to less than 30 percent of the credit line. Do it quickly and it will boost your score, and preserve that availability of credit in case you need it in the future.

In other words, in your quest to get rid of your debt you want to be careful not to inadvertently lose access to credit. Especially if you have no savings built up.

There's another twist on the old-school advice to pay off the card, cut it up, and then close it. Be prepared for your credit score to drop. This shouldn't matter to you if you are not in the market to borrow money. But if you are planning to buy a car or a house in the next six months, you may need to keep those cards open for a little while longer.

CUTTING UP THE CARDS

Emily is a young woman who e-mailed me that she doesn't carry huge balances from month to month but has many cards and various interest rates. She wants to be a homeowner in the next two years, but she has been listening to all our warnings about new creative fees, more stringent requirements for down payments, and credit scores, and wants to get her stack of credit cards in order before she's ready to buy a home. She doesn't want any surprises, and she feels overwhelmed by the purse full of department store cards and credit cards.

> I have a lot of store cards—Saks, Bloomies, Gap, Macys, Banana, Victoria Secret—the list goes on and on I use the Saks, Bloomies, Gap card pretty frequently—I like the store benefits. But I don't really use

the others anymore (Banana, Victoria Secret, I think I had a Nordstrom at one time—but haven't used it in years, so not even sure). Can I get rid of some of those cards? Are they hurting my credit?

Emily thought she was being savvy by opening a store card before a big purchase and getting the instant 20 percent discount. Now she can't even remember how many store cards she has and she's worried about potential inactivity fees. She could make a purchase every month to avoid a fee, but then she would be spending money that she is trying to save.

If Emily closes the cards, does she lose available credit and her credit score drops? Is it worth it to keep the credit available (some of these cards she has had a long time) to make her credit score look better?

First things first: Emily needs to visit www.annualcreditreport.com for her free credit report. She needs to scrutinize it for any mistakes and make a list of all the open credit lines that she has with different stores.

Not surprisingly, credit experts have differing advice for Emily, depending on what she thinks is most important. If she really wants to buy a house and keep the credit score as high as possible, she should keep all the cards open. If Emily really wants to simplify her wallet and remove the temptation of spending money she doesn't have, she should keep the cards with the longest credit histories or biggest credit limit that she actually *uses* and ditch the rest.

Emily, thankfully, is not running up huge balances every month, so her credit utilization ratio is not hurting her credit score. But if she starts closing accounts and losing access to credit lines, even if she doesn't spend anymore her ratio will start to hurt her. She'll need to be mindful of this the closer she gets to potential homeownership.

The fact that Emily sat down, listed the cards, and sought advice on what to do is the first step. FICO's public affairs director, Craig Watts, agrees that she is in a good position. She should get her credit score, check it for errors, and scrutinize all outstanding credit cards and close the cards she is not using. With a two-year horizon to applying for a loan, she has plenty of time to clean up any mistakes on the report and build up a solid—and more simple—credit history.

"You can get a good credit score with a single credit card. You don't need a pocket full of cards and an auto loan and all that. If you've been managing one credit card for 20 years, you are likely to have a really fine credit score," says Watts.

He says that Emily should focus on the card that works best for her life, and get rid of the others. And he says she shouldn't worry too much about which card she has had the longest.

"There is a widely held myth that you lose that history from the credit score and that if you have a really old card in the bottom of your purse you need to keep it open," he says. "That's not true. The FICO score pays attention to both old and new cards on the credit report. That old card will stay on there for 10 years even after you close it. In Emily's case, don't worry about the length of credit."

Emily's smart that she doesn't have the more common problem of numerous credit cards with numerous big balances to go along with them. I am no longer shocked when viewers write in to tell me that their credit card debt is the size of a small mortgage. At least when you are taking out a mortgage, student loan, or car loan, the volume of paperwork gives you pause and clearly indicates that this is a huge financial responsibility. But with credit cards, borrowing money was as simple as using the card. Just remember, it has to be paid back.

DEBT REVOLT

Ann Minch decided she wasn't going to pay it back.

She became an Internet sensation with her moral stand against her credit card company.

After the financial bailouts but before credit card reform became law, many banks raised interest rates on customers like Ann.

When her interest rate went from 12.99 percent to 29 percent on a Bank of America credit card with a $5,900 balance, she looked into a webcam and told the world she would not pay the bill. As a taxpayer she had bailed out the banks, and now she was washing her hands of their "evil" ways. She fired the first salvo in a debtors revolt that shows the depth of the anger against the financial institutions that pushed credit cards and credit on Americans for 30 years, and then began preaching about creditworthiness for the little guy once they almost brought the world economy down.

Ann's rant played 'round the world. More than 350,000 people clicked on her moral stand against the banks and she became, for an Internet moment, the face of the outrage against credit cards.

"There comes a time when a person must be willing to sacrifice in order to take a stand for what's right," she said. "Now this is one of those times and if I'm successful this will be the proverbial first shot fired in the American debtors' revolution against the usury and plunder perpetrated by the banking elite, the Federal Reserve, and the federal government."

She refused to pay the balance until Bank of America lowered her interest rate. She sent a letter to the CEO demanding he watch her by-then viral YouTube rant.

She told us the bank contacted her, told her she had been late on a couple of payments, and tried to negotiate a 16.99% rate with her. She refused.

That interest rate change was not simply an obscure number buried in the fine print. That rate increase meant real money. It would make it decidedly more difficult to pay off the card. Becoming debt free on Ann's $5,900 balance would cost her $8,900 at 29 percent interest, $1,745 more than she would pay in total at 12.99 percent (see Table 5.1). All of this assumes she can religiously pay the right amount each month for three years with no new purchases and no late fees.

Her outrage resonated (or maybe it was the bad PR) and the bank lowered her rate back to the original 12.99 percent.

A bank spokeswoman told us all customers get advance notice of a rate hike and can choose to close the account and pay off the balance at the current rate.

But Ann in her online rant pledged to NOT pay.

Ann beat the bank and while I admire her spunk, I'm afraid she's the exception. It's not practical advice for just anyone with big balances, big anger, and a webcam. Yes, the banks got bailed out for their risky behavior, and the little guy gets stuck with sky-high interest rates and brutal fees—and

Table 5.1   Debt Free in Three Years on $5,900 Balance

| 12.99% | $198.77 a month for 3 years | $7,155.72 total |
| 29% | $247.24 a month for 3 years | $8,900.64 total |

that's even *after* Congress passed laws to clamp down on egregious credit card practices. She's right to take a stand and close her account, but she's responsible for the bill. If you think you are in line for a personal financial bailout, think again. Yes, fight for a lower interest rate. Ask the bank to clearly state why your interest rate is rising. But pay your bills. The only one you're hurting in the end is yourself. And know that if you have been late with two minimum payments, you have given the bank ammunition to raise your rate.

BORING IS BETTER

Bravo. You pay off your cards in full each month. You are never slapped with fees and you walk an extra two blocks or drive an extra mile out of your way to avoid a $3 ATM fee. You have a perfect record and an enviable credit score.

In the world of credit, boring is better.

People with the highest credit scores tend to be the most predictable—they use credit carefully and are impervious to those credit card mailers and neat financial products that lenders try to sell.

"The people who have outrageously high FICO scores are sparingly frugal users of credit and they have terrific scores," says FICO's Craig Watts. They use cash for most purchases and credit for the big ones and pay down their debt quickly.

ROMANS' NUMERAL

712

Median FICO credit score, mostly steady over four years.[10]

Believe it or not, the recession hasn't hammered the median credit score. According to FICO, it's about 712—half of Americans have scores higher than that, half are lower. FICO's Watts explains that there has been "a migration to both extremes." Foreclosures and unpaid bills have pushed many people lower, but many others have responded in the opposite way. They are paying down more debt and using credit more sparingly. For them, their credit scores are rising. "For all those who have fallen off the turnip cart an equal number have hunkered down and are reducing balances on cards and doing all the stuff that comes naturally" in a crisis, Watts says.

Figure 5.1 shows that the greatest number of people—27 percent—already qualify for the best interest rates when borrowing money. Their scores are in the 750 to 799 range, according to FICO. Only 13 percent have the coveted, gold star 800 or higher. FICO's Watts says these are people who rarely use credit—except to make a big purchase—and then pay it down quickly. The best credit scores belong to farmers for example, who use cash for everything except a huge equipment purchase or truck purchase every now and then.

But even if you are an overachiever with perfect credit, it doesn't mean the New Normal won't affect you.

Credit card companies are cutting credit limits, even on people who pay religiously and in full each month.

Or maybe you are so diligent with your budget you put everything you can on your cards and manage your entire spending through them to maximize the miles or the rewards. You might be surprised to know that can hurt your credit score—you look maxed out and living to the edge of your available credit.

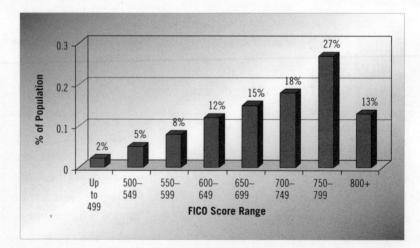

Figure 5.1 National Distribution of FICO Scores

Consider the Type-A planner who manages her budget through her credit card—preschool tuition, clothes, groceries, gas, everything—so that she can accrue miles or rewards. She knows exactly how much she spends every month. At the end of the year, she can see precisely what she has spent per category (vacations, restaurants, grocery stores, education), and she uses a web site like mint.com or personal finance software to manage all her budgets. Sounds smart, right?

Well, she's ready to buy a house and the mortgage banker tells her she doesn't qualify for the best interest rate because her credit utilization ratio is too high. She is gobbling up too much available credit each month. Even though she pays the balance off in full, and she is managing her finances well, she looks like she's living too close to the credit edge.

If she's close to a home purchase or a new car, she might consider making credit card bill payments twice a month, instead of once. Her credit-utilization ratio will look smaller then, and she can time the payments to paycheck days to make the bill-paying even easier. Or she can use a debit card for some purchases. It could make the difference between a credit score in the low 700s to something a little higher that gets a better interest rate.

Of all the credit score mishaps, this counts the least against you, but it makes a difference. According to FICO, someone with a 780 credit score who maxes out a credit card then pays it off would see the score drop to 735 to 755. (You need 760 for the best mortgage rate.) Someone with a 680 score would drop to 650 to 670.

For more comparisons on how different credit missteps hit your credit score, check out www.myfico.com/creditEducation/Questions/Credit_Problem_Comparison.aspx

Bottom line: You want to be that overachiever who looks boring to the credit scorers.

Now for the other extreme.

DEBTOR BEWARE

You're not boring, you're buried.

You can't pay it off. This debt is an immovable mountain. You would sleep in your car between jobs like the Hildebrandts in Wisconsin, except you don't have a job and you are about to lose your car.

For you, you are trying to pay something—anything—to get yourself out from under the debts and you are bombarded with ads promising "your federal credit card bailout."

If it is too good to be true, it probably is. There is no credit card bailout for you: What is there? An explosion of debt-settlement scams trying to get big fees from you to help settle those debts.

Here's how it works.

Debt-settlement companies promise to negotiate a settlement for you so you can pay your creditors less than you owe, if you pay fees up front. They can charge, ultimately, up to 20 percent of what you owe.

The debt-settlement company sets up an account you deposit money in, with the idea that money will be used to pay your negotiated settlement. In reality, it can take six months or longer to fill that account up enough so you can actually pay anything off and in the meantime you are still racking up late fees and interest charges. Not only that, you risk getting hauled into court by your creditors, even as the debt-settlement company sits on your money. Your wages can be garnished and your credit score will take a big hit if you aren't paying the bills.

Some companies are legit, others never even bother to contact your creditors.

The Better Business Bureau warns consumers against unscrupulous debt-settlement companies, and the Government Accountability Office says its undercover investigation of these companies found scams galore—fraudulent, deceptive, and abusive practices that pose a serious risk to consumers.

The industry is growing fast, and attempts to regulate it are just starting now. Senators Chuck Schumer and Claire McCaskill have introduced legislation to regulate this industry. The FTC has waged 20 lawsuits over the past seven years against scammers disguising themselves as nonprofit credit counseling firms, debt settlement services, and debt negotiators.

There are legitimate debt-settlement companies. But for two reasons, you should be wary.

1. Many firms are making promises that are simply too good to be true.
2. You can do it more cheaply on your own.

DECEPTIVE DEBT RELIEF WARNING SIGNS

- High upfront fees.
- Promises your debt can be cut in half.
- It's fast, easy, painless!

Working with a debt-settlement company will cost you potentially hundreds of dollars in fees. Fifteen percent of your total debt is their typical fee—20 percent if they reach a settlement. And legitimate credit counselors and the credit card companies say you won't do any better with an agency than if you do it yourself.

Gail Cunningham, vice president of public relations at the National Foundation for Credit Counseling, says most people assume it is easier to hand over their problems to a debt-settlement company than do it themselves. She says the people seeking debt-settlement relief help through her office, on average, have incomes of $43,000 and unsecured debt of $26,000.[11] They have seven maxed-out credit cards, and many consumers assume that they can't handle all the paperwork and calls themselves.

"They think, 'Oh, I can't tell my story seven times over' and they are overwhelmed in the debt," says Cunningham. But paying a debt-settlement company could top $4,500. It's worth the time and effort for that much money. "There is the real money cost and the cost to your credit report and score," she says. Worse, some of these firms are not even contacting your lenders much less paying the settlement in the end.

It's going to be hard work, but you racked up all that debt, now you must think of it as a small part-time job to dig out of it.

"What really bugs me here is that these companies are preying on people who really want to pay their bills, to do the morally right thing," Cunningham says. While you are negotiating with the debt-settlement firm, your bills are left unpaid and you are increasing your balances owed with late fees and penalties. They can even send you to a collection agency well before the debt-rescue company gets you any help, stopping the whole process in its tracks.

- **Go directly to your credit card issuer**. "That issuer knows more about your financial status than you do, so don't think this is going to be a newsflash to them. They have seen that you have had some financial hiccups, you lost a job, you're limping along, you borrowed money to pay off another debt . . . they know what's going on. They know if you are a candidate for a settlement and they are the only ones who can arrange a settlement," Cunningham says.

  If the credit or begins to negotiate, understand that they will try to get the most they can from you. Do your homework. What are your baseline living expenses? That's mortgage or rent, plus car payments and insurance, childcare, prescriptions, and food. Tell the credit card issuer above and beyond those baseline living expenses you can begin to pay a portion of your debt.

  Cunningham says be frank with the credit card company and ask them, "Tell me what my settlement options are."

- **Pay your bills**. You have a better chance if you have legitimately tried to keep up with your bills. Your credit card issuer is much more likely to sue you if you have not been paying your bills. If they can see that you have made an effort, they know that you will more likely hold up your end of the deal.

  For more information on how to settle your debts on your own, check DebtAdvice.org.

- **Taxes**. If you successfully dodge the bill collector by getting the credit card company to settle part of your balance, your bill problems haven't disappeared just yet. If your credit card company or other creditor settles your debt, any forgiven debt over $600 will be reported to the IRS and will be treated as income.

  When you are assembling your documents the next spring for taxes, you should be ready for form 1099-c to come in the mail from the IRS. Don't let it be a surprise. When you are in the process of settling with your creditor, be clear up front whether you will have to pay taxes on the forgiven debt. Too many times, cash-strapped consumers think they have wiped away a chunk of their debt forever, only to get in trouble again nine months later when the tax form arrives in the mail showing the forgiven debt as income they must pay taxes on.

There's a credit score hit, too. A credit card settlement will show up on your credit history and knock your credit score down 45 to 125 points.[12]

The Federal Trade Commission (FTC) also warns about ads promising to help you wipe away your debts, fix your problems and keep your property. The Federal Trade Commission warns that often these are enticements that will cost you money and land you in bankruptcy.

The FTC says be wary of this language:

- Consolidate your bills into one monthly payment without borrowing.
- STOP credit harassment, foreclosures, repossessions, tax levies, and garnishments.
- Keep Your Property.
- Wipe out your debts! Consolidate your bills! How? By using the protection and assistance provided by federal law. For once, let the law work for you!

Often, these ads appear to be offering debt relief but are pushing bankruptcy, which should be the last resort for anyone with debt problems. It's hardly relief—it stays on your credit record for up to 10 years and makes it harder if not impossible to buy or sometimes even just rent a home, get insurance, borrow money, get a credit card.

And if you have bad credit or no credit, be wary of any offer that "guarantees" you access to credit before you even apply.

THE PAYOFF

Credit cards are an American way of life.

Most of you are paying your cards on time. Millions, though, find themselves overwhelmed by their relationship with their cards. To find out if your cards are a convenience or a crutch, ask yourself these questions:

- How long would it take me to pay off my balances?
- Is it possible to be credit card debt free in three years, and what would I need to pay every month on the cards to do that?
- Is the interest I am paying to carry a balance worth it?

And if you are worried about your credit score, spare the expensive credit-monitoring services and the agonizing about a number over which you have limited control.

Clear up any mistakes on your credit report by checking for free at www .annualcreditreport.com. Pay down your debt and pay your bills on time. The longer you do this, the higher your score. And remember, unless you are in the market to buy a car or a house or to otherwise borrow money, the credit score shouldn't matter to you anyway.

The only bill more important than the credit card bill is the mortgage payment. Read on for the pulse of the housing market, and the value of your biggest asset, your home.

CHAPTER 6

Home Sweet Home

24 Percent

Nearly one in four home loans is "underwater," meaning that the homeowner owes more to the bank than the home is even worth.[1]

Your home is likely your biggest asset and your biggest expense. Millions of Americans see buying a house as the pinnacle of financial responsibility, the culmination of the American Dream, and full admission into the economy.

But the relentless quest for record homeownership, propped up by the government and aided by record low interest rates, has come at a terrible cost. Millions of people who thought they were attaining the dream of homeownership have instead found themselves in the nightmare of a spreading foreclosure crisis.

More people this year will receive a foreclosure notice in the mail than will buy their first home.

In the wreckage of the housing market, there will be once-in-a-lifetime opportunities for some who are finding affordable homes for the first time in their lives. For others it will take careful planning to keep their homes and still plan and save for the future.

In this chapter we explore a housing bubble that is still popping, and what it means for your rent, your mortgage payment, and your chance to buy a first home. Some are holding on to a house that is eating up ever more of their pay. Should they become renters? Many first-time buyers are scared to jump because they are worried about the jobs market. But are historically low interest rates about to end and with it a golden opportunity? Contractors are hungry, but is it the right time for a high-end kitchen and bath remodel? What investments in your home pay off the most and what renovations are just throwing your money away? In the bubble, none of these questions mattered. Home prices rose so quickly and so indiscriminately, it didn't take a genius to make money. Today, you have to be smarter than ever to make the right moves regarding what is likely your largest expense, so homeownership becomes a privilege again and not a burden.

First, here's where things stand.

Home values are down 27 percent over the past three years, according to Fiserv, a division of Moody's Economy.com. Other gauges show home prices, on average, down 40 percent or worse in some places. So, even if you never took out an exotic home loan, even if you have your job and are faithfully making mortgage payments, you have lost value and opportunity. Why opportunity? If you are underwater and owe the bank thousands more than the home is worth, it is harder to move for a new job or a promotion. Depending on where you live, chances are you have neighbors whose home is worth far less than what they are paying every month. Table 6.1 shows just how underwater some of the worst states are—led by Nevada where 70 percent of all homes are worth less than the mortgage. If your neighbors

Table 6.1   Negative Equity aka "Underwater"

State	% of loans underwater
Nevada	70
Arizona	51
Florida	48
Michigan	39
California	35

Source: CoreLogic.

are underwater, they are more likely to face foreclosure. If they foreclose, your home value goes down, too.

Underwater means that you can't sell your home without writing a big check to the bank, and most people after the stock market crash of 2008 don't have tens of thousands of dollars sitting around to cover the value they've lost in the house to get out from under it. Underwater also means that your bank is reeling in the low-interest home equity line of credit many homeowners enjoyed in the 1990s and early 2000s. For some, that was the back-up plan to pay for college. For many others, that money has already been spent and now must be paid back even though the house is worth less.

The assumption has always been that most homeowners who are underwater will ride it out. But this time is different. Some homeowners are just walking away, turning the keys over to the bank, or, in some areas, leaving the home altogether before the foreclosure process begins and renting elsewhere while they still have good enough credit to rent a decent apartment. Yes, a foreclosure destroys your credit score and hurts your ability to get a new credit card, to rent an apartment, and to borrow money. A foreclosure is financially and personally devastating.

Even if you work out loan forgiveness with the bank, you could end up owing taxes on that forgiven loan. So even after the house is foreclosed, the financial fallout is immense.

Yet there is the creeping feeling that because the banks were irresponsible in their lending and were bailed out, homeowners bear less responsibility when they walk away.

Credit counselor Gail Cunningham says never in her 24-year career has she seen a situation where people are actively considering walking away from their most important financial contract.

"People once did anything to keep their homes, it was a flag of honor they waved. Becoming a homeowner was the American Dream . . . and a great wealth-building tool," she says.

But if the banks were such bad actors, why are battered homeowners held to a higher standard?

"Corporate America should not be our model," Cunningham says. "We're in trouble if we model our personal behavior on them."

One in 10 people with a mortgage is behind on their payments, according to the Mortgage Bankers Association. Of those, 12 percent are so-called "strategic defaults"—people who can afford to pay, but because the value of the home has fallen so much they have decided to live in the house for free and then walk away when the bank forecloses. For these people, a house was simply a gamble that they lost.

But for millions more, they aren't paying the mortgage because they don't have the money. Cunningham says that the stresses for many families are glaring—a real challenge for a country that for years valued paying the mortgage above all else. "Fast forward to today and we see people paying their credit card bills before their mortgage."

Giving credit cards priority over the mortgage shows severe financial stress. It means these customers have significant cash-flow problems and essentially can't afford the lives they lead. It also bodes ill for the health of the housing market going forward, suggesting that millions of Americans are on the verge of default, if not defaulted already. A study by data and credit analysis TransUnion finds troubling new patterns of behavior that go against conventional wisdom. Table 6.2 shows that 6.6 percent of consumers are late on their mortgage bill, but at the same time current on their credit cards, up sharply over the past two years. The bottom line—you can't put gas in the car with a mortgage. So people are making sure they have the use of their credit cards and are keeping those up-to-date first.

Of course, on top of being a huge danger sign, paying the mortgage late means incurring a late fee.

Cunningham's advice if you are routinely paying a late fee so you can juggle the big monthly bills: "I would change around my due dates and create a cash-flow chart," to better balance the monthly bills. She says that you should call your creditors and ask to have your mortgage due date or credit

Table 6.2   Late on Mortgage but Current on Credit Cards

6.6%	Q3 2009
6.3%	Q2 2009
4.9%	Q3 2008

Source: TransUnion survey February 2010.

card due date changed to balance them out better with your paychecks. You might have a one-time payment of some extra interest, but it's worth it to avoid those late fees and be current in both the mortgage and the credit cards. But bottom line, if this is you—triaging these important bills every month and routinely paying credit card bills before the mortgage, it means you can't afford your life. Cunningham reiterates her cardinal rule: Spend less, earn more, or both.

Financial adviser Ryan Mack, president of Optimum Capital Management, tells clients to keep their housing costs below 35 percent of their gross income. You will hear a variety of advice on this topic. Table 6.3 outlines housing cost rules of thumb. Some money managers say the smart homeowner or renter limits all their housing expenses to 28 percent of their take-home paycheck. Others, like Mack, use 35 percent of their gross income. The government's own housing rescue programs modify loans so that total housing expenses (principal, interest, taxes, insurance and homeowners association or condo fees) are 31 percent of gross monthly pay. Take your pick, but remember to include the monthly payment, taxes, utilities, and to be safe, some people even put all phone and Internet service in this category, too. In high-tax states in the Northeast and high-home value cities on both coasts there is the temptation to ignore these rules. Do so at your own peril. One six-figure job loss or a couple of foreclosures in a "nice" neighborhood will be devastating to someone who's paying well over 40 percent of their income on their housing expenses.

For example, there is no way Kevin Huhn's housing expenses can fit into any of those rules of thumb. He makes $3,500 a month living in Denver working two jobs, and his monthly mortgage bill is $2,200 a month. "You do the math on that," Huhn says. "It just doesn't add up." The mortgage alone is almost 63 percent of his take-home pay. A former deputy sports editor at the *Rocky Mountain News*, making $80,000 "living in a nice house in

Table 6.3   Housing Cost Rules

Conservative	25%–28% of take-home pay
Most financial planners	33%–35% of gross pay
Government programs	31% of gross pay

a nice part of town," he went on unemployment when the paper folded. He was out of work from February 2009 to October 2009, when he took a job administering drug and alcohol tests to felons. That job gives him full health benefits (an incredibly smart move by Kevin) and coupled with a freelance editing job, he brings in $40,000 a year—half what he made two years ago.

"I can't even come close to paying the bills," he says, matter-of-factly. He religiously paid his mortgage (essentially diverting his unemployment check to the bank) and begged his bank to work with him. No response, he says, until he was late on a payment in February 2010 and did not send in the March payment.

"My family values are that you pay your debts," he says. He bought the home in 1998 with a plain-vanilla mortgage. He refinanced in the low 5-percent range a few years ago and rolled in his credit card debt. He says because he already refinanced at a historically low rate, he doesn't qualify for government relief programs. He put his house on the market in Denver for $419,900. "If I get $410,000 then everyone gets paid and I walk away with about $2,000 in my pocket. If that doesn't happen. . . ."

A former landlord has offered him a beautifully rehabbed apartment to rent for $600 a month. He's moving into it, one way or the other.

"I have no ethical problems walking away," he says. "I could do that with a clear conscience even though my dad will roll over in his grave that I left a debt like that. But that's the way this country is going right now. In my mind it's a strategic default—a business decision. It's just a business decision."

POP!

How did it come to this?

It once was standard to pay 20 to 25 percent down for a home. The rule of thumb was that housing costs should be more than a third of your income. More conservative buyers budgeted no more than a quarter of their income for their housing expenses. The only mortgage available was a 30-year fixed-rate loan. And the mortgage you wrote sat in the bank, with the banker who wrote it, for the course of the loan.

The only big decision you had to make after you took the loan was whether to pay a 13th mortgage payment every year so you could pay it off earlier. Then things got really complicated.

The financial market innovation of the 1980s and 1990s meant that loans were packaged and sold to investors. As home prices rose, Wall Street banks were hungry for more loans to package in ever more exotic investment vehicles. Your own 30-year fixed-rate loan, or the seven-year adjustable rate mortgage, was sliced up and sold in little pieces all over the world. We all know what happened next. The typical U.S. home loan became ever more complex. Mortgage giants invented new types of loans one after the other: The interest-only loan, the negative amortization loan, numerous adjustable rate loans with low teaser interest rates, even the dreaded NINJA loan. NINJA—*No Income, No Job, No Assets*, no problem.

At the same time we started building bigger homes, and moving farther and farther away from our jobs. We spent less time at home but at the same time, built more garages than we had drivers in the household and bought more cars than people to drive them. We added media rooms, and craft rooms, and extra bedrooms. We popularized the "great room" but still kept the family room and the living room and a finished basement and what was the result? The size of the average U.S. home jumped 49 percent in a generation. With it came higher heating bills, higher credit card bills to fill this house with stuff, and longer commutes. It also meant that it took two incomes to afford the payments. In 1970, Census data show that a single-family home was 1,525 square feet. By the peak of the bubble, new homes were a whopping 2,277 square feet. This, indeed, was the late twentieth- and early twenty-first-century middle class—an economic mirage housed in a home larger than families actually needed, paid for with credit and a bet that it could all go on endlessly.

With home prices rising, these risky products that helped the middle class supersize their lives were sure bets. When home prices began to fall, it all came unglued.

The entire real estate market is now adjusting. Millions of families are trying to stay in homes that are gobbling up a huge portion of their income. Their teaser rate loan has reset, and suddenly the house payment has leaped out of their reach. Fancy financial products masked the true cost of homeownership. Next came a jobs crisis that threw millions more into the more traditional path of foreclosure—loss of income.

Numerous government programs have failed to stem the problem because there are simply too many people who will never be able to afford the homes they are in.

We'll be lucky if half of the housing crisis is behind us. As mortgage servicers sort out those who have a chance of affording payments and staying in their home from those who are financially too far gone, the foreclosure docket will remain chock full.

322 per Hour

ROMANS'
NUMERAL

R ate of new foreclosure notices in 2009.[2]

One in every 45 homes received at least one foreclosure filing in 2009, up 21 percent from 2008 and double 2007.

Most people who are underwater on their loans have income and savings and will stay in their homes for all the right reasons—their jobs, the neighborhoods, the schools, and convenience. Others have sucked the equity out of their home and spent it, or their home costs are rising because of teaser loans, or, like Kevin in Denver, they've lost a job and *can't* stay. They are either fighting the foreclosure process or tempted to walk away. Over the next 18 months, as this continues, it will mean a real estate market still under stress.

The number of foreclosures promises to remain stubbornly high as prime borrowers join the ranks of distressed homeowners over the next two years. Poor borrowers with bad credit were the first wave of foreclosures. Then the middle class was drowning in underwater loans. Now it's the "millionaires-on-paper." Today, the fastest growing group that is falling behind on loans is homeowners with big mortgages. According to real estate tracker CoreLogic, the default rate on million dollar plus mortgages *tripled* from 2008 to 2009, to an astonishing 12 percent. That's twice the rate for mortgages worth $250,000 or less.

It's why comfortable, even affluent borrowers are having more trouble securing a jumbo home loan these days. It was too easy to do it in the bubble and too many of those paper millionaires either lost a big job or were in over their heads to begin with. An affluent borrower today—like everyone else—should plan on at least 20 percent down and a very good credit score. The bigger the property, the richer the buyer, the more the bank might demand. You might even hear of loan-to-value ratios of 60 or 50 percent. That means you put 40 or 50 percent down. (Think of it: On a million-dollar house, that's up to $500,000 down!)

AFFORDABILITY

There is opportunity. Three years of plunging home prices and dirt-cheap mortgage rates means for some homebuyers, homes have never been more affordable. Throw in free government money of up to $8,000 for anyone who has not moved in the past few years, and thousands of families shut out during the bubble found value for the first time in more than a decade.

From the peak in 2006 and 2007, home prices have tanked, worse in some places than others. The median price of a new home sold today is $198,400,[3] down $49,500 from 2007.

Sunbelt speculative bubbles like Fort Myers-Cape Coral, Florida, Miami, and Las Vegas have seen a third to a half of home values evaporate (see Table 6.4). Home prices in Phoenix lost 51 percent in three brutal years. Its foreclosure crisis is now an epidemic. Nevada, Florida, California, and Arizona accounted for all top 20 foreclosure-blighted cities in 2009, according to RealtyTrac, an online marketer of foreclosed homes. In Nevada, what happens in Vegas gets a foreclosure notice in Vegas. A whopping 12 percent of housing units in the city received a foreclosure notice in 2009. That's five times the national average. Cape Coral-Fort Myers, Florida, is close behind. Merced, California, and Phoenix, Arizona, round out the list of foreclosure leaders.

Fiserv forecasts even more price pressure for those markets into 2011 simply because of the volume of foreclosures. The same firm forecasts home prices nationwide down another 6 percent through autumn 2011.

These cities were the canaries in the coalmine for the housing crisis. Now foreclosures are spreading to other regions and to borrowers with good credit histories. Provo, Utah; Rockford, Illinois; Fayetteville, Arkansas, and many others now show higher than average foreclosure rates. The problem

Table 6.4   Worst Home Price Declines

California	Q3 2006–Q3 2009
Bakersfield, CA	−55%
Merced, CA	−72%
Salinas, CA	−65%
Stockton, CA	−60%
Florida	**Q3 2006–Q3 2009**
Cape Coral-Fort Myers	−59%
Miami	−48%
Punta Gorda	−55%
Port St. Lucie	−53%
Nevada	**Q3 2006–Q3 2009**
Carson City	−29%
Las Vegas	−56%
Reno-Sparks	−36%

Source: Home price forecasts February 2010, Fiserv.

now is job loss, not wild speculation with borrowed money that drove the Sun Belt debacles.

Clearly, these price declines came after years of unrealistic price appreciation. In some parts of the country frankly even a 50 percent collapse in home prices leaves the house out of the reach of average Americans, especially if they don't have a job. The number one component now for a recovery in home prices is a recovery in the jobs market. If jobs growth is slow, so, too, will the housing market be slow.

That said, for the first time in a long time, there are opportunities for the brave, the solvent, and the bold. If you have a job, and you have savings, and you are confident in your future, and approach a home as a place to live and not a place in which to invest, this is a perfect time to buy. Why? Record low mortgage rates, lower home prices, and a larger availability of homes. Opportunities, no matter where they are, are for people with good credit, money to put down, and a steady income. Come to the table with a retro approach to buying a home. If you are a two-income family, don't stretch for a home that will take both your incomes to support. Before you buy that house, calculate how long you could pay the mortgage if one of your incomes vanishes. Live below your means and buy a home below your means. Do not let the mortgage broker or the real estate broker push you into a higher price bracket than you can afford. Since the frothy frenzy of the early 2000s is over, that means you should buy a home with solid resale value because the field of solvent buyers is much smaller today than it was even three or five years ago.

What are the most important factors—besides price—to consider when buying a home in a down market? Location, location, location.

- ❑ Quality of the local schools.
- ❑ Length of commute.
- ❑ Property taxes.
- ❑ The size of the property.
- ❑ Proximity to grocery stores, your place of worship, and shopping.

Subzero refrigerator, Viking stove, multiple Jacuzzi tubs are decidedly not on this list. More on this later in Table 6.14. (Hint: You get the least return on your investment for these things.) Census records show migration from the exurbs back into the nearer suburbs to be closer to jobs. Smart homebuyers purchase the smallest or oldest or most tired house in the nicest neighborhood or on the biggest lot, never the nicest house in a less desirable neighborhood. (The former has the best chance of price appreciation, the latter does not.) Just as your grandparents always said, you make your money on a home the day you buy it, not the day you sell it. Old rules, old advice, all thrown out during the bubble are back today.

For buyers, this steep recession in home prices (depression in some places) means three-quarters of all homes are now considered "affordable," according to data from the National Association of Home Builders and Wells Fargo. What makes it affordable? If a family making the metro area's median income spends no more than 28 percent of take-home pay on all its housing costs. No surprise, as Table 6.5 illustrates, in general, the middle part of the country boasts much better affordability than either of the coasts.

Table 6.5   Major Metro Areas' Affordability

Most Affordable	Least Affordable
Indianapolis	New York
Detroit	San Francisco
Dayton, OH	Honolulu
Youngstown, OH	Santa Ana, CA
Akron, OH	Los Angeles

Source: NAHB and Wells Fargo quarterly survey.

Rust Belt cities tend to dominate this list, but that doesn't mean you can move there and get a job the next day. Often the most affordable place offers the least job opportunity for outsiders. The reality for most of us is that we deal with the affordability of our own region and you can count on paying more for your housing needs on both coasts than in much of the rest of the country. It's bittersweet reviewing the statistics on home affordability. Yes, finally millions of properties are within reach after the bubble. But more than 11 million Americans today are paying their bills with unemployment checks and for them, housing affordability is meaningless. There are more Americans on food stamps than in college today in this country. It's an upside-down world right now and as long as this is the case, the overall housing market could remain under pressure.

For smart investors, yes, there are opportunities in foreclosures and in distressed real estate markets. (More than a few economists have told me they personally are eyeing for retirement Miami condos or Arizona golf course casitas that have plunged in value.) Average Janes and Joes tried the speculation game in the bubble and either made money and walked away, or made money, then doubled down and got burned. In the New Normal, housing is a domicile, not a speculative investment. There may be terrific opportunities for landlords who want to buy properties on the cheap and rent to the legion of foreclosed-upon former homeowners. If that's your business, fine. But if you are a teacher, a police officer, a writer, a lawyer, a software engineer, or a truck driver, leave the real estate game to the players and focus on what you can do best and do your best at the job you have. Buying foreclosed properties is full of pitfalls and quite time-consuming.

The easy money in real estate is over. It was finished four years ago. The opportunities for the rest of us are for the solvent and the bold who want that perfect little place in Tucson to retire in 15 years from now, they can enjoy it in the interim, and they've watched the price fall 40 percent. For them, the advice is different. Pounce. Buy what you know and what you can afford.

30 Years Old

ROMANS'
NUMERAL

Median age of a first-time homebuyer in 2008 and 2009.[4]

First-time homebuyers—who plan to live in and commute from their residences—make up just less than half of home sales right now. According to Walter Molony at the National Association of Realtors, in 2009 some 2 million first-time homebuyers qualified for the tax credit that was part of the economic stimulus plan. For 2010, he estimates another 900,000 will buy their first homes. But there is some concern among real estate watchers that the tax credits have attracted the qualified buyers and cleared out the quality, reasonably priced starter home stock. Tax credits only go so far when almost 10 percent of the population is unemployed. And those tax credits are temporary.

No doubt all real estate—like politics—is local. In a sea of cities facing stagnant to lower home prices through 2011, as forecast by Fiserv, there are a few metro areas where higher home prices are forecast. Some examples are shown in Tables 6.6 through 6.12.

Table 6.6   San Francisco

Median home price	$675,000
Lost value since 2006	25.7%
Gain forecast through 2011	4.8%
Jobless rate	10.1%

Source: Fiserv, BLS December 2009 jobless rate.

Table 6.7   Pittsburgh

Median home price	$122,000
Lost value since 2006	0.8%
Gain forecast through 2011	2.2%
Jobless rate	7.8%

Source: Fiserv, BLS December 2009 jobless rate.

Table 6.8   Rochester

Median home price	$119,000
Lost value since 2006	5.2%
Gain forecast through 2011	2.2%
Jobless rate	8.0%

Source: Fiserv, BLS December 2009 jobless rate.

Table 6.9   Memphis, TN

Median home price	$108,000
Lost value since 2006	19.9%
Gain forecast through 2011	1.0%
Jobless rate	10.3%

Source: Fiserv, BLS December 2009 jobless rate.

Table 6.10   Birmingham, AL

Median home price	$152,000
Lost value since 2006	6.0%
Gain forecast through 2011	0.4%
Jobless rate	9.8%

Source: Fiserv, BLS December 2009 jobless rate.

Table 6.11   Oakland, CA

Median home price	$318,000
Lost value since 2006	48.1%
Gain forecast through 2011	0.4%
Jobless rate	10.1%

Source: Fiserv, BLS December 2009 jobless rate.

Table 6.12   Seattle

Median home price	$371,000
Lost value since 2006	15.2%
Gain forecast through 2011	3.8%
Jobless rate	9.1%

Source: Fiserv, BLS December 2009 jobless rate.

MORTGAGE RATE VERSUS HOME PRICE

If lower home prices, or stagnant at best, is what we are in for, shouldn't we just hold out for better prices in another year or two? Not so fast. A word here on holding out for lower prices ahead—*Beware* of rising mortgage rates and higher monthly payments.

If interest rates rise, as many economists expect, mortgage rates will rise, too. The Fed this spring stopped repurchasing mortgage-backed securities, a measure that initially was an emergency move to help the market during the crisis. Now as the Fed begins withdrawing support in the Treasury market it could eventually mean higher interest rates. Further, the U.S. government is borrowing record amounts of money and at the same time running huge fiscal deficits. (Essentially, it is borrowing money to spend money it doesn't have.) Many market watchers think it is inevitable that the investors and countries who loan the United States all that money will eventually demand higher interest rates in exchange for the risks they are taking. Rising interest rates make it more expensive for you and me to borrow money, too.

So far, this hasn't happened. The rate on the 30-year fixed mortgage was a record low 4.58% at the end of the first half of 2010. But many think higher rates are coming.

It doesn't take much for higher mortgage rates to negate any advantage of lower home prices. You can buy a house for a little less, if the interest rates rise, the house will cost you *more* over the course of the loan. Wait too long and those lower home prices will cost you more.

Consider this: You have a down payment set aside, a 720 or higher credit score, and you're ready to buy. You find the right home for, say, $177,500, about the median existing home price in the United States last year.

If you buy it now, for argument's sake, let's say the mortgage rate on this home is 5 percent. Over the course of that 30-year loan, this home will cost you almost $310,000 when you add in interest.

Examine Table 6.13. Here's what happens if you decide to wait and buy that home for $19,000 less—you nab it months later for just under $158,000 instead of $177,500. Your down payment will be less, that's good. But interest rates have risen over that period to 6.5 percent. Your monthly payment will be higher and over the course of the loan, the lower-priced house will actually cost you more.

Like everything in real estate, there are plenty of variables: Can you pay the mortgage off early? Will interest rates go down later so you can refinance the home? Will home prices fall substantially and outstrip the effect of rising interest rates? Also, you get to deduct the interest on the loan on your taxes. Consider all these variables carefully when weighing mortgage rates versus home price.

Bottom line, if you can afford the house, rates are low, and it is the house you want in the neighborhood you want, it doesn't pay to wait.

Table 6.13   Does It Pay to Wait for Lower Prices?

Mortgage Rate (%)	Home Price ($)	Down Payment ($)	Monthly Payment ($)	Total Home Cost ($)
5	177,500.00	35,500.00	762.29	309,923.21
5.75	167,737.50	33,547.50	783.10	315,462.21
6.5	157,975.00	31,595.00	798.81	319,165.72

Source: Bankrate.com mortgage calculator.

Greg McBride, senior financial analyst at Bankrate.com, says mortgage rates could rise to 6 percent by the end of 2011, but cautions that higher mortgage rates won't be the biggest impediment to buying a home. He believes the main hurdle for homeowners will be a higher down payment requirement—at least 20 percent down to get the best terms on a loan. He says that if you think you can't afford a house at 6 percent mortgage rates, you shouldn't be buying a house. You should be saving money to get yourself in a position to buy later.

Another rule of thumb that might not work right now for homeowners—the long-held smart advice to make 13 mortgage payments a year to finish the loan earlier.

It was wise—and worked—when the mortgage rate and the cost to borrow money for a long period of time were higher. But your home loan interest rate, if it is fixed, is probably still low, for now. For some homeowners, it no longer makes sense to make the extra mortgage payment every year. If you have high-interest credit card debt, you should plow that extra payment into paying off your cards. And if you are worried about losing your job or have lost your job, obviously, that extra payment should not go *to* the bank but stay safely *in* the bank in case you need it to live on.

GETTING A LOAN

It was too easy to get a home loan for too long and now it will be too hard for a while. That's the nature of the cycle.

The two most important ingredients today are money in the bank and your credit score.

You need money in the bank for a 20 percent down payment. You need more money in the bank to cover up to six months of mortgage, insurance, and property taxes. (Some loan officers are insisting on this, especially in high-tax states. Be prepared for your local utility company to demand six months of heating expenses paid up front, too.) Lower down payments come with FHA-backed loans (often 3½ to 5 percent down) and those loan limits are much smaller.

Once you have the cash on hand, then you need good credit.

It's truly awful that Americans have become beholden to their credit scores—that this number is vitally more important in financial decisions than a social security number or annual income! It's not fair, but it is what it is. Often, the formula for the credit score can seem mysterious. There are lots of great tools to follow for strategies on how to manage the score ahead of a home purchase.

Bankrate.com's McBride says it is imperative to review the reports from the three credit bureaus, free from www.annualcreditreport.com. "Leave yourself some time to correct any errors," he advises.

Six months ahead of a home purchase, pore over your credit reports for any mistakes. Take special care not to close out any large credit limit credit cards in the year or so before a home purchase. This can knock your score down. Make sure that you have all your bank documents showing that you have money in the bank. The lower the credit score, the higher the interest rate and the more money you will have to put down.

Get prequalified for a mortgage. To do that you will need to have all your financial documents together: paystubs, tax returns, account statements, and a breakdown of debts and assets.

If you are trying to buy a home in the foreclosure process, consider getting prequalified from the bank that owns the home. It might streamline the process and put you slightly ahead of other bidders.

For all potential homebuyers, "Be careful where you step in terms of your credit score. Don't close out any cards whether you use them or not, pay down your credit card debt, aim to keep the balance below 10 percent of your available credit," McBride says. Anything above 30 percent will hurt your credit score. In other words, if your available credit on all your cards is $30,000, make sure that you are not carrying a combined balance of more than $3,000.

Bottom line: The days of buying a house with no money saved are long gone. Getting ready to buy? "There is no substitute for cash in the bank," McBride says.

And for God's sake, pay your credit card bills on time. Even one late payment can knock your credit score by as much as 110 points.[5] If you can't pay your routine bills on time, no way will a mortgage lender think that you can pay your mortgage on time. Why are you late? Examine why and fix it. The banks will be merciless on this point.

Assuming that your credit score is solid and you have a good payment history on your other bills, make sure to get the loan that is right for you.

In the bubble, the so-called experts said the 30-year fixed-rate mortgage was obsolete. It turns out that old dinosaur was the safest instrument to be in when the housing market crashed. Real estate agents will tell you that the average person lives in their home seven years, so a shorter-term adjustable rate mortgage will do. (And indeed, some smart homebuyers are finding their seven-year ARMS are resetting to *lower* interest rates! Not all of these products were toxic.) But interest rates could rise, and Americans are moving less today than any time since World War II, meaning that there are fewer potential buyers when you need to sell. Safe and steady wins the race. If rates are rising and the economy stays stagnant, boring is better.

Part of getting the right loan for you is getting the right size loan for you. I have long worried that even the most respected online "how much house can I afford" calculators are too optimistic. It's impossible to factor into those equations the malaise in the housing market or the unease in the jobs market. Go safe and smart and borrow less than the calculators recommend.

THE FANCY KITCHEN DREAM

So maybe you're staying put, hunkering down instead of trading up, and you want to spruce up the house to sell later on. Be strategic with your renovations. The return on the renovation investment has been declining for four years in a row. If you must have the new kitchen or the shiny marble bath, do it because you are going to live in the house and enjoy it, not because you think you'll get the money back when you sell the house down the road. It's getting harder to get your money out of these improvements when you sell. (Although some prospective buyers are asking their real estate agents to show them only properties with recent upgrades to kitchen and baths. They're hoping to find distressed sellers who have spent a fortune on their home but now need out fast, for whatever reason. They don't plan on paying up for these improvements, however, just nabbing them cheap.)

An annual remodeling cost versus value report from Remodeling magazine suggests large, high-end kitchen remodels are about the worst investment a homeowner can make. Buy the Subzero fridge or the Viking range because you are a culinary guru and will get hundreds of dollars of enjoyment each time you use it, not because it is an investment. In 2009, the average cost of one of these high-end kitchen jobs was $111,794. The Remodeling magazine report found[6] that only $70,000 or so of that is "recoupable value" when you go to sell the home. In other words, that investment (not counting the Grand Marnier soufflés you'll no doubt expertly prepare with such expensive equipment) is only 63 cents on the dollar. Do you really need commercial-quality home appliances? Really?! Is that more important than a semester of college tuition tucked away or an extra month or two of savings in the bank?

In the peak of the high-end remodeling frenzy in 2005, a homeowner could recoup 80 percent of the cost of a state-of-the-art kitchen. But today the value you get out of big renovation projects is falling, and falling fast, unless you are adding a basement bedroom or doing a high-end siding replacement to fiber cement (see Table 6.14). Not as sexy, but more valuable in the long run. Those improvements recoup more than 80 percent of your cost of renovations and in a neighborhood with lots of homes for sale it may be the difference between selling your home or the neighbor's.

The post-bubble rule of thumb is that exterior remodeling, small or strategic improvements—door and window replacements, for example— might give you the best bang for your buck. Home-office remodels and sun-room additions added the least resale value to a home.

Finishing a basement or an attic bedroom or adding living space with a new deck are among the upgrades that return more of your investment,

Table 6.14   Best Renovation Return

Project	Cost ($)	Value Added to Home ($)	Recouped at Sale (%)
Avg. remodel job	50,908	32,497	63.8
Attic bedroom	49,346	40,992	83.1
Fiber cement siding replacement	13,287	11,112	83.6
Foam-backed vinyl siding replacement	13,022	10,285	79.0
Steel entry door	1,172	1,470	128.9
Wood deck	10,634	8,573	80.6
New vinyl windows	13,862	10,601	76.5

Source: 2009–2010 Remodeling Cost vs. Value Report, © 2009 Hanley Wood LLC. Complete Cost vs. Value data is available at www.costvsvalue.com.

but it depends on where you live. Obviously, window replacements in the Northeast deliver better results than they do in warm climes, and in the South Atlantic region, it is generally better to add more living space. (One theory is that the more space you add in the Northeast or in the Great Plains, the more it costs to heat.)

Some renovations are needs and not wants. (Plumbing disaster ruins a bathroom floor, termite damage in the hardwood floors around the fireplace, an infestation in the kitchen, an old drafty attached garage that needs insulation to lower your energy bills, for example.) But in general, remember, in a tough housing market the renovations that make the most sense are the improvements that add curb appeal.

RENTING

Maybe you are tired of the homeowner experience altogether. Some "investment!" Your home value is falling, your taxes are atrocious, and you could get more for your money by renting—and still put a little away for a rainy day.

Rents across the country are falling. More apartments are vacant than at any time in the past 30 years. By the fourth quarter of 2009, almost 8 percent of all rental properties were vacant in this country, as young jobseekers delayed moving out until they could get a job, people sought roommates to cut costs, generations moved in together to save money, and a quaking jobs market filtered into the rental real estate market.[7] Furthermore, a flood of new apartment buildings financed during the peak came on line in big American cities—coming to market just as the economy was coming apart. Some 28,000 newly constructed apartments became available to rent just in the last three months of 2009.

Analysis by real estate research firm Reis shows the largest decline in rent prices last year since they have been tracking the data. Whether rents keep falling depends on whether the labor market improves and workers are confident enough to sign a lease and move out from their parents' and friends and into an apartment.

In the nation's largest rental market, New York City, almost 60 percent of apartment rents fell in 2009 and nationwide rent prices fell 2.3 percent, also the largest decline in 30 years.

If you are older and cashing out of a home you have lived in for years, the rental market is your friend. If you are young and saving to move to one of those high-growth cities (Pittsburgh, Seattle, and so forth) you may be able to rent a better apartment today than you could a few years ago.

In Colorado, Sharon Riley is a single 38-year-old attorney who happily sold her duplex to become a renter again.

"I got a lot of pressure, 'You're a grown-up now, you really should buy,'" she says, so two years ago, "I bought a little duplex in a cute part of town," with a monthly mortgage payment of $1,600.

"Everybody tells you, 'Oh, you've got to buy, you've got to buy,' and it was great when the market was better but now I don't know," Sharon says. She never saw huge tax savings, only $2,000 a year, she says, and she's not much of a gardener, doesn't like to shovel snow, and she likes to spend her money on travel. The mortgage payment was manageable with her $110,000 salary, but $850 a month in law school loans kept the budget tight. Finally, when it became clear the next-door neighbor had stopped paying his mortgage and foreclosure was inevitable—"it was a race to the finish" to get out before his foreclosure knocked down prices in the whole neighborhood.

"I knew it would be easier to sell than in two years," when there could be other foreclosures, too.

Sharon closed literally one day before the neighbor's foreclosed house sold for $25,000 less than hers.

It wasn't without pain. She had to write a $15,000 check at the closing to cover some roof repairs and closing costs.

Sharon is now renting a room in a friend's three-bedroom apartment for $600 a month until she digs out of the hole from the closing, and then she will rent an apartment for $1,000 to $1,200 a month, freeing up $400 to $600 every month in cash flow. Plus, she'll get more space and amenities by renting.

"I want a nice little cushy place with a pool and an exercise room where I won't have to do any work!"

Sharon wasn't sure she had made the right choice—"It killed me that I had to come to the table with 15 grand"—but her doubt was erased when a homeowner friend had to come up with $6,500 for a new sewer line for her home.

Says her friend—"I have to admit I am a little jealous of her."

This trend won't last forever. As people leave their homes because of foreclosure, the competition to rent will pick up. But for the next year or two, there will opportunity for renters who haven't the money to buy or who want to move out of their expensive loans. The best opportunities are close to city centers with a minimal commute and no burden of the long list of homeownership costs.

There are countless online calculators to help you decide whether renting makes more sense than owning. A good start is the rent versus buy calculator at www.bankrate.com, but don't limit yourself to one calculator and remember, there is little margin for error in this economy. Go with your gut. If homeownership for you has become more of a burden than an investment, and your housing costs are eating up half or more of your pay, it might be time to rent again and build up your savings once more. And don't forget, if you need to pay off high-interest credit cards or variable rate loans in a rising interest rate environment, cash is king and renting gives you more flexibility.

LOSING A HOME

ROMANS'
NUMERAL

Up to 200 Points

The hit your credit score takes with a short sale or deed-in-lieu.

Five years ago, foreclosure was a rare event tied to job loss, medical catastrophe, or ugly divorce. Few could imagine a tsunami of foreclosure activity swamping the nation the way we see it today. Right now hundreds of thousands of homeowners will not keep their homes. In most cases, these people are not technically even homeowners. The bank owns the majority of the home, and falling home prices mean that your share of this asset is falling. Beginning in 2005 and 2006, I began reporting that technically homeownership was rising to records, but that most homeowners owned not even half of the house—some owned nothing at all—and the bank was really the owner. In hindsight, it was a powerful foreshadowing of the housing bubble popping that, at the time, was dismissed by most economists, policy makers, and pundits as overly pessimistic in what appeared to be a roaring economy. In too many cases, under no circumstances will people be able to afford the payments. Sometimes the owner has "no skin in the game" having put nothing down, or paying an interest-only mortgage that means they were never building equity. In many cases, they are in a home they will never afford, either because of a rotten mortgage sold to them that was never right for their situation, or because a job loss has put them impossibly behind on the payments. Only you know whether you are going to be able to keep the home. But never before have so many people gone to bed at night asking the question, "Can I *ever* afford this house?"

The Mortgage Bankers Association says a record number of home loans are late, some 7.9 million of them by the start of 2010. If millions of Americans are late on their most important financial contract, it is almost certain that foreclosure and distressed sales are with us for some time. If you have one of those bad loans, what's in store for you? And if your neighbor is one of these statistics, how he or she navigates will affect your home price and the value of your neighborhood.

"There is no clean way out of a bad mortgage, unfortunately," says John Ulzheimer, credit guru at Credit.com. Here are the choices:

- **Sell the house** for a loss and write a check at the closing. This preserves your credit scores because the lender has been made whole and isn't losing a dime of money, Ulzheimer says. This is much easier if you put money down when you purchased the house or have owned it a long time and the housing collapse hasn't fully wiped out the appreciation of the property. But it still hurts to write a check to the bank.

- Negotiate a **deed-in-lieu of foreclosure** with the bank. Essentially, you turn over the deed and avoid the hassle of a foreclosure and the certainty of your credit destroyed for seven years. The bank avoids the drama and cost of repossession. This can be the quickest way out of the house, but if the lender eventually sells the house for less than what you owed, the bank can get a deficiency judgment against you. Also, it has the same negative effect as a foreclosure, without the scene. "Really, what you are doing is exiting the house in a more noble manner," Ulzheimer says, "Meaning the sheriff won't show up at 6:30 A.M. demanding that you get out."

- You have a buyer for a lower price than you owe so you convince the bank to agree to a **short sale**. The lender takes a loss on the loan and you walk away with a 150 to 200 point hit to your credit (if you had good credit to start, says Ulzheimer. If your credit is shot to begin with, the hit will likely be less). It is still as onerous as a foreclosure because it will likely be reported to the credit bureaus as a settlement or a charge off, but you probably won't be shut out of borrowing mortgage money for three to five years like you would have had the lender foreclosed.

- A **bankruptcy** is no guarantee you'll save the house, but it can delay foreclosure if you are trying to hang on. Foreclosure proceedings halt at the moment bankruptcy is filed, buying you enough time to get current on the loan, if there is still a chance that can happen. This is especially helpful if you have missed only a few payments. Declaring Chapter 13 can help you stretch out the missed payments over time. You may be able to keep the house in the end, but bankruptcy stays on your credit report for up to 10 years.

- In a **foreclosure**, you lose all equity in the home, it is padlocked, and repossessed by the bank. "And in the ultimate embarrassment, the local sheriff can escort you and all of your belongings out of the home and you have no say in the matter," Ulzheimer says. There can be further judgments against you for your unpaid debts and your credit is essentially destroyed for seven years.

By the beginning of 2010, foreclosures were still high but slowing. It's not because homeowners have suddenly come into money to pay their bills. It's because foreclosure prevention programs were slowing the process as lenders searched for buyers who had a chance to keep the house, and helped them modify those loans. By and large, homeowners still report difficulty working with their lenders, trouble getting calls returned and trouble qualifying for a loan modification.

The government is still focused on helping homeowners who have a chance of keeping the home, with a subtle new shift. The government will now begin paying lenders and borrowers for a short sale, or a deed in lieu of foreclosure. The goal is to help the troubled borrower leave the home and return to the rental market and nudge the lender into accepting less than the bank is owed. (So far, many lenders have been slow to agree to short sales because they have to take the loss on their books.) It's called the Home Affordable Foreclosure Alternatives program (HAFA), part of the Treasury Department's Home Affordable Modification Program (HAMP).

Short Sale Bonus Eligibility

- Principal residence and first-lien mortgage
- Serious delinquency
- Unpaid balance under $729,750
- Monthly mortgage over 31 percent of gross income

The borrower receives up to $1,500 in relocation assistance to stabilize them so they can rent for less and begin to rebuild their savings. The loan servicer receives $1,000 and the knowledge that the home won't be left to be vandalized and rot, empty, further hurting its value and prospects. Surprise, surprise—there are numerous restrictions and the program is not for everyone. Check the official government foreclosure rescue web site at www.makinghomeaffordable.gov for all the details, including a checklist of which borrowers qualify for the program, http://makinghomeaffordable.gov/borrower-faqs.html.

For every tale of success in these government programs, there are dozens of stories of frustrated homeowners who do not qualify for one reason or another. At the end of February 2010, Treasury said that more than a million borrowers were saving money with trial modifications of their loans, with a median savings of $500 a month.[8] (That's on average about 36 percent less than they had been paying when they couldn't afford the mortgage and ran into trouble.) Still, with millions of borrowers in arrears and with foreclosure filings expected to reach 8,219 every *day* this year, by the end of February only 170,000 homeowners have qualified for permanent loan modifications through the government's program.

One foreclosure bright spot—when homes are foreclosed and finally get back on the market, they are selling quickly, often with several bids, reports Rick Sharga from real estate tracker RealtyTrac. It shows that if the price is low enough, there is opportunity even in the toughest real estate markets.

THE INEVITABLE SCAMS

Wherever there is financial distress there are scammers. The FBI opens new cases every day where homeowners thought they were saving their home only to realize they have been scammed out of it. Often, the scammers are quite clever, with foreclosure rescue schemes mailed on letterhead that looks like an official bank or government document. Mess up the URL of your bank or the Treasury rescue programs by just one keystroke and you can be diverted on the Web to a site that looks just like a legitimate real estate site, but is really a scam.

- Basically, anyone who is asking you for money to help you with the government's home loan modification or refinancing programs may well be cheating you. The Treasury Department warns: "There is never a fee to get assistance or information about Making Home Affordable from your lender" or from HUD, or a HUD-approved counselor.
- Watch out for any person or group that demands a fee for housing counseling services or a loan modification. "Do not pay—walk away!" the government warns.
- Never transfer over the deed of your home to someone or some group that promises to rescue your home for you if you sign it over. You must be working directly with your mortgage company to manage or forgive your debt.
- Beware of people who say they can "save" your home if you sign or transfer over the deed to your house.
- And finally, Treasury Department officials warn: "Never submit your mortgage payments to anyone other than your mortgage company without their approval."

THE PAYOFF

The payoff for you comes with managing the simultaneous roles of your house as a home, a debt, and an investment.

To get the most out of your house:

- Remember you make your money the day you buy the home, not the day you sell it. Think about the ease of commute, the quality of the schools, and the taxes.
- The best interest rates on mortgages go to people with credit scores above 760. Pay your bills on time, save 20 percent for a down payment, and clean up any mistakes on your credit report.
- Carefully examine the renovation returns in your area. Something as unsexy as a steel entry door gives you more bang for your buck than a Viking stove.
- And remember, mortgage debt—like student loans—is "good" debt when it is treated with respect. The house is no longer the piggy bank. It's a place to live and a long-term investment.

More on investments in Chapter 7.

7

Save, Invest, Retire

75 Million

The number of Americans who have not put even one penny toward retirement.[1]

On one day in May, riots in the streets of Greece were playing on televisions on trading floors, in office buildings, and living rooms across the country—an entire European nation in need of a bailout to keep from going bankrupt. At the same moment, U.K. elections looked headed for a hung Parliament. And across the world, the Chinese government was slowly putting the brakes on bank lending to slow rocket ship growth in the Chinese economy. The stock market had been up for 14 straight months without a pause at all and certainly without a meaningful correction. Suddenly, in a matter of minutes, the Dow Jones Industrial Average tumbled more than 998 points for its worst one-day point decline in history and ended the day down 348 points, the worst performance since the bad old days of spring 2009. The rise of high-tech and superfast electronic trading exacerbated an already very volatile market.

What's an ordinary investor to do?

Absolutely nothing.

Nothing, that is, if you are making the smart and consistent choices with your investments and how to prepare for retirement.

There's an old saying on Wall Street: "Don't just do something, stand there."

Studies show that decisions made in the panic and fear of market mayhem can be hazardous to your portfolio health. And these rash decisions also belie the fact that you might not really be comfortable with what you're doing in your investment and retirement planning. By the time you are reacting and bailing out, it's too late. The volatility and uncertainty of the stock market is a timely reminder that you need to have your saving, investing, and retirement planning in order—to ride through times like these no matter what happens.

"If you are a long-term investor and you are set up properly, you don't care about a 1,000-point drop in the stock market," says certified financial planner Doug Flynn. In fact, he says, after all the chaos of the past two years and a huge stock market rally that many investors missed because they were too afraid to get back in the market, it might actually be time to buy stocks. But it depends on your time horizon for retirement, how much money you have to invest, and what your personal tolerance for risk is.

A word here about all the volatility—there's no reason to think that wild days aren't here to stay for a while. Experts like Doug Flynn and Ryan Mack say never look at your portfolio just in times of crisis. If you do that, you'll be making emotional decisions based on factors beyond your control, and not managing your long-term money for the right reasons. Keep cash on hand for times of uncertainty and to cover your bills in the event of a job loss, so you don't have to touch the investments that are down in value or, God forbid, touch the 401(k). After all, retirement savings is for retirement. Not to afford a down payment on a house. Not to raid to pay the bills or

---

WILD MARKET ACTION PLAN

- Turn Down the TV Volume.
- Understand Where You Are Invested.
- Make Adjustments as Necessary.
- Revisit Your Portfolio in Six Months.

buy a new TV or car. It is money that is the most illiquid of all. You are not going to touch it until you are 67.

If you find yourself in the midst of a stock market rout and you are so uncomfortable about the status of your investments you need to make some changes, fine. But make those adjustments knowing that you will revisit the situation in exactly six months and make more adjustments as necessary to smooth things out.

Don't just react and run!

Just like everything with your money—earning it, saving it, and spending it—investing it takes discipline. It takes self-awareness and smart money sense. What are your money goals? How can you get your money to work for you for the long haul? How much risk can you take and still sleep at night? What are you going to do if stocks fall 10 percent in a week?

In this chapter we look at how much you should set aside for a rainy day, versus how much to sock away for the next 20 years or more to fund a happy and healthy retirement. We discuss how to profit—whether stocks are rising or falling—by making sure that you are diversified and balanced for your age and your risk profile.

If you're saving, spending, and building retirement in the right mix, these wild swings mean little to you and you can sleep well knowing you've got the right plan in place.

Sleeping well, after all, is a good way to spend the decades until retirement, not worrying about whether you'll have enough money once you get there.

What happens in the markets is outside your control. That makes it all the more important to control what you can. There are three steps to building peace of mind and wealth: budgeting, saving, and investing. Except for the price of stocks and bonds, everything is up to you.

GOOD STEWARD

Do you consider yourself a good steward of your money? It's where wealth accumulation begins—in the daily management of your cash and the thousands of small decisions you make that are the precursors for the big ones.

Financial planner Ryan Mack says that not everyone is destined to be a million dollar wage earner. Not everyone will be able to earn $100,000 a year and get bonus awards of stock options and the like. Mack counsels his clients that wealth is not how much money you make but what you do with the money you have.

"The good steward is the guy who was interviewed by CNN who never made over $13 per hour his entire life but was worth over $2 million after the age of 70," he says.

No matter how much money you make, you can build wealth. First comes the smart daily decisions about spending your money. Then comes saving what is left over.

How much should you save?

Mack was advising that clients keep six to nine months liquid assets in savings long before the financial collapse. He is correctly known for preaching that investment in the future comes from savings right now.

THE PROVERBIAL RAINY DAY

ROMANS' NUMERAL

30 Percent

Percent of adults who report they have no savings.[2]

It is said that what separates anarchy from civilization is putting away provisions for the future. In the generations after caveman times, the communities that shared and planned and gathered and put away stores for the winter survived. Rules and governments grew and society could be protected and prosper. In modern times, we think of this putting away for the future as saving. And the most tremendous threat to our civilization and way of life came when as a group, we stopped saving and putting away for the future.

We learned that lesson the hard way, and now smart families everywhere are not only making sure they are saving properly, but making sure they are saving enough for a new reality. The average length of unemployment is more than 35 weeks, taxes are likely rising, as are tuition and energy prices.

"Savings in a time after a recession is crucial because cash is king in this economy," says Mack.

"There are many individuals who I personally know who are earning $300,000 per year as a household, who are not living as well as those I know who are earning less than $100,000 in the household. This is because as their income has increased . . . so has their debt, living expenses, taxes, and irresponsible giving," and they fell away from the fundamental truth that savings is the basis for it all.

How much should you save? In normal times, experts say three to six months of your expenses. But if, as some economists predict, it could take until 2015 to replenish the 8-plus million lost jobs, obviously three to six months just isn't enough. A safer cushion is six to nine months, with an additional semi-liquid three months more in case of a prolonged job loss.

What is liquid? And where can I stash it? Not in the mattress, of course, but putting it in the bank almost feels like the same thing. It's a terrible time for savings in this country because low interest rates mean you're not getting paid much to give your money to a bank and the proliferation of bank fees and maintenance costs on accounts means that if you are not smart, you could end up paying the bank to hold your money for you.

Walk the extra block or drive the extra mile for an ATM machine that is in your network. If you don't, you are literally paying the bank for the use of your money. This is the smartest thing you can do today, right now, with virtually no effort that will mean savings and more money when you retire.

Seek out fee-free checking accounts at your bank of choice. Make it clear you do not want an account that will charge you money just for holding onto your cash. If you have thousands of dollars instead of just hundreds of dollars to deposit, you can seek out passbook savings accounts or money market accounts within your bank that do not have fees and pay a slightly higher interest rate. You can also quickly check and compare bank deposit interest rates at bankrate.com to find the best deal for holding your money. Checkingfinder.com offers comparison-shopping on free checking accounts. And credit unions are incredibly popular with depositors because they are covered by federal laws to protect your savings up to $250,000, and at the same time they have less onerous fees and fine print. These are all what is known as liquid assets. It means that you can use them right away in an emergency to cover living expenses like the mortgage or rent, car payments, taxes, school tuition, food, utilities, cell phone and Internet service, and gas bills.

Some smart savers believe three months liquid is not enough and keep six months on hand. Others prefer to keep three months of their living expenses in the bank and put up to six months more in a place they could get to it with a little more effort, like a taxable mutual fund account, a brokerage account with a discount stock broker, or a shorter-term certificate of deposit.

Having all your cash at the ready in a bank account earning 1 percent interest at the most is maddening when so many financial markets are on the move and creating opportunities. No matter where it is, if you need it to live on, make sure that you can get your hands on it in a matter of weeks. We relied for too long on the money invested in our houses and that pot of savings has disappeared.

The smart scenario to be in is this: You have six months of your living expenses in a bank and you want to save a little more but would like to put it into a taxable stock market account to see if you can earn some higher dividends from stocks or grab a rally should stocks rise. It's a great problem to have. Do what's right for your own risk profile. Can you sleep at night knowing you could lose some of that money? (If you can, then yes, move into the stock market with the savings you have beyond six months.) Do you want a guarantee that the money is going to be there in a year because you are getting closer to retirement? (Then no, you probably shouldn't.)

Q: I have no money. I am literally starting over. Advice?

There is no money in the bank. Your 401(k) is shattered. Your job is on the line. Your spouse lost a job and you've stopped contributing to the kids' college funds. You have thousands of dollars in credit card debt. How can you save and even think about retirement when you are trying to stabilize to get to the end of the month?

Or worse, you literally have nothing and all this talk of saving for a rainy day and investing in the future is irrelevant. How can you put away for the future when the right now is barely funded?

Financial planners say you must start somewhere or there is no doubt you will end up with nothing.

You have to do something. Certified financial planner Doug Flynn says you must live on 80 percent of what you make, no matter how big or small that income is. The other 20 percent must be allocated for your financial goals—savings and retirement. If you want to give 10 percent to charity, you'll have to live on 70 percent.

Look, it's tough if you are strapped and starting over. But you can start small and build quickly.

Flynn says start by putting away 5 percent of your earnings. If you can't manage that, then take 3 percent of what you make and put that away. Begin by building the cash cushion you need for daily survival, and then start funneling that money into retirement savings.

"Every time you get a raise take half for yourself—you've earned it—and put the other half toward your savings and investments," Flynn says. "Over the course of time you will be notching ever closer to the 20 percent—or 30 percent—and it won't feel like it."

You don't go from zero to saving and investing 20 percent overnight.

"But, you have to begin somewhere. And getting started is the hardest part," Flynn says.

If you are living on an unemployment check, by all means, begin saving 3 to 5 percent of that immediately. It will last, in extreme cases, up to 99 weeks. If you have one spouse working and the other collecting unemployment, save every single penny you can.

Without savings, you are at extreme risk for building up credit card debt and further delaying your retirement goals. The 30 percent of Americans who report they don't have any money saved at all are ripe for even more financial distress when the inevitable financial emergency arises. Something as small as a car repair, a hospital visit, or a leaky faucet could push them even further behind in their goals. Of the 75 million Americans who have nothing saved, one in four say they would put any emergency cost that arises on a credit card bill or take out a loan (29 percent). All this does is add to the debt load with another big bill to pay.[3]

GETTING STARTED, STARTING OVER

ROMANS'
NUMERAL

18 Percent

The share of Americans expected to meet all their financial needs in retirement.[4]

Are you in that number? If not, how are you going to get there?

Most people weren't in that number even before the stock market crash of 2008. You've been battered and bruised by the housing crisis that led to a market crisis. Investors are angry and cautious. But the question to ask now is not where have you come from, but how are you going to get where you want to go?

After savings, the next step is investing for retirement. Before you can start, here are a few important loose ends to tie up and some important questions to answer.

First, are you out of credit card debt? Or have you at least reduced it to manageable levels? On the surface, it's silly to put money away—even tax-free and matched by an employer—when you are paying 29 percent interest for the credit cards. But financial planner Mack says that for some investors, it's understandable to start saving and investing *before* they cut all the credit card debt, just so they can get started and get inspired.

It helps combat "fiscal fatigue," he says. "This is where you focus on paying down credit card debt only month after month and when you look up you still have a mountain left with no progress in any savings/investments. This results in a lot of discouragement and can lead somebody to just say 'forget it!'"

Don't forget it—slowly but surely, you can get there.

Second, do you have health insurance, life insurance and disability insurance for your family?

Third, are your estate plans in order? Do you have a will spelled out for the care of your children?

Now, do you have a working budget? You have to know what is coming in and going out before you can slot money for investments and retirement goals. Write them down, track them and make realistic goals and be consistent.

Next, Mack wants to see a **FICO score improved to 750**. Paying down big amounts of credit card debt and never being late on your bills can accomplish this more quickly than you think.

Then make sure that you have **savings in a high-yield savings account** for emergencies, Mack says.

After you've completed this checklist, then comes the big fun—the retirement investing.

"It is important that when you do start investing you have a solid foundation that allows you to weather life's uncertainties that are guaranteed to show up," Mack says.

Uncertainties like the financial collapse and horrific recession that struck in 2008.

FINDING YOUR MAGIC NUMBER

ROMANS' NUMERAL

$10,000

43 percent of people have less than $10,000 saved for retirement.[5]

Retirement planning doesn't just happen. It's something you do and it starts with a simple question.

How much do you need to retire?

If you're like most people, much more than you have right now (see Tables 7.1 and 7.2) and the reasons are clear—most say they can't put away for the future because they can't afford it right now.

Pension plans are dwindling and workers are switching jobs several times throughout their careers. The whole model for how you work and retire has changed, and that means the burden and responsibility is on you to make sure that you are saving and investing enough for your future.

Table 7.1   Most Not Ready for Retirement

% Share of Workers	Retirement Savings
43	Less than $10,000
66	Less than $50,000
11	More than $250,000

Source: Employee Benefit Research Institute, excluding the home and pension plan.

Table 7.2   Reasons for No Retirement Savings

% Share of Workers	Why Not Saving?
79	Can't afford it
6	Other priorities
5	Haven't found the time
4	Plenty of time until retirement
5	Other

Source: Employee Benefit Research Institute.

It used to be that the pension was automatic. But the share of private sector workers receiving a pension dropped from 50.3 percent in 2000 to 43.6 percent in 2008.[6]

Millions of us invest instead in 401(k) plans. New rules will make enrollment automatic and that will encourage more people to start saving younger, but the burden is now on the employee to make sure that a part of each paycheck is going toward the future.

Pretty much the best advice you can give a young person is to steer them immediately toward saving for retirement. Without a mortgage and a family, they are least likely to notice 10 percent out of their take-home pay and the tax advantage of that savings accumulates richly over the years. The same principles of compound interest that bedevil anyone with credit card debt enrich smart young savers who start saving young. Most people need to be saving 6 to 10 percent of their pay for retirement. The younger you start, the more money you have at the finish.

Ryan Mack, president of Optimum Capital Management, isolates three phases of your life for retirement planning purposes:

1. **Accumulation:** "You are in your twenties and you are young, full of vigor, and the unprecedented ability to sustain risk," Mack says. "You have almost 40 years and multiple market cycles to go before you are going to retire. If you have a portfolio that has 80 percent to 90 percent in stocks, and . . . can tolerate that high amount of risk then by all means have at it!"

2. **Conservation:** These are workers in their thirties and forties who now have a nest egg they have been working for years to build and they

don't want to lose it. It's time to start edging back slowly and taking the raw risk out of the equation and diversify. Mack says to start putting gold in the portfolio to hedge against inflation and the possible weakening of the dollar. Mack says both of those things—inflation and a weak dollar—are likely, so he recommends a 10 percent position in a gold exchange traded fund (ETF) and a maximum 50 to 60 percent position in stocks.

3. **Distribution:** This is not the time to *start* paying attention to the 401(k) for the first time in years. "If you are one of those who hasn't looked at your 401(k) seriously in the past 15 years then shame on you," Mack says. Anyone at age 55 with 80 percent in stocks needs a stomach of steel and better be in good health. If the market turns against you you'll be working for many more years when your contemporaries are relaxing in retirement. Where you should be in your fifties: 50 percent bonds, 10 to 15 percent gold, and the rest a mix of stocks and world stocks, Mack says.

The right mix, as you know, is called asset allocation and it depends on your age, goals, and risk appetite. Ten minutes with a retirement and asset allocation calculator online and you can get a good idea of where you stand.

Retirement Calculators

http://cgi.money.cnn.com/tools/retirementplanner/retirementplanner.jsp

http://fc.standardandpoors.com/calculators/jha/prex/calculator.jsp?
   toolid=000634

The wreckage of the past few years makes it all the more important to build the foundation for the future. It's hard to even think of it now, with your retirement portfolio likely down 25 percent since 2007. Many smart planners thought they were well situated for retirement until recently. And now they are revisiting these calculators to see if they have to save more, work longer, or lower their living standards.

That's the brutal truth of the crash of 2008 and the market volatility of 2009. It has set us all back in our goals and made us less confident of getting where we want to go.

This is where the optimists tout the advantages of buying stocks on the cheap. In the year-plus since the crash, steady investors have been adding low-priced stocks to their portfolio. The hope is, the longer the time horizon, the more your nest egg can recover, and your goals that seemed elusive in November 2008 and March 2009 seem attainable again.

When you consistently and methodically invest for your retirement—or if you are investing in a taxable investment account—you are doing something called dollar-cost averaging. You are buying stocks, bonds, and other assets at all different prices levels. It averages out your exposure to violent swings in the market and protects you from volatility. And if you are using a company's 401(k) plan that has matching money for your investments (which you are crazy not to use if it is offered) then you are receiving more free money toward your retirement, which also helps smooth out day-to-day swings in the market.

Two points—you must be contributing to a tax-advantaged retirement plan. And second, you've got to make sure that you are making the right assumptions about how much to save. Most people, believe it or not, simply guess how much money they'll need (see Table 7.3).

So how much?

Factoring in inflation and post-retirement medical costs, Hewitt Associates forecasts that Americans need, on average, 15.7 times their final year's salary saved to get them through retirement.

Quick math—that means that if you make $60,000 a year, you need to have just shy of a million dollars saved and invested to last you through retirement at roughly the same standard of living today.

If you make $100,000 a year, you need well over $1.5 million saved.

Table 7.3   Figuring Out Retirement Needs

Guess	44%
Make my own estimate	26%
I ask a financial adviser	18%
I read it somewhere	9%

Source: Employee Benefit Research Institute.

Hewitt says Social Security benefits will cover some of that, so employees are responsible for accumulating savings and retirement plans valued at 11 times their final year's salary.

"Employees have been able to recoup a good portion of the retirement assets they lost due to market volatility, but unfortunately most workers are still falling significantly short of meeting their retirement needs," says Hewitt retirement expert Rob Reiskytl.

Hewitt's research shows that the average American saving for retirement is on track to meet 85 percent or less of his or her retirement needs. Employees who are saving for retirement only through a 401(k) are on track to meet less than three-quarters of their retirement expenses.

It's a wake-up call for employees, no matter how far off retirement is. There are only two choices. Either save more today, or plan on dramatic cuts to your living standards in retirement.

It won't happen by just relying on the 401(k) or the employer-sponsored plan. It was never designed to be the sole retirement savings. That, coupled with Social Security and other savings must carry you through what could be 20-plus years of retirement.

FIXING YOUR 401(K)

Fixing it doesn't have to be overwhelming. You don't have to go from zero to 60 mph in 5 seconds or less. In fact, little changes and tweaks can make a big difference right now.

Hewitt recommends some immediate small moves that can get you closer to your retirement goal.

> **Start saving right now**. Hewitt's research shows that 26 percent of workers are not participating in a defined contribution plan like a 401(k). These people, on average, will retire with less than half of what they need. That means they will be forced to work into old age, move in with friends or family, and will not have financial health to enjoy retirement.

> **If you are young, go for it**. A 25-year-old making $30,000 a year can achieve all retirement targets by contributing 11 percent of pay on

average each year, assuming that the employer is matching 5 percent of the investment in the retirement account. If you wait until the age of 40, you need to contribute 17 percent of your pay each month to meet your goals. Hewitt says to disregard the old advice that 10 percent savings for retirement each year is sufficient. "Unfortunately," Hewitt's Reiskytl says, "that old rule of thumb is no longer true given the general erosion of employer-provided benefits and the reduction in employers providing subsidized retiree medical plans."

Up the contribution amount. Every little bit counts. Raise the amount you are contributing to your 401(k) by 1 percentage point each year for five years and you can close the gap between what you have saved and what you need dramatically. Many employers even offer this automatically. Check your plan's specifics.

Work longer. Hewitt research finds delaying retirement until the age of 67 cuts the savings shortfall. Putting off retirement by two years puts a comfortable retirement within reach for people who have not saved early enough."

"Social Security benefits are increased, there's more time to accumulate retirement savings, and assets will be withdrawn for a shorter period of time," Reiskytl says. "In addition, workers can continue to receive healthcare coverage under their employer—which can save employees a significant amount of money during that time."

SABOTAGING YOUR RETIREMENT

If you are like most people, the damage done to your retirement nest egg wasn't your fault, but the market's. If you are in your thirties, it is quite possible that you have been saving and investing for retirement for 10 years now and you have lived through the first time in our lifetimes that the return on the S&P 500, including dividends and interest, is actually negative.

$66,200

Your family's share of the stock market value lost in the financial crisis from September 2008 to the end of 2009.[7]

At least in stocks, you feel like you don't have much to show for it. But look at it this way: If you have a company match to your 401(k), you have been getting free money that has softened the blow, and you have probably not been exclusively in stocks, but also buying a little bit of bonds over the years in your 401(k).

Now that the economy begins to heal, smart investors are extra careful not to sabotage their retirement planning themselves. There are a half-dozen things that people do every day that are surefire ways to sabotage their retirement planning.

1. **Ignoring your 401(k).** You decided what proportion of stocks, bonds, and international funds to put in years ago and have never looked at it again. By not reallocating your assets periodically, you risk getting off track with the right asset allocation for you. A young person should have more stocks and fewer bonds than someone approaching retirement. Along the way, you want to take profits in the asset classes that have performed well and add slightly to the others at lower prices to keep your assets in balance and keep your money working for you. It doesn't have to be every quarter. You can decide to reallocate every six months or every year. Just do it.

2. **Don't underestimate your health-care costs**. Nursing homes, assisted living, and so on, will not be completely covered by Medicare and Social Security. According to Fidelity Investments, you need $250,000 in retirement for health expenses outside of your retirement savings. You will spend vastly more money on health care in the last two years of your life than the rest of your life combined.

3. **Starting too late**. $2,000 saved in your twenties is more valuable than $10,000 saved in your fifties. Here's why: The miracles of compound interest. That $2,000 in your twenties grows to more than $20,000 by the time you retire. Invest five times that in your fifties, and it is worth less than $18,000 on retirement. The goal is to start early and invest every year. The most important advantage you have is time.

4. **Cashing out the 401(k) early**. It's why it is so dangerous when young people cash out the 401(k) early. They think that the few

thousand dollars they have in there is inconsequential, but necessary to pay bills. Consider this: $5,000 cashed out at age 25 is $75,000 of retirement savings you have sabotaged. A recent study by Hewitt Associates found a majority of young people cashing out their 401(k)s. Even if it is only a few thousand dollars, it seriously jeopardizes retirement. When you are young, time is on your side. The longer you have to go, the more that money works for you. And cashing it out means taxes and a 10 percent penalty. Cash out $5,000 and you'll take home half of that and rob yourself of tens of thousands of future retirement dollars. It is simply not worth it. Retirement money is for retirement, not for paying bills.

STAY FOCUSED

Certified financial planner Doug Flynn says to think of your investment planning as an annual physical exam, only an annual *fiscal* exam. Just like you go to the doctor for routine wellness visits and to check your blood pressure, you need to do the same with your money. He likes to do it at the beginning of the year. You can also set a date to do this for your birthday every year, to take stock of where you are and how far you've come over the past 12 months. That doesn't mean you can neglect your financial organization in the interim.

People who are consistent with their bill-paying ritual save money in the end and tend to be better prepared for savings and retirement. The sheer amount of accumulated financial paperwork can be daunting with a 401(k) or two, savings accounts, car loan materials, and the like. Stay focused and keep the paper moving. Everything is available online these days, but some things you need to keep at hand for your own peace of mind and for future planning.

> **Pay your bills on time:** Set up a place on your desk or a file in your home of all the incoming bills to pay. Keep it in the same place, and give yourself electronic reminders on your BlackBerry or via e-mail to pay them. Pay them a few days before the due date. You can set up automatic online payments for your credit card and mortgage payments.

Keep for less than one year and then shred: Bank records. Check when they come in the mail that they match your online records and your balance and then keep them until the next month. After that, you can shred them. Same with credit card bills unless you need to keep the receipt and the monthly bill for a charitable contribution you need for your taxes. Keep a separate file for charitable contributions. As for the quarterly statements for your investment and 401(k) accounts, keep them until the next quarter's arrives and then shred them. *Consumer Reports* "Money Advisor" recommends keeping the annual statements until you sell the investments. I like to keep the annual statements anyway, compiled in a three-ring binder, to use as a gut check for how my goals have changed over the past few years.

Store away: Receipts for large purchases like home furnishings and electronics and the warranty information and instruction manuals for your appliances. Keep any receipts for anything related to the improvement of your home, especially documents relating to any energy efficient improvements that may qualify for tax credits. (Tuck these away in a filing cabinet.) Save your loan-closing documents for cars, student loans, and the house if you have paid them off, preferably in a safe-deposit box, along with any savings bonds you have. It is relatively easy to convert the paper savings bonds to an electronic version by visiting www.treasurydirect.gov.

Save forever: Birth certificates, marriage licenses, divorce decrees, Social Security cards, military papers, wills, trusts, and power of attorneys, pension plan documents from your employers, and life insurance policies. Some of these are perfectly safe in a locked, fireproof cabinet in your home. Other documents you may want to safeguard with valuables in a safe-deposit box.

As you manage the daily and weekly flow of cash and bills, the 401(k)—or the 403(b) and the IRA—and the bigger picture comes into clearer focus. Periodically take a look at where you stand, not just when all hell is breaking loose.

You can do this online, easily and quickly. There is simply no excuse not to. Technology has made this so convenient. There is no reason to think of the 401(k) statement as something that comes in the mail and needs to be opened and examined with dread. The idea of waiting for the quarterly 401(k) statement to come in the mail is archaic. It's just as easy to take a snapshot of your net worth at any moment as it is to check the weather or sports scores. Smart investors make it a habit, and they profit from it.

ETF

30 Percent

ROMANS'
NUMERAL

Share of Americans' retirement wealth held in IRAs because people are leaving jobs and rolling over their 401(k)s into IRAs.[8]

You've heard of them before—exchange-traded funds or ETFs—just another exotic phrase in the alphabet soup of finance. But this little acronym is really a simple and slimmed-down way to buy or sell just about anything you want exposure to as an investor. Do you think gold is going to keep rising beyond these record levels because the U.S. public finances are a mess? There's an ETF for that—SPDR gold shares. The ticker symbol is GLD.

Do you think stocks are going to keep rising as the global economy recovers and you want exposure to the entire stock market? There's an ETF for that, too. Vanguard Total Stock Market or VTI.

Are you convinced that the world's hunger for oil and raw materials will only grow as middle classes evolve in India and China and the world's factories come back to life? How about ishares S&P Global Energy IXC?

I'm not recommending these. I'm a journalist, not a financial adviser. But you can type in those symbols to any finance web site and learn more about what they do and what they cost. What you buy depends on what you think will happen in the world. (And there is much happening. The next few years will provide incredible challenges and opportunities for investors. The financial crisis is over, but the adjustments to countries, companies, and consumers are just beginning.)

Essentially, ETFs are the low-cost version of fancy mutual funds that have managers who are paid out of your returns to manage your money. If you want plain vanilla, easy investment, and low fees, this might be a nice way to get started investing or—if you have a large nest-egg in a taxable account—protect yourself from fees over the long term.

If you want to pay a little for a seasoned fund manager to pick and choose stocks and bonds and other instruments in the categories you are interested in, then mutual funds might well be worth the price.

Mitch Tuchman is an evangelist for ETFs and cites his own research over a lifetime, higher-cost mutual funds will suck away a chunk of your investment gains, he says.

Tuchman says that rich people and wealthy university endowments *stay* rich and wealthy by following three rules:

1. Have the right asset allocation. That means the right mix of stocks, bonds, commodities, and cash.
2. Keep the fees down to a minimum.
3. Rebalance the portfolio regularly to make sure that they have the appropriate asset allocation at all times.

Fees are key. By Tuchman's math, if you are filling an IRA with mutual funds, you could be losing in the neighborhood of $1 million in fees over the course of a 41-year investment horizon. Sounds impossible?! Here's his math. Starting at the age of 35, contributing $4,000 a year to an IRA with a 7.5 percent annual return, you'd have a mutual fund portfolio worth just over $2 million by the age of 76, a million dollars less than the lower-fee ETF portfolio. Add in a mutual fund portfolio managed by an adviser and the loss, he says, is even more dramatic.

"Since ETFs are managed by computers not by Harvard MBAs who need a Lexus and a beach house, that's why ETFs are cheaper," Tuchman says.

If you want to try to manage this portfolio yourself (and remember, lots of successful investors are quite happy leaving the big decisions to experienced

IRA contributions
Age 35/ $4k/yr at 7.5 percent annual return

Age	Mutual Fund Portfolio	ETF Portfolio	Returns Lost to Fees
76	$2,039,000	$3,148,000	$ (1,109,000) 54.4%

IRA contributions
Age 35/$4k/yr at 7.5 percent annual return

Age	Mutual Fund Portfolio and Advisor	ETF Portfolio	Returns Lost to Fees
76	$1,432,000	$3,148,000	$(1,716,000) 119.8%

financial planners and well-known mutual funds—they feel the fees are worth it) you need the right mix for your age and goals.

For a 25-year-old investor with little experience and a high risk tolerance, who has a little money to invest in a discount brokerage account or in an IRA retirement account, Mitch recommends a portfolio that looks like the one in Figure 7.1.

Obviously the portfolio would be different for an older investor who is closer to retirement. For that investor, with good investment experience but low risk tolerance, a more appropriate ETF portfolio would look like the one in Figure 7.2, Tuchman says.

You can easily research ETFs to fit these categories on your own through your IRA manager, a discount broker, or at CNNMoney.com.

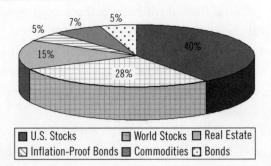

Figure 7.1   ETF Investments for 25-Year-Olds
Source: www.MarketRiders.com.

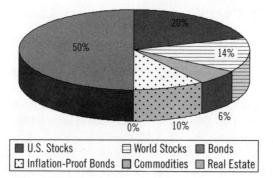

Figure 7.2   ETF Investments for 55-Year-Olds
Source: www.MarketRiders.com.

Tuchman recommends these for starters.

U.S. stocks

Vanguard Total Stock Market (VTI)

World StocksVanguard FTSE All World (VEU)

Real Estate

SPDR Dow Jones REIT (RWR)

Commodities

SPDR Gold Shares (GLD)

ishares S&P Global Energy (IXC)

Inflation-Proof U.S. Bonds

ishares Barclay TIPS bonds (TIP)

Bonds

Vanguard Total Bond Market (BND)

SPDR Barclays Capital 1–3 month T-bill (BIL)

"There is a revolution going on with respect to how to invest. You don't have to be Warren Buffett to be a do-it-yourself investor anymore," Tuchman says. "Your trades through a broker used to be hundreds of dollars, now they are $8." Five years ago you couldn't invest in emerging markets without paying analysts and fund managers for their research and access to the region. Today you can buy any number of emerging market stocks funds for a few dollars, depending on your broker.

THE PAYOFF

There are three steps to building peace of mind and wealth: budgeting, saving, and investing.

Once you have paid off your debts and built at least six months of savings, it is time to start investing. As an investor, you have a simple checklist to research and follow: (1) How much money do I need to retire? (2) What is my risk tolerance? (3) Choose an asset allocation; and (4) rebalance periodically.

The payoff for you comes by living on 70 percent of your pay, saving and investing 20 percent, and giving 10 percent to charity. You'll sleep well at night along the way. And in retirement.

CHAPTER 8

Family Money

ROMANS'
NUMERAL

54 Percent

Percentage of parents talking to their kids more about money in the wake of the financial crisis.[1]

The brutal recession has shocked parents of all ages into the realization that their kids are not prepared to handle even the most basic money matters. These parents are now talking to their kids more about personal responsibility with their money than they are about physical fitness, religion, alcohol and drug use, marriage and sex.

Three things that polite people are told never to talk about around the dinner table: religion, politics, and money. I say pursue the first two at your own peril, but the third is an essential part of every family's conversation. Maybe not around the dinner table, exactly, but certainly as a running conversation as you raise your kids. And it's not just your kids: Boomers need to have frank conversations with their own aging parents on issues of cash flow, health needs as they age, and estate planning.

Whether you are a couple just starting out in a relationship, or frazzled young parents juggling two jobs and a new family, or married folks getting ready to retire: Family money is at the center of family life. It's a silver lining of the financial crisis that families are beginning to talk about finances, responsibility, and expectations in a way that recent generations have not.

It's well documented that not having these conversations only leads to misunderstandings and financial hardship in the end. Yet only a small minority of families is financially literate in part, because money has long been viewed as a grown-up subject. But you don't wake up one day at 21 and magically have the tools you need to make smart money choices.

Being money smart is much like playing a musical instrument. You don't suddenly know how to play "Minuet in D" on the piano. Often, it's something that was introduced to you young and gradually and as knowledge and ages build, so does the skill. Money is the same way. Your child will go to college with a sound financial footing only if you have laid the building blocks through the years. That means everything from how you reward your kids for a job well done on grades, whether you expect your child to do chores, and what sort of allowance arrangement you give.

In this chapter you'll learn why being honest and frank about money early in a romantic relationship is critical, because too much debt can ruin a marriage. We'll explore why kids who take out the trash grow up to be financially responsible, and we'll ask how young is too young to learn about saving, investing, and budgeting. You'll see why Generation Y is in debt and out of work, and examine smart rules for the sandwich generation who is managing the finances of their debt-ridden college grad kids and their elderly parents at the same time.

And, of course, talking together about money doesn't have to mean sitting down at the dinner table with the *Wall Street Journal* and poring over the quarterly earnings of Berkshire Hathaway. (Although if you find yourself with a little Alex P. Keaton, encourage it.)

LEAD BY EXAMPLE

It can be as simple as fixing a meal together instead of going to a restaurant. Make money a part of the conversation, and use saving money as a means to connect with your family.

The best example of this comes from a woman I met named Paula, who is an evangelist for the notion that believing in yourself and hard work will bring you success. In 1989 she was a single mother of two teenaged boys, dead broke with her last $20 bill, a crippling fear of going outside the house, and a pile of bills.

At the time, Paula was by her own account, miserable, but wallowing in self-pity wasn't going to feed her kids or pay the rent. So she examined the two things going for her—her sons and her cooking. Instead of being a bag lady, she started a little "Bag Lady" business, making gourmet sack lunches in her kitchen and delivering them to dentists and doctors' offices. Her young sons were her delivery boys, her sandwiches were divine, and she built that little business feeding doctors to feed her sons into the family empire that is Paula Deen, the queen of Southern cooking.

"My boys sold that food," she says in her slow Southern drawl, pinching her younger son's cheek. "They were so sweet walking in to those office buildings. Y'all, the women just loved them."

Paula involved her children in a conversation about money because she had to. She's as quick to talk about money—and getting value out of your dollar—as she is to talk about butter and coconut cake. (She's not a fan of the organics craze and thinks middle-class families waste money on organics when there is no way to know if the ingredients are different or better.)

She says the Great Recession has forced families to look inward and talk about money and values again. If you want your kids to be raised with a good understanding of how to earn a dollar and what it means, you have to do it at home.

Paula Deen's recipe? Perhaps not surprisingly, the author of 16 cookbooks says stay home with your kids and cook.

"If you go to a real nice restaurant it can be $30 or $35 and you can do it so much cheaper at home. The same thing as with a good steak," Deen says. "Ya know if you want a good steak, do it at home. It's a wonderful way to get reacquainted with your teenagers who are on the go all the time. Encourage them to come help prepare the food—it's just a win-win for everybody."

TAKE OUT THE TRASH!

6 Percent

Kids who learn about money and finance in school.

That means it's up to you. Granted, you already have a long list of things to teach your kids including:

- Look both ways when you cross the street.
- Wear your seatbelt.
- Eat your vegetables.
- Don't hit your brother.
- I said, don't hit your brother.
- Wash your hands and brush your teeth.

Here's something simple to slip into that list that will pay dividends when your little darling gets old enough to have a credit card or a school loan: *Take out the trash.*

Children who have chores growing up are more likely to be better with money down the road. The kind of kid who takes the trash out twice a week, or changes the water in the fish tank, or has the special job of folding the towels and making sure they are delivered to the bathroom——that kid grows up to be more diligent about money.[2] The theory is: Early and consistent expectations about the contributions a child must make in the home translate into responsibility with money later on.

Should you give the child an allowance for those chores? That's a subject of endless debate among financial literacy experts. An allowance is appropriate for some older children, say middle school age kids—and they should be monitored closely how they spend it. But certainly all kids should have some level of chores and household responsibilities that they don't get money for. It's part of being in a family.

The reason why the allowance debate is so spirited is because kids are born with different wiring about money. Some respond to financial incentives, some don't. Some understand quickly the value of the dollar and what it buys, some kids take much longer. But like everything else, the habits they learn from their parents and family work with that wiring to create what type of spender, saver, and investor they will become.

Look no further than your own family for proof. My mom would pile her three kids into the car in the late 1970s and early 1980s and head to

Duck Creek Mall or the Ben Franklin Five and Dime in my tiny hometown. Each of us was given $5 to spend. Not an allowance per se, just a five-dollar bill that we could buy something with. I would carefully browse for an hour, figure out what to buy, compare prices, and then buy my item at the end. (Most likely Laffy Taffy and a Barbie dress.) My brother would put the money in his pocket and never spend it, but share my candy in the car ride home. My sister would spend all of it on the first thing she saw and spend the rest of the hour regretting that she didn't wait. A trip to the mall was like the movie *Groundhog Day* for us, because that's the way we were all wired about money. We have the same parents and genetics, but our philosophies about money were different from the start.

The exercise taught us a lot. Today my sister is the best budgeter I know and my brother is still incredibly smart about money. And I still share my candy.

Looking back, I admire my mom for letting us figure it out on our own— it was a valuable exercise for us together as a family, exploring our values about what to buy and how to share it. We certainly learned the value of a dollar— candy today that's gone tomorrow? Or save for the Legos pirate ship kit? My mom let us make the choice (with some urging and guidance) and she'd gently point out that the candy wrappers were empty before we even get home and we weren't any closer to the big toy we wanted. She also could see exactly how we were spending our money.

For kids today it will be harder. There is just so much—kids have too much—and most have never had to save up for anything.

Globalization has made consumer goods cheap and prolific. Over the past 30 years we've grown accustomed to having whatever we want, when- ever we want it. In the 1970s and 1980s, parents didn't buy their kids toys every week on credit. Birthdays and Christmas and a few times in between came big, satisfying gifts that kids looked forward to. Three things stand out for me: a tape-recorder for Christmas in fourth grade. A yellow banana seat bicycle in second grade, and a Barbie Dream apartment (with an elevator!) that I had to share with my little sister. (C'mon, anyone 30 or older reading this is remembering right now the stand-out gift, right?!)

Will kids today grow up and remember vividly three or four perfect, coveted gifts? I doubt it.

In the pithy words of one CNN viewer, Sid: "When it comes to savings, the average American can't help themselves. Americans have a compulsion to spend. The one with the most toys at the end wins."

Will we pass this compulsion onto the next generation or nip it in the bud? Spending money is the first financial lesson kids learn, yet for years we have spent money so freely that it is almost a meaningless lesson. And that undermines an already shaky record of teaching kids about money.

Which brings me back to the allowance debate.

Parents should discuss their personal philosophy about allowances, decide how much and what responsibilities are involved, but always remember to monitor how they spend it and make sure that there are also some chores that are just expected, not reimbursed. The older your child is, the more you can give them, but with caveats. Some parents insist that a percentage is given to church or charity. Some designate half for spending now and half for saving for college. The benefit of an allowance is lost if it is essentially parents giving money to their kids in exchange for no contributions at home so the kid can buy an expensive video game.

Education Secretary Arne Duncan has just started his kids, aged 6 and 8, on allowances. Treasury Secretary Tim Geithner says for high school aged kids, it's more about what you say than what you pay.

"You want to talk to them about things you got right and things you didn't get so right," Geithner says. As a parent and a top administration money man, there's plenty to talk about with his kids! He famously prepared his taxes incorrectly earning the ire of those who opposed his confirmation to treasury secretary. And he couldn't sell his house in Larchmont, New York, when he moved to DC to become treasury secretary, renting it out for less than the mortgage.

Debt counselor Gail Cunningham recommends keeping an envelope in your purse or briefcase for each kid, and at the store, when they see something they want, tell them to buy it and give them their envelope. "Most of the time once they realize they are spending their own money, they decide they no longer want the item," Cunningham says.

When they want trendy tennis shoes or jeans, have them contribute their own money. "It'll put a whole new perspective on spending."

Gail says to teach your kids 80-10-10. They can spend 80 percent, save 10 percent, and give 10 percent to charity.

The point of the allowance, of course, is to teach kids that money isn't free.

Jase is 25 years old and says his allowance taught him the value of money. When he was 13, he did the dishes every night, took out the trash, and mowed the lawn, all for $20 a week. He had always done those chores, but his dad "started paying us as he got raises, so in that sense I respected where it came from."

Jase got an allowance and was taught that this was coming right out of dad's paycheck, not out of thin air. It's an important anecdote as you consider how to structure an allowance for your kids.

But how to raise kids with good money skills goes well beyond the age-old question of whether to give an allowance or not. More than an allowance, your kids are watching and learning from you.

If you curse, chances are your kid will drop a bomb every now and then, even if it's behind your back. If your smoke, your kid has a greater likelihood of becoming a smoker. If you're good with money, you have a better chance of having a kid who learns how to follow you and be good with money.

If you buy things you don't need with money you don't have, you've got an excellent chance of raising kids who do the same. Same if you value possessions over experiences.

And you shouldn't think someone else is going to teach them this. Just like drugs and sex, unless you are in there controlling the message, someone else will be and it's a good bet that what they are learning isn't compatible with your values.

Economist Bill Rodgers at Rutgers University says to teach kids good money habits you need to start 'em young, by making sure there are books in your story-time or bedtime routine that lay the groundwork.

"Want to help stimulate the economy, spend time with your child and reduce the chances that the financial crisis occurs in the future?" he asks. Read to them from books that cleverly and subtly teach money lessons about saving (*A Chair For My Mother*, by Vera B. Williams), entrepreneurship (*Jack of All Tails*, by Kim Norman), and differentiating wants and needs (*The Giving Tree*, by Shel Silverstein).

Rodgers suggests a free resource for choosing books for your young children that speaks to individual money ideas. The web site http://econkids .rutgers.edu/ lists the top five children's books for dozens of categories, including job loss—a touchy and important subject for all families living in a time of nearly 10 percent unemployment. Chances are, someone in your family has lost a job and if not your family, then a child's playmate has a parent out of work. Money for kids is more than about what they get. It's also a strained conversation happening around them all the time.

Once was, 20 years ago, parents opened a savings account at the local bank for their child to deposit their birthday money into and watch it grow. Many of you of a certain age probably still have the little passbook, stamped with your deposits. But today, interest rates are so low and checking and savings account fees for small accounts can be so high, it doesn't make sense anymore. Credit unions are your best bet for small balances and teen accounts. Check your local credit union for fee-free savings accounts for kids or better yet, start a state-sponsored 529 education savings plan.

A word here on credit cards for young people. Avoid credit cards for young people until they have learned how to manage a low-cost credit union checking or savings account. They don't need them and credit card reform means that they can't get one on their own anyway. A debit card attached to

---

SMART MONEY KIDS CHECK LIST

Your Child Should . . .

- Have routine chores for which he or she is not paid.
- A next level of chores for which there is a modest allowance that you monitor.
- Save at least some birthday and holiday money.
- Be raised with high expectations—you *will* go to college and we are already planning for how to pay for it. You will be expected to help.
- Not get every material thing he or she wants. Make your child contribute to expensive or trendy items.
- Open a checking account at a credit union to keep track of their money.

your account for emergencies and a prepaid card or a checking account with checks is the best way to start them slow. With many debit accounts you can get automatic text alerts and e-mail notifications of purchases, so you can see every last $1.07 iTunes purchase your kid makes. You can even put their modest allowance in there automatically.

Even a college freshman doesn't really need a credit card. Judging from the trouble so many college kids have found themselves with plastic, don't risk it. There is a reason that kids under 21 are restricted from access to credit cards under the recent credit card reform laws. Debit cards, pre-paid cards, or cold hard cash is just fine when they are starting out. They have a cellphone, right? If there is a true cash emergency they can call you and explain why they need the money.

1 in 5

ROMANS'
NUMERAL

Number of people aged 18 to 34 who have been denied a credit card or other loan.[3]

This age group is more likely to be turned down for a loan than any other, so building a responsible credit history is quite important. A secured credit card may be the answer for a young person. How does it work? You deposit money in a savings account, and the amount in the account is the credit limit for the secured card. After 18 months of responsibly using the card and paying it off with the money in the account, you're on track to get a real credit card. Cardratings.com lists lenders that offer secured credit cards.

Be wary of any with fees that top $35 and search for secured cards with annual fees more like $20 to $25.

Aside from you, the mom and dad, how else is your kid getting money? How about a job? For years, parents pushed their kids into extracurricular activities and away from the job. Perhaps rightly so, many parents wanted their kids to focus on schoolwork and building up their "resume" for college applications instead of delivering pizzas. Over the past decade, youth summer employment has tumbled from 60 percent of kids working, to only 47 percent of kids working. One reason, parents have been giving their teens everything they need. Another reason, the economy. Teens in the past two years are now competing with other people out of work for jobs and small businesses are cutting back to save money.

As the economy starts to turn again, what a perfect time to get your little cost center out there to start earning his or her own spending money for college and at the same time start teaching them about money.

Some ideas for teens: Be an asset to small businesses in the neighborhood by offering (for a fee) to set up and manage that little company's online presence via Twitter or Facebook. Get together with a few friends and put together a work squad to shake down babysitting jobs, yard work, house cleaning, pet sitting, car washing, tutoring and rudimentary tech support. (Call the school, the local cemetery, even the local Department of Transportation to see if there are freelance jobs to mow or tidy up public areas.) For more formal jobs, try Craigslist, CoolWorks.com, SnagAjob .com, or Teens4Hire.com.

Forget this notion of "my child has his whole life to work. I want him to focus on being young. I want him to focus on being a teenager and having fun." Hogwash. Nothing teaches a kid about money better than earning and knowing just how hot those pizza ovens are or how long you have to sling burgers to afford a new iPad. You're doing your kid a favor.

GENERATION Y

80 Percent

Percent of the college graduates of the Class of 2009 who moved home with their parents after graduation.[4]

Generation Y could also be called Generation "Why?" As in, why don't you have a job and why do you already have so much debt?!

It's also known as the boomerang generation, because after striking out and finding their independence in college, many end up living back at home under one roof with their parents.

The so-called millennials (born 1980 and after and coming of age in a new millennium) are having a much tougher go at it than the generation that came before them, the Generation Xers. Generation X hit the strides of their careers before the job and housing market came crashing down in 2008. They started out after the much milder recession of 1991 and were well established by the time the Great Recession rolled around. Raised by the oldest Baby Boomers, Generation X was more likely to have had a summer job, save for their own college, and pay their own way after graduation.

By contrast, Generation Y was brought up in the go-go days of easy credit and now they live in the shadow of a popped bubble, sky-high joblessness, and crushing credit card bills.

This generation had at least three credit cards in college and bought expensive tech gadgets with no income. Often, their tuition was paid for by the home equity in their parents' houses (home equity that doesn't exist anymore) and they have been told again and again to do what they love and not worry about money. There are 50 million of them and they are the most educated generation in U.S. history. Three-quarters of them have a profile on a social networking site and 4 in 10 have a tattoo.[5] They are also the group most likely to be out of work, least likely to pay their bills on time, most likely to cash out their 401(k) savings and the least likely to have health insurance. They could well be the first generation in history to wind up less well-off than their parents.[6]

They are writing their own rules and they are fiercely independent, in their politics, their expectations for themselves, and their views on religion and social mores. Pew Research Center also estimates that they are less religious than prior generations and they trust authority less. A third

GENERATION Y STATS

60 percent have cashed out their 401(k)s after a job loss (Hewitt Associates)
Only 58 percent pay bills on time (National Foundation for Credit Counseling)
39 percent have no health insurance (Pew Research Center[7])

of millennials are parents, and more than a third of 18- to 29-year-old women who gave birth are unmarried, far more single-parent births than in prior generations.

USA Today calls them "teens and twentysomethings known stereotypically for their coddled upbringing, confidence, opinionated dialogue, free-spending habits and openness to change."[8]

They are independent in everything, it seems, except for money. This generation is the most likely to be supported by Mom and Dad. The very parents who were independent themselves well before 25 are now supporting their children all the way up until 30.

A recent survey by the Charles Schwab Foundation found that more than a third of parents said their kids were more reliant on them today than they were on *their* parents when they were young, and at least one in five of those parents thought their twentysomethings have a sense of entitlement absent in prior generations.[9]

Certainly college debt and a lack of job opportunities are the major reasons these kids are in debt and out of work. But their attitudes about money didn't happen by accident. These same parents have raised their kids to believe that they are unique, that their opinions are paramount, and that they should pursue what they love first, financial success second.

It's a fine philosophy when jobs are abundant, but after a bruising recession, it's a difficult strategy for these millennials who are out of work, up to their necks in debt, and aren't getting paid to do anything.

Retailers love this category—they have been a dependable market for music, clothes, and gadgets. And human resource experts find this group fascinating: For the first time ever there are four generations at work and Gen Y has completely different expectations and work habits. Gen Y workers could well transform the U.S. work experience with their knowledge of technology, their flexibility, and their open-mindedness—once they are no longer stopped in their tracks by the recession. It's a generation brought up after Columbine and during two wars whose largest cultural influences are terrorism and technology. And their differences are remarkable (see Table 8.1).

Table 8.1   What Makes Your Generation Unique?

Millennial or Gen Y (Born 1980 to 2000s)	Gen X (1965 to 1980)	Boomer (1946 to 1964)	Silent (1928 to 1945)
1. Technology use	Technology use	Work ethic	WWII, Depression
2. Music/pop culture	Work ethic	Respectful	Smarter
3. Liberal, tolerant	Conservative/ traditional	Values/morals	Honest
4. Smarter	Smarter	"Baby Boomers"	Work ethic
5. Clothes	Respectful	Smarter	Values/morals

Source: Pew Research Center survey based on respondents who said their generation was unique.

PARENTS OF GENERATION Y

TOP THREE THINGS THEY SAY THEIR KIDS NEED TO LEARN ABOUT MONEY

Living within their means	48 percent
How to save	42 percent
How to invest wisely	33 percent

Source: Schwab 2010 Families & Money Survey.

Millennials are the only generation that doesn't list a strong work ethic as a distinctive characteristic. That may be because their parents are still taking care of them.

The parents who raised these millennials are trapped in a contradiction of their own making. Parents of twentysomethings report that they should have taught them more about budgeting and living within their means, yet they are still supporting them financially. These parents worry that their kids are not saving early enough for retirement, not saving money for emergencies, and carrying credit card debt from month to month, but these parents are raiding their *own* retirement and savings to help their kids.

PAYING FOR COLLEGE

69 Percent

Parents of Generation Y who tell their kids to choose a profession they love even if it means they won't be able to pay the bills.[10]

The majority of parents of millennials are willing to subsidize their kids indefinitely, according to research from Charles Schwab, and an alarming percentage think that financially supporting their kids is nearly as important as preparing for their own retirement.

That'll be some shock for both generations. The same moms and dads who are so committed to helping their adult kids now could well be living with them and *off* them in 20 years.

Here's that cardinal rule again for you: You can borrow for a kid's college, but you cannot borrow for retirement. Always pay yourself first. If that means Junior needs to get loans for some or all of college, then so be it. It also means that Junior needs to choose a degree course that matches his skills and interests and will allow him to quickly start earning a living to pay down his debt.

A viewer from California—let's call her Nancy because she doesn't want to advertise her situation—told me that she and her husband had taken money out of their house and had taken out a second mortgage to pay for college tuition for three children. Two more were still at home. She and her husband both struggled to pay their own college and did not want their kids to have to do the same.

And they also promised that their children would be able to go to the school of their choice. The first went to a state school. The next two went to out of state.

Today that couple, in their late fifties, is painting and fixing their modest house to sell it so they can pay off their debts. Thankfully, they bought real estate in California after the bust of the 1980s, but they have sucked tens of thousands of dollars in equity from it. They may be able to break even when they sell. That means they will spend their years before retirement in a rental apartment. They have still not funded their retirement and two kids still need to get to college.

Nancy and her husband made mistakes from day one. They didn't realize that *their* early struggle (to pay for their own college) was an investment. They would work, raise a family, save money, and build a retirement. Their children would do the same. That college debt, if properly managed by a financially literate young adult, is a powerful tool and motivator. I have talked to hundreds of high school and college students who have debt and manage it wisely. They are motivated to get a better-paying job or follow a more lucrative field because they know they have bills coming due. Nancy didn't save her children from the struggle she had. She just gave herself more expensive struggles and less time to pay it off.

The second mistake was private school. You cannot on a middle-class income give five children a free checkbook for college. It is irresponsible of *you*. Take the long view. Many state schools are wonderful. Nancy and her husband would have saved at least, by my calculations, $100,000 by using the resource their taxes already help pay for.

The third mistake was taking money out of the house to pay for this expensive education. Like millions of other families, the real estate boom gave them bubble-vision. As the home values soared all around them, they thought the money in their house could be tapped like an ATM. Now, that money is spent on expensive college educations, and the bill is still due.

The house money is gone, folks. The days of tapping it to pay for sky-rocketing tuition costs are over. Time to get creative.

- If your little darling wants to be a biomedical engineer (one of the Department of Labor's fastest growing fields for the next 10 years) then send her to state school for her undergraduate degree, because you will be bankrupt if she decides on a master's or another degree.
- Make them pay. If you have your heart set that they not struggle like you did, then you can cover three years. They pick up the fourth year with loans. Heart set on becoming a doctor? Fine, you'll pay for the undergrad, they have to get loans for med school. But only if you can afford it. If you haven't funded your retirement, they should be heading straight to the financial aid office.

I am at odds with my own parents on this, who paid for a state school undergrad degree for each of their children. I even offered to pay my dad back once, and he was appalled. "My parents sent me to college, I will send my kids." He took that generous line, to a degree. He was already saving for his retirement, so he wasn't robbing himself to pay for us. And he expected us to kick in our summer savings and more. I worked two or three summer jobs at a time, and earned money at the student newspaper during the year. When my dad helped me do my taxes junior year, he laughed out loud. I had earned enough to pay for room and board and a semester of state-school tuition and the next year, I did.

It was absolutely the right thing for him to do. With three more kids headed to college, he had to think of his household cash flow first. And certainly I was less likely to blow my hard-earned money on something stupid when I knew exactly how far it went at the bursar's office.

SANDWICH GENERATION

But that anecdote is so Generation X, isn't it? And Gen X had an advantage—we were graduating into a period where 20 million jobs were created. Eight million jobs vanished over the past three years for Generation Y.

That means that today's graduates are unique, tech-savvy, tattooed, and indebted but living at home again. If you've got one of these under your roof, you are halfway to becoming part of the so-called Sandwich Generation—the millions of Americans with an adult child who depends on them and your own aging parents are still living, as well.

These are Baby Boomer parents with financial ties to their children and to their parents at the same time. It puts added stress on Boomers' own retirement planning. Forty-one percent of Boomers today are providing at least some financial support to their kids, and 1 in 16 Boomers is also supporting an elderly parent. Their parents, by and large, have prepared much better for their later years, in part because they are much more likely to have a pension. And they do not have a long history of living beyond their means. (Remember? That's the generation in Table 8.1 that was defined by the lessons of the Depression and World War II.) But it's a trend that is growing as we (and our parents) live longer and our kids have fewer opportunities in the economy.

11 Percent

ROMANS'
NUMERAL

Boomer parents with the real fear that their adult children will never be financially independent from them.[11]

Think of it this way—more than 1 in 10 parents has the sinking feeling that their well-educated, thoughtful, and opinionated kid won't hack it in the real world without money from home. You'd play the lottery for a 1 in 10 chance wouldn't you? The most important thing you can do is set some real limits on how much help you are giving the kid. Have an open conversation about how you are balancing your responsibilities to grandma or grandpa, to your own retirement, and then to your child. You might be surprised that your college-educated back-at-home adult child just doesn't realize that you do not have an endless pot of money. If you have always given them whatever they wanted, how would they know?

It's ironic that the real strain for these sandwich parents is less their own elderly parents with finite resources and health concerns, but their healthy able-bodied children with the future stretched out before them.

If you are under one roof with your adult, college-educated child, everyone involved needs to realize this is a close-ended commitment. Some personal finance experts recommend making the kid pay rent. In reality, the reason they are living at home is because they have no money or a job that doesn't pay much. Another strategy is to collect "rent" from the young adult each month and safeguard it for the first and last month's rent they will need

---

UNDER ONE ROOF

- Close-ended commitment.
- Pay rent *or* forced savings for apartment deposit.
- Job search progress reports.
- Make it clear that you are not a luxury hotelier and you expect help and contributions to the household. Clearly define those contributions and stick to it.

when they get out on their own. Essentially, you are making them save and invest in their moving expenses for when they can leave. Some parents make the kid pay for cable and Internet service—making some financial contribution, at least, to the household. Don't fill the refrigerator with the expensive bottled imported beer he or she loves. (You'd be surprised. . . .) You want them to grow up and become independent, not live in a luxury bed-and-breakfast.

Encourage your adult child to fill the time with activities that fill the resume. Volunteer work, budget traveling for charitable work, finding organizations that need your kid's skills—all are ways to fill up the time and the resume. That's the toughest part—finding what constitutes experience on a resume, when 37 percent of Generation Y is unemployed. If this kid lives with you, you have every right and responsibility to insist that they are spending their time in a constructive way. Even if you are just starting to do it now for the first time in their lives!

There's a new trend emerging—college graduates fighting for unpaid internships, just to get an inside track at a company or at least a line on their resume that could be relevant when hiring of young people resumes.

After all, the competition among these kids is intense. Today, the class of 2010 is competing with the class of 2009 for the same jobs. And depending on the degree, there may be less chance of success in landing a job.

In some families, multiple generations under the same roof makes economic sense. In fact, for the first time since World War II we are seeing an

QUALIFIES AS WORK EXPERIENCE

Internships	62 percent
Part-time jobs	50 percent
Volunteer work	40 percent
Class work	31 percent
School organizations	23 percent

Source: CareerBuilder.

JOB OUTLOOK FOR COLLEGE GRADS

Same as a year ago	50 percent
Slightly better	28 percent
Much better	12 percent
Worse	10 percent

Source: Challenger, Gray & Christmas.

BEST CHANCE OF SUCCESS

Health Care	26.0 percent
Business	18.0 percent
Computers	11.0 percent
Accounting/Finance	10.0 percent
Liberal Arts	5.5 percent
Education	3.0 percent

Source: Challenger, Gray & Christmas.

increase in multiple generations under one roof. It can save a lot of money, and help families weather the moribund housing market. When it is a family choice made on purpose to save money on day care and housing costs or because you love each other, embrace it.

But set boundaries, and remember, as soon as you set a precedent, there is no going back. When you are under one roof you need rules.

Whether it is your elderly mother or aunt or your college-educated son, arrange ahead of time who pays the mortgage, who pays for utilities, upkeep and maintenance, who buys groceries, and who gets to keep the car in the garage.

CARING FOR A PARENT

ROMANS'
NUMERAL

59 years old

Nearly three-quarters of U.S. residents consider 59 "middle-aged" compared with only 13 percent who say 59 is "old."[12]

There you are—a baby boomer in the prime of your life, still working and hopefully looking into the not-to-distant future for a healthy, well-funded retirement. It's supposed to be the sweet spot of savings and investment. Your kids (in theory) are educated and raised. Yet you could be one of 30 million Americans taking care of an elderly parent, either financially, or overseeing their health care. Studies show that while your adult children are likely to be a larger burden right now on your finances, there is no question that aging parents need an incredible amount of attention and care from their boomer children. Just the complexity of the health-care system alone means caring for Mom or Dad is infinitely more difficult today than a generation ago.

> **The conversation:** This should come well before a health scare or a financial crisis. It should come today if you have not done this already. Be sensitive and frank. Talk to your parents about how they have prepared for their own later years and whether they have saved enough. What are their intentions if there is a health emergency? Don't do it right away, but after you are comfortable having this conversation a few times, get authority to act on their behalf. You want a durable power of attorney to pay bills, sign checks, and manage the day-to-day finances of your parent should they be hospitalized and you want to be designated the health-care proxy so you can make medical decisions for them. (Contact the National Academy of Elder Law Attorneys to find a lawyer specializing in this near you, www.naela.org.) Insist that your parents draw up living wills outlining their final wishes in a life-and-death situation. If, God forbid, this conversation is happening in a hospital, talk to the hospital's social workers. A good hospital system will have an "advance directives" form—a simple document that your parents can use to lay out their wishes clearly. It doesn't need a lawyer.

> **The money:** How will you pay for assisted living, extended home-based care, or a long-term stay in a nursing home? Does your parent have long-term care insurance and how much will it

cover? Chances are it won't cover everything. A top-quality, safe assisted-living facility can cost more than $4,000 a month. Expenses in the final years of life can easily run $50,000 to $100,000 a year or more. The average length of stay in an assisted-living facility is 28.5 months.[13]

Medicare and some HMOs cover home care, but home-care rules are strict. Plan on needing money saved to cover these and other expenses.

Ask questions and take notes: Appoint a family advocate, or share the responsibility with other siblings and diligently take and share notes with family members about Mom or Dad's care.

Get help: The U.S. Administration on Aging can connect you with local agencies to help you find programs to help—www.eldercare .gov covers everything from adult day care to talking to your elderly parent about driving and finances. Contact the National Association for Home Care & Hospice, www.nahc.org, for information about hiring someone to care for your parent at home. The Consumer Consortium on Assisted Living (CCAL), www.ccal.org, lists tips for choosing a high-quality assisted-living facility. The web site for the National Association of Professional Geriatric Care Managers has a treasure trove of news stories and advice on dealing with the financial and health challenges of aging parents, www.caremanager.org.

See Chapter 9 for more on health-care expenses, including details of the new initiative passed under health reform that could help you save money for your own long-term care one day.

The financial choices and stresses come long before you have an elderly parent who needs care just as you are trying to figure out your own retirement goals. And long before you have a highly educated boomerang back home.

In fact, the most important financial relationship is not between you and your kid, or you and your parent, but you and your spouse.

'TIL DEBT DO US PART

ROMANS'
NUMERAL

30 Percent

Couples who disagree about money once a week are 30 percent more likely to divorce than couples who fight about money less frequently.[14]

Thrifty couples are happiest and too much debt can kill your marriage.

Jeffrey Dew studies couples of all incomes and assets and has found that the more debt a couple has the more likely they are to be unhappy. In fact, too much debt is right up there with cheating and drug or alcohol abuse as a source for divorce.

"When you look at how much couples fight or their marital happiness or their likelihood of divorce, basically, consumer debt is particularly problematic," Dew, an assistant professor of Family, Consumer, and Human Development at Utah State University, says. "It increases the frequency that couples fight and it certainly increases the conflict in marriage."

Dew calls consumer debt "an equal-opportunity marriage destroyer. It does not matter if couples are rich or poor, working class or middle class," he says. "If they accrue substantial debt, it puts a strain on their marriage."[15]

He studied couples of all income levels and found, no matter how much money they make, if there is overall debt, it hurts the marriage. In fact, he found lower income couples with $200 to $600 set aside in savings were happier in their marriage than their middle-class and high-income counterparts with nothing set aside.

"From my research, it doesn't matter what you make but what you do with that income," Dew says.

Even modest assets—and no debt—can increase a couple's marital happiness.

Debt causes marital strife in obvious ways. Sometimes, one spouse has more prolific spending than the other. Sometimes, one spouse is hiding debt they have brought into the marriage. Working to pay off big debts means working longer hours and making more sacrifices in terms of quality of life, which can make couples stressed. It can be difficult to get over feeling that your spouse is spending money foolishly, and you are working harder to pay it off.

Newly married couples grappling with big debts have the most trouble. The longer a couple has been married, it seems the more they understand each other's spending patterns and habits.

Figure 8.1 shows the relationship between disagreements over money, and the rate of divorce.

Dew's analysis of married couples in the recession found that couples managing together through the crisis and paying down their debts actually strengthened their marriages.

"When you manage your finances well, it gives your relationship a more solid foundation, with respect to stability and peace of mind," Dew reports. But he says at the crux of all his research is one central finding: "Debt is problematic for couples."

Bottom line: money can't buy happiness, exactly, but being careful how you manage it can make you happier.

First comes love, then comes marriage, then comes the baby in the baby carriage. Okay, maybe not in that order in the modern United States, but let's start with romance first and work our way up to marriage and babies.

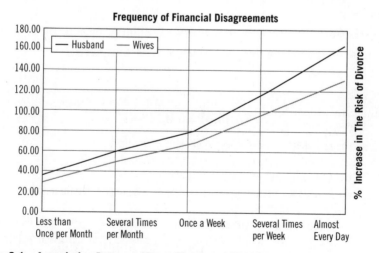

Figure 8.1   Association Between Money Fights and Divorce
Source: Bank On It: Thrifty Couples Are the Happiest.

The extent of most couple's conversations about money stops after deciding who pays for the movie tickets. Do you switch off? Go Dutch? Does he always pay? Does she pay for the movies, he pays for dinner? If it were only as simple as that!

The potential for money trouble in marriage or in a serious relationship is well documented and can't be overstated. Ironically, often it is financial opposites who attract. Many couples think it's impolite to talk too much about money while courting. Often, one partner's "generosity" while dating can be seen as free spending while married.

When savers marry spenders, one spouse can be on the hook for the stereotype of overspending. Sometimes people hide their debt, and you don't know the true picture until you marry and try to borrow money together. From the perspective of the spender, sometimes the saver appears too frugal and not very fun. And when spenders marry each other, it can be a debt disaster.

Men and women often think differently about money. Surveys show that women tend to be more organized with their financial paperwork than men. According to a survey by *Consumer Reports* "Money Advisor," 58 percent of women surveyed had a better idea of where their important financial documents were than their spouses did and only 30 percent of married men thought *they* had a better idea where the paperwork was. Being disorganized with paperwork brings the inevitable late fees and missed deadlines, and exacerbates the obvious strain between spouses over financial matters. (For more on organizing financial paperwork see Chapter 7.)

'TIL DEBT DO US PART

- Be honest about your debts with your significant other.
- Make big purchases together and don't hide your spending.
- Strive to be debt-free on your credit cards.
- Build savings for a rainy day. Studies show that savings bring financial stability and reduce fights.
- "Don't spend more than you earn," advises marriage and money expert Professor Dew. "Recent research has shown that happy couples often cite spending less than what they earn as one key to their success."

That same survey found that 5 percent of people in a relationship admitted to having secret accounts hidden from a spouse or significant other.[16] Hiding debt or hiding accounts is a time bomb ticking away. (Can you say trust issues? Or guilt about your own poor spending habits?) Address the problem and come clean on the accounts and debt.

All matters regarding money demand openness, patience, and forgiveness. That's easier said than done, if you look at divorce statistics.

The perception that one person is overspending or is not making as much money as the other can cause real trouble.

The University of Virginia's Marriage Project report, "State of Our Unions," found men, in particular, were increasingly unhappy in their marriages because they were losing hours and economic status to women.

This recession has been dubbed a he-cession or man-cession, because of the disproportionate effect of job loss on job categories held by men.

Men are 61 percent less likely to be happy in their marriage if they work fewer hours than their wives, and the report concludes that the "man-cession" will strain marriages in working class communities and widen a divorce divide. What is the divorce divide? The more education and less debt a couple has, the more likely they are to stay married. The less education and more debt they have, the more likely they are to have trouble.[17]

The stress is not just on men. From 2004 to 2009 the number of professional women with nonworking husbands jumped 28 percent—a result of the man-cession and of women's reluctance to drop out of the workforce— even for a short time—for fear of difficulty getting back in.[18]

It might be one reason why the Great Recession has reoriented financial attitudes of women more than men. A survey by Citi found that young women aged 18 to 39 are now more focused on acquiring money smarts over materialism. For women of this age group, it's the first downturn they have felt firsthand.

Women (72 percent) were more likely than men (65 percent) to say that if they were to somehow get extra money, they would save it or pay bills with it.[19]

Women were also more likely than men to be conservative about buying big-ticket items and 61 percent of young women said they were focused on cutting down their debt over the next six months. One thing at the top of the list of both men and women for lessons learned from the crisis is a better understanding of valuing their family. Yet women (38 percent) say that they learned to value family, friends, and experiences over materialism, compared with 28 percent of men who said the same thing. What's clear is that women and men—and savers and spenders—think differently about money, and debt can be the root of all sorts of conflicts.

But as stress about money is up, divorces are down during and since the Great Recession. It's not because suddenly people are more in love, but more likely, according to the Marriage Project, "The challenges of job losses, foreclosures and depleted retirement accounts may be driving couples to stick together."

It could also be that couples are just delaying the inevitable, because they can't sell the house or they just don't have the money.

Look, it's painful enough to decide to divorce. Then to find out you *can't* because of the economy?!

BREAKING UP IS HARD TO DO

At the trough of the recession, the American Academy of Matrimonial Lawyers found that 37 percent of attorneys polled reported fewer divorces.

Some are proceeding with divorce, but living together in the same house because of the economy. Either they can't sell the house, or with kids they simply can't afford two households even though they don't want to be married any longer.

When Sallie Frederick's marriage was ending, she was still living with her husband of 15 years. And not because they wanted to.

"My husband lives in the guest room and he comes home on Wednesday nights early to have dinner with the kids and the other nights he comes home late to give me my space," Sallie says. "It's not perfect. It's been difficult."

Boston-based divorce financial planner Gabrielle Clemens says many couples just could not afford the $3,000 to $5,000 to initiate a divorce. "If you can't even retain a lawyer and you have nothing to divide up except for debt, then I think you're better off to wait. I think that's what a lot of people are doing."

As for Sallie—a stay-at-home mom and aspiring life-coach—and her husband—a commercial real estate executive—they eventually switched from two divorce lawyers to a less-expensive divorce mediator instead. Once the divorce became official, they still lived under the same roof.

"Right now there are 20 houses in town on the market that are in our price range and there are no buyers, so my broker pretty much prepared me that the house is going to sit for a while."

Divorce lawyers first reported to me a dramatic drop in divorces at the beginning of the recession, then later they saw a pick-up in business from families reworking child support agreements and divorce agreements to adjust for one spouse's lost income or new lower income once they found a job.

Some attorneys are aggressively trying to rework alimony and palimony agreements based on permanent losses to retirement wealth and income.

Divorce financial planner Clemens says most critical is making sure the family is covered by one ex-spouse's health insurance. Next comes adjusting an agreement to new cash-flow realities.

And as we settle into the months of recovery after the recession, Clemens says, "pent-up demand for divorces" will bring couples back to court.

"Everybody is just tired of feeling like a deer in the headlights and now they are accepting their circumstances and they are starting to move forward."

In many cases, "they never changed their mind to divorce and now they are closer than they were a year ago."

First step, if you are untying the knot, is an assessment of your net worth. That's assets minus liabilities. If there is only debt left in the marriage, the debt will be divided, depending on the circumstances. Clemens recounts the story of one client who made $350,000, her husband made $75,000. The couple had no assets, and in dividing the debt a judge assigned her to pay his student loans instead of paying him support after the divorce.

Clemens says that some couples are surprised in divorce proceedings that they have to divide the 401(k) between the spouses, even when one spouse was not contributing to retirement savings but spending the paycheck instead. Remember, in divorce proceedings, the 401(k) assets will be divided.

If you are already divorced and lost your job, tell your ex immediately. The most important thing is to make sure that there is health care for the children. Try to keep it amicable, on both sides.

Clemens also says that whenever negotiating a court divorce settlement, think five years out and plan for every contingency. What if one partner loses health care? What if someone loses a job? Who pays for the kid's college? Are you prepared to pay child support to one parent even as you are also paying for college tuition (in many states the custodial parent still receives a child support check even when the child is full time in college). Good planning and contingencies on the front end will keep you out of court (and more legal fees) later on. You can research divorce financial planners in your area through the Institute of Divorce Financial Planners and the Association of Divorce Financial Planners.

UNTYING THE KNOT

- Prepare a net worth assessment.
- Decide who pays health care.
- Make contingencies in case one spouse loses job.
- Think five years ahead.

THE PAYOFF

- Be honest with your spouse about money.
- Spend less than you earn, pay down your debt, and you might have a more happy marriage.
- Make your kids take out the trash and do chores. Responsibility at home is a precursor to financial responsibility later on in life.
- Always fund your retirement before paying for your kid's college. You can borrow for college, you can't borrow for retirement.

CHAPTER 9

Health Care

$250,000

How much cash retired seniors need to cover their portion of health-care costs in their last 20 years.[1]

Health-care reform does not mean that U.S. families can stop saving for health-care coverage. It means more and better access to health care. For most of us, it does not mean it's free.

Since 2002, Fidelity Investments has estimated how much a retiring couple, aged 65, would need to save to cover all their health-care costs through the rest of their retirement. Fidelity assumes that they qualify for Medicare and are not on an employer's plan that covers retirees. Why does Fidelity crunch these numbers? To help companies plan for their own expenses related to employee benefits.

Fidelity found that retiring couples will spend about $10,000 a year per year through their retirement on their costs. Only 3 out of 10 retirees while they were working socked money away specifically for health-care costs in retirement, Fidelity found, and 47 percent said that once retired, they found that their health insurance premiums and out-of-pocket costs are higher than they had planned for.

It's a frightful number. As an average figure, it will obviously be distorted by different realities for different people. But Fidelity found on average that retired couples spend $535 a month on health-related costs—a significant chunk of their average total monthly expenses of $2,842.

So what do you do about it? Are you saving today to pay for $535 a month in health costs in retirement?

Health experts, economists, doctors, and personal finance experts argue over the reasons for rising health-care costs and the ultimate fallout of health reform on how much you will pay out of pocket in your retirement for health care. (To say nothing of the quality of that care.) But it underscores the financial importance of staying in good health during your working years. Call it the fiscal fitness of physical fitness. Stay healthy and you'll save tens of thousands of dollars. Make small investments in wellness early for you and your family, and the dividends pay out richly later on. After all, you will spend most of your health-care dollars at the very end of your life. There is a focus on wellness in health reform, but as consumers we all need to take control of wellness and get serious about staying healthy. When I ask health economists, doctors, and administrators what is the best thing families can do to prepare financially for their health-care spending, the answer is unanimous. Stay healthy and stay out of the hospital.

That's obviously not possible for everyone, so this chapter explores new health-care laws meant to guarantee access to the health-care system for you and your family.

The rules are still being written. Lobbying continues on how the different players will interpret and how the government will enact the law. These epic—and still emerging—reforms in the law, are coming amid significant changes in how we already use and access health care.

We're living longer, we want more out of retirement, and we have thousands of new procedures to help us live more comfortable lives and treat the creaky joints and maladies long associated with slowing down and getting old. The good news is that there is no need to slow down. We have artificial hips, cholesterol-lowering medicines, antidepressants, and stents. The bad news is that it all costs money and we have to pay for it somehow. Many health-care economists and fiscal experts say the rising costs of health care are not adequately addressed in health reform. The cost of drugs and procedures are still rising. The law guarantees access first and foremost. If you are low- or middle-income (that's a family of four making $80,200 or less), there will be subsidies to help you pay for that access to health care and there will be penalties and fines for people who don't buy into the system.

Health care matters to you in many ways. The most obvious—you are a consumer of health care. In this chapter, we break down health care from the point of view of you the patient, you the taxpayer, and you the worker who may find valuable opportunities in the growing health-care arena.

REFORM AND YOU

Congratulations! The nation has health-care reform. You can't be discriminated against for a preexisting condition, children cannot be denied insurance coverage, your kids can stay on your insurance until the age of 26, and new health-care exchanges in the next few years will give you more choice for how to buy your health insurance. A few provisions happen immediately, the rest will roll out over the next four years as the rules are written and the new architecture of health care is built.

Immediate Changes

- No lifetime caps on insurance coverage.
- Can't deny coverage for kids with preexisting conditions.
- Temporary high-risk insurance pools for people who can't otherwise get covered.
- $250 drug rebate for seniors to begin closing the Medicare doughnut hole.

Before it can go into action—the rules have to be written. From 2,000-plus pages of health-care reform law, the government must now interpret and write thousands more pages of rules. As you read this, these details are being worked out and we are just beginning on the long path to a new health-care system in the United States.

You're still probably not saving enough money to cover your portion of the costs of health care in retirement—premiums are expected to rise in the coming years for people who have work-based plans, and there may be unintended consequences as policy makers and medical professionals actually put reform into action. (Big legislation always comes with big unintended consequences. Already, the projected costs of health-care reform are rising, as the cost to implement the programs gets clearer.)

The key word here is access. The biggest winners are people who currently want health insurance and can't get it, either because they can't afford it or because no one will insure them. But because that means millions of people with underlying health problems could be entering the pool of the insured, it means costs for everyone else could rise.

People with the most to gain are those with preexisting conditions who have been shut out of the health system. (And by extension, society wins because people who are ill are now entering the health-care system before their conditions are chronic and extremely costly to taxpayers.) When you lose your job and with it your employer-sponsored health care, you can't be rejected by insurance companies because you have high blood pressure, diabetes, cancer, or heart disease.

People with the most to lose—it's a moving target and it depends on how the reform is implemented—but most health experts agree it's the people with employer-sponsored health care and couples who make $250,000 or more a year. The former will likely immediately see their employers or insurance companies push more of the cost of health care onto them (a process, to be fair, under way well before health-care reform). And wealthy Americans will pay higher taxes to help pay for reform.

Starting in 2013, couples who earn $250,000 or more (or $200,000 for single earners) will pay a few hundred dollars more in taxes. It's an added 0.9 percent tax on so-called earned-income and 3.8 percent on investment income.

There are thousands of provisions. Let's start with those you will feel first.

UNDER 26 YEARS OLD

Beginning in 2011, young people will be able to stay on their parents' health insurance until the age of 26. The government is perfecting the rules on this much-talked-about aspect of health reform. A third of these young people have no health insurance—the highest rate of any age group. Their parents agonize over the risk of huge bills for these "young invincibles" if something should

1.2 MILLION

Young people who will stay on their parents' health insurance plan by 2011 because of new health law.

happen to them. At the same time, health economists say healthy young people need to be in the insurance pool to make true reform fair and even.

For years, once a kid graduated from college, there could be an uncertain gap when he or she rolled off their parents' coverage and headed out into the real world. Now, even when kids get in that real world they are having trouble getting insurance. With high unemployment for young people, when they are finding jobs they are often temp jobs, part-time work, or full-time positions that do not offer insurance.

For young people, the new rules offer peace of mind and continued access to their parents' health plans. According to the Department of Health and Human Services, one in six young people has a chronic condition like cancer or diabetes, contrary to the myth that all young people are healthy and don't need insurance.

Here's how the new rules will work.

Starting September 23, 2010, insurance plans that already cover dependents must cover the children of their policyholders until the kid turns 26.

It's not just if your kid lives with you or is still in college. Even if you can't claim your young adult child on your tax return, you are still eligible to put him or her on your health insurance at work. As long as the under-26-year-old doesn't have access to another employer-sponsored plan, they can reenroll on mom or dad's plan.

Even if your child is married and has a family of his or her own, they can still be covered under the parent's work plan. But their spouses and kids cannot. And the insurers must treat each dependent the same. They can't hike up rates or limit types of coverage based on age. Essentially, there will be no difference between a 15-year-old child and a 25-year-old child.

Insurance premium costs are expected to rise by 0.7 percent for parents with children in their plan next year. The government estimates those premiums will rise another 1 percent in 2012 and 2013.

Just like everything in health-care reform, it's about access first and foremost. One in five uninsured in the country is under the age of 26, so this helps get more people into the system.

How much will it cost employees to add their adult kids? The Department of Health and Human Services estimates $3,380 for each dependent in 2011, $3,500 in 2012, and $3,690 the next year.

There's an important wrinkle if your young person is currently covered by you under the military's benefit plan.

Barbara: "My husband is retired from the Navy. Will our dependent daughter keep her TRICARE under age 26 also? She is 22 and will lose her coverage in one year."

The way the rules are written today, Barbara's daughter will not keep her TRICARE military insurance coverage.

Nothing changes for members of the military or retirees. Their TRICARE plan is intact. But because Congress did not touch military benefits in its remake of the health-care system, the dependent children of active military members and retirees will *not* automatically continue on their parents insurance until the age of 26. They will still age out of military health benefits at 23. (As of this writing, the VA and the Department of Defense were working with committee staffers to craft a solution to this loophole. But for now, the young adult children on military health benefits will roll off at 23, not 26.)

Another provision for young people creates a special catastrophic insurance policy for the so-called "young invincibles," the under-30 crowd that is healthy and makes up one-third of the uninsured population. For health reform to work, as many people as possible need to be in the new system, so that healthy people are also paying and spreading the risk around.[2]

The details and rules are still being worked out, but many think it will have a relatively high deductible—almost $6,000, but low monthly payments and offered through the state insurance exchanges to young people who do not have insurance through work and don't qualify for Medicaid. Getting young, healthy people into the system is critical to the success of reform. The Congressional Budget Office forecasts that overall health-care premiums will be 7 to 10 percent lower if young people are included in the coverage pool.

STATE HEALTH EXCHANGES

By January 1, 2014, the states will have marketplaces where consumers can go to buy their own health insurance, if they do not qualify for health care through their employers or expanded Medicaid. By 2019, an estimated 24 million Americans and legal residents will purchase their health insurance through one of these so-called health "exchanges," plus another 5 million or so employees of small businesses whose employers allow them to purchase a plan from an exchange.

The HHS secretary is writing the rules on how these will be constructed, but basically, they must cover four levels of policies (bronze, silver, gold, and platinum). Each policy has the same covered benefits but will offer various options for premiums, co-pays, and deductibles. All plans will have the same maximum out of pocket expenditure. States will offer a variety of plans to meet whatever your family's needs are. If you can't afford it, there are taxpayer subsidies and tax credits to help cover the costs.

To pay the premiums for the insurance, low- and moderate-income people will receive a tax credit in return, starting in 2014 for individuals and families whose income is 133 percent to 400 percent of the poverty level. What does that mean? The poverty level in 2010 was $22,050 for a family of four, so that means that families who earn between $26,600 and $82,000 will be eligible for tax credits to help pay for their insurance.

Starting in 2014, if you fail to buy health insurance the government will fine you $95 or 1 percent of your income, whichever is higher. The penalties rise each year beyond that, as a prod to get people covered. By 2016, the penalty rises to $695 of 2.5 percent of your income. The combination of fines and subsidies is meant to drive as many people as possible to buy insurance.

For most of us, there will be few obvious immediate changes. The Congressional Budget Office forecasts that until 2019, some 160 million Americans will be getting their health insurance coverage through their jobs.

But there are some provisions that received little attention that you could feel right away.

CLASS ACT

$5,500

Average family's out-of-pocket costs for support for an elderly or disabled relative.[3]

You will probably need more money than you think for long-term care. Even before you go to an assisted-living facility or a nursing home, the costs pile up. You need someone to prepare a meal. You need transportation to a senior day-care facility. You'd like a home health aide during the night, in case of emergency.

Long-term care is not an individual issue, it is a family issue. Usually someone emerges as a team leader in the care of an elderly or disabled relative. It often means juggling your own bills, work schedule, and family with the care for someone else.

The CLASS (Community Living Assistance Services and Supports) Act is a voluntary savings plan to put money away to save for the nonmedical expenses you will need to cover home health care or adult day care in old age or disability.

We are getting older, living longer, and will undoubtedly need more money in old age than previous generations. The law is meant to help people stay in their homes and communities as long as possible, and give relief to family members who are struggling to pay their own bills, work a job, raise a family, and care for an elderly or disabled relative at the same time.

Further, costs can be less for someone with a few limitations to stay in the home with some help, rather than enter a nursing facility where the national average cost in 2009 was $79,935 a year, according to MetLife (see Table 9.1).[4]

Here's how it works. It's meant to give up to $27,000 a year on average in benefits to keep people in their communities but help them with their long-term care needs.

Table 9.1   2009 MetLife Survey of Nursing Home, Assisted Living, Adult Day Services Costs

Nursing home, private room	$79,935	Up 3.3% from 2008
Nursing home, shared room	$72,270	Up 3.7% from 2008
Assisted living	$37,572	Up 3.3% from 2008
Home health aides	$21 per hour	Up 5.0% from 2008
Homemaker/companion	$19 per hour	Up 5.6% from 2008
Adult day services	$67 per day	Up 4.7% from 2008

National average rates 2009 versus 2008.

While you are working, you can, through payroll deductions, start putting money away to draw on when you need it for long-term care later on. Participating employers will automatically enroll employees who will have money deducted from their paycheck and deposited into a trust fund held at the U.S. Treasury. It is voluntary—employees can opt out.

After you have paid into the system for at least five years, you become eligible to draw from it when you reach the physical or mental limitations that mean you need care. It's a cash benefit of at least $50 a day, depending on the patient's condition and needs. It's not meant to be the primary savings or insurance tool for long-term care costs, but it's meant to help address the costs of chronic diseases and disabilities. Like many of these provisions, it is completely new, the rules have yet to be written, and it will not begin to pay out to eligible beneficiaries until 2017.

Eligible for CLASS Services

- Home health care
- Adult day care
- Assistive technology
- Home modifications
- Transportation
- Home-health aide services

"It is for practical support," explains Larry Minnix, president of the American Association of Homes and Services for the Aging. "Eighty percent of long-term care goes on in families' homes. On any given day there are 11 to 12 million people over the age of 50 who have disabilities at home, and their families are spending out of their own pockets $5,500 a year on average for practical support like transportation, meals, and medications."

Most of these people do not have long-term care insurance. For anyone not covered by Medicaid, these are out-of-pocket expenses borne by the family.

He says the program will help put money back in the family budget, and the money can also be used when moving to an assisted-living facility or a nursing home. The program offers counseling on finding home health providers and making decisions on what sort of care is appropriate.

The rules are still being written and the program won't begin for a couple of years, but eventually, supporters hope it will be a viable insurance plan to help pay for what are sure to be big out-of-pocket costs for families. Minnix (and the Congressional Budget Office) say the program will eventually save the public health system money by keeping older people at home longer—either in their own homes or in a relative's home—and by helping younger disabled people work a job with a little help getting ready for work and getting *to* work.

Fifty dollars a day will not pay for all your long-term care costs, make no mistake. It doesn't mean that you can stop saving for these out-of-pocket costs. It's just another way to try to tackle what are sure to be huge costs in late retirement, or disability.

FSA CHANGES

$2,500

Ew limit to tax-free money in your flexible spending account, starting in 2013.

Get ready for new restrictions on your flexible spending account (FSA) and say good-bye to using it to buy saline solution and Ibuprofen at the pharmacy.

For years smart savers and investors have used their health-care flexible spending accounts to soften the blow of rising health-care costs, more co-insurance or co-pays. That account allows consumers to put away money before paying income taxes on it, to draw from for the year's out-of-pocket health-care expenses, including over-the-counter medicines, contact lens solution, and baby medicine. In the past, many employers allowed their covered employees to put away up to $5,000 tax free for the FSAs.

People with chronic conditions and small children use these tax-free funds routinely to help pull down their costs.

This new cap is already causing consternation among smart consumers who religiously max it out to save money on their health-care costs. It might seem like a relatively small change in the grand scheme of health reform, but many smart viewers who use this tool to handle their health costs were outraged.

"I am now taking out the maximum for my family and fully expect to use the whole thing, so for me this means a big tax increase," e-mailed Robert in Georgia, after a segment aired on the changes.

When you put money away tax free to pay your health bills, it is essentially a nice little tax cut for you. But that's changing.

Beginning in 2013, smart savers can only put $2,500 away in pretax money, but another aspect of the rule will be felt immediately, when you make your elections for how much to withhold from your pay check *this year.*

Starting in 2011, you can't use the FSA to pay for pharmacy bills that are not prescriptions.

No more tax-free money for over-the-counter medicines like pain relievers, antihistamines, saline solutions, acne drugs, and wart removers.

Health experts say the government had to find ways to raise revenue in health reform, and this is one of those measures.

Other measures include a new 10 percent tax on tanning beds and new rules that chain- and fast-food restaurants post calorie and ingredient information about the food you are buying. The hope is that people will cut back on the empty calories even a little, ultimately saving the system costs from treating chronic obesity, heart disease, and diabetes.

HOSPITAL RESPONSIBILITY

$25 Billion

Unnecessary costs each year because of preventable hospital readmissions.[5]

Hospital-acquired infections. Complications from surgery. Unnecessary procedures. Wrong-site surgeries and the ensuing complications. These and dozens of other routine problems in the chaotic health-care system drain billions from patients, insurance companies, and taxpayers and despite years of attention, little progress has been made. If you have successful open-heart surgery but come home with a nasty MRSA infection, the hospital is paid twice, first for the heart surgery stay and next for the ensuing readmission.

Part of health-care reform is designed to protect you by denying health-care providers revenue when a hospital readmission is preventable.

Starting in 2012, the government for the first time will require hospitals to track and report preventable readmissions. That year, Medicare will stop reimbursing hospitals for preventable readmissions tied to pneumonia or heart failure and by 2014 four more areas will be added to the list. And later, the government will begin reporting each hospital's record on medical errors and infections of Medicare patients. Eventually, the hospitals with the worst scores will be docked Medicare reimbursement from taxpayers.

It's all meant to bring some accountability and awareness, and save revenue in a system that gobbles up dollars whether the health care is successful or not.

HEALTH CARE AS LIVELIHOOD

30+ Percent

Rate of job growth projected for "wellness" careers, including fitness trainers, dental assistants, aerobics instructors, and skin care experts.

Don't think of health reform only as a patient, but also as a job seeker.

People want to look good and feel good. Wellness is part of the national conversation, and health-care reform means jobs, jobs, jobs!

Health care is the fastest growing part of the economy, with nearly 16 cents of every dollar spent in the health system. It is also the fastest growing segment of the jobs market. Indeed, even as labor markets were melting down for almost two years, health-care jobs were consistently added month after month. Where are the job opportunities in health care? Anything that involves the patient, or the equipment, information technology, and supplies used to diagnose and treat the patient.

Figure 9.1 is a snapshot of what the health-care field looks like right now—the larger the sphere, the more jobs. And the higher up the scale, the more money that job pays.

Here's where the Department of Labor says it is going. Table 9.2 shows that the government estimates more than half a million jobs will be created in nursing by the year 2018, but the real growth is in home health care and personal care aides—an explosion really of more than 800,000 jobs. The low pay, long hours, and scant benefits packages of these jobs

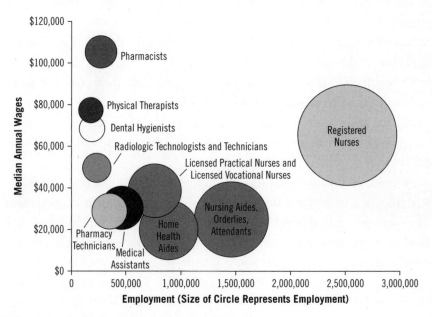

Figure 9.1 Health-Care Jobs Growth Next 10 Years

Source: Bureau of Labor Statistics.

Table 9.2   New Jobs 2008–2018

Job title	# of New Jobs	2008 Median Wages ($)
Registered nurses	581,500	62,450
Home health aides	460,900	20,460
Home care aides	375,800	19,180
Nursing aides, orderlies	276,000	23,850
Physicians, surgeons	144,100	193,780

Source: Bureau of Labor Statistics.

though is a serious concern for the economy. For many people with little education or for many newcomers to this country, they will be the first step into the U.S. workforce. But many of these are not "ladder" jobs like nursing, where on-the-job experience brings opportunities for continuing education and moving up the income and skills ladder. Unfortunately, economists note that there will be huge job creation in the lower-skilled ranks of health care and those jobs will not have the pay or benefits of the manufacturing jobs that were long the first rung in the labor market for unskilled workers without a college degree or a foothold in the economy. Still, health care is an incredibly diverse field and there are numerous niches to fit different skill sets, education levels, and interests. And many workplace and retraining experts tout the locality of these jobs—there are health facilities in all neighborhoods and regions, close to your own support base.

Obviously doctors, pharmacists, optometrists, dentists, and chiropractors are going to load up on the schooling—and the student debt—before they can practice in this field. But as health-care demand explodes and new areas develop, experience and training opportunities mean big bucks for some fields that do not require a four-year degree (see Table 9.3).

The key in all of these jobs is continuing education and on-the-job training and experience. Many of these careers have good benefits packages and job prospects. Clearly, as the country remakes its health-care system and ensures more access to it, there will be new opportunities for you as a worker, not just a patient.

Table 9.3   Good Pay, No Four-Year Degree

Medical Jobs	Median Pay ($)	Top Pay ($)
Radiation Therapist	77,100	101,000
Senior Charge Nurse	72,200	101,000
ICU Registered Nurse	71,900	108,000
MRI Technologist	68,700	90,700
Medical Equipment Repairer	68,600	95,000
Ultrasound Technologist	66,700	91,200

Source: PayScale.com.

THE PAYOFF

Even as millions of Americans gain access to the health-care system for the first time, it doesn't mean it is free. For most of us, health care will require more than we are saving, and we will all face important—and expensive—decisions about end-of-life care. Have those discussions with your family when you are healthy.

- Stay healthy. "An ounce of prevention is worth a pound of cure." This could well be a financial decision for your family and part of your family budget. The cheapest food in the richest country in the world also happens to be the worst for you. You might have to pay more for a healthy diet and healthy lifestyle. Health experts say it is an investment. Eat right. Exercise. And participate in your insurance company or employer wellness programs.
- Figure $10,000 per year per couple in retirement for out-of-pocket health-care costs.
- Consider long-term disability insurance through your employer and through the government's new CLASS program to keep you in your home as long as possible when you become elderly or disabled.
- Look for health care for employment, too. There are jobs in every metro area.
- If you are retraining for a job in health care, make sure it is a "ladder" job with upward mobility. Millions of low-paying jobs with little advancement are being created. Choose wisely.

Health-care reform will be big business over the next decade. For a look at the landscape for small business, read on.

CHAPTER 10

Small Business

1,718 Every Single Day

The number of small businesses created amid the recession in 2008.

The Great Recession hasn't killed the United States small business spirit.

As the banking system was crumbling around us, Rob Redfearn was making plans to expand his restaurant in Lumberton, North Carolina. In one commuter town in New Jersey, 60 small retailers teamed up to encourage local shoppers to visit Main Street instead of the big box stores. In Washington, DC, two sisters shocked their parents and quit their jobs to open a cupcake bakery with their life savings and no loans. And a baby and bath care company got its big shot—a huge order from a major drug store chain—and learned from its early mistakes in the worst retail environment in 70 years.

When bank funding dried up, creative entrepreneurs found new start-up incubators, borrowed money online from strangers, and shook the cushions for every penny they could find to keep going.

Some didn't make it. Many others did. And still many more have changed their business models forever to adapt to a new reality.

SMALL BUSINESS BY THE NUMBERS

- 64 percent of jobs in the past 15 years have been created by small businesses.[1]
- Just over half of small businesses are based in the home.
- Small businesses hire 40 percent of the high-tech workers in this country and produce 13 times more patents per employee than large firms.

There is nowhere in the world better to run a small business with an idea, a business plan, hard work, and a dream. That's still true, although not without new challenges: like wary customers and less availability to the credit so many small businesses depend on.

In this chapter, you meet these small business owners—and others—and learn from their challenges and mistakes, and hopefully, get a good sense of where the ideas and job creation are coming from in this economy. You see where they are turning for funding, including some creative new ways of financing. These businesspeople are decidedly divided on how economic stimulus and the bailouts have helped them, and they acknowledge that the years ahead will be uncertain and difficult as they adapt to health-care reform, less credit, and the prospects of a more restrained American consumer.

But to a person, they want to grow and are looking high and low for ways to make that happen. Because small business creates more than 60 percent of all new jobs in the United States, that's a sentiment that matters to you.

21 Percent

ROMANS'
NUMERAL

Small business owners who say that their companies are healthy and growing.[2]

There's no question that small business is the key to an economic recovery. But no one said it was easy. An American Express poll of owners of firms with 100 or fewer workers found only one in five small companies consider themselves healthy, nearly half of small businesses described themselves as "staying afloat" and one in five said they were "sinking."

Similarly sobering, the chief economist of the National Federation of Independent Business gave this assessment after surveying 950 business owners this spring: "Poor sales and uncertainty continue to overwhelm any other good news about the economy," said Bill Dunkelberg.[3] These small businesses are not cutting as many jobs as they were a year ago, but they have not stepped up the hiring, either.

Until lending improves, small business owners are cautious about making capital improvements, hiring more workers, and expanding.

In short, the recovery you're hearing about on Wall Street and in the economy in general has yet to visit most businesses on Main Street. If you believe the statistics, most businesses are vacillating between survival mode and stasis.

Here's why.

THE DISAPPEARING BANKER

39 Percent

ROMANS' NUMERAL

Small business owners that report they can't get adequate funding for their business, up from 22 percent in August 2008.[4]

Small business suffered a credit shock that is not easy to survive.

Big banks that received the most bailout funds from taxpayers sharply cut their small business lending in 2009, cutting lending by $12.5 billion in the last half of the year.

Basically, big banks whacked their lending to small business during the recession, even though they received billions in taxpayer funding. Simply put, taxpayers bailed them out with no strings attached and they pulled in their lending from small business.

"Big banks pulled back on everyone, but they pulled back harder on small businesses," says bailout watchdog Elizabeth Warren. Her committee overseeing how the bank bailout helped restore credit to small businesses found that it simply failed.[5]

Again and again, the data have shown that credit for small business has dried up.

Entrepreneur Jeff Baker owned a small textile company with his brother in Buffalo, New York. When the economy started to heave in 2007, he approached his bank about restructuring his debt to make it through.

"We weren't asking for more funds, we just needed to consolidate longer term debt and the bank looked at us cross-eyed," he says. "It makes me wild [that] they crushed me and my brother with one hand and they took bailout money with the other hand."

That sentiment resonates among many established small business owners who have been vaporized by the recession. Baker started a group called "I Need a Freakin' Job" and put that slogan on a billboard in Buffalo as a way to urge the country not to become complacent about near 10 percent unemployment.

On the group's web site he vents his frustration at the disappearing banker to small business.

"Cynical is what you become after witnessing the destruction of American exceptionalism and realizing you are a casualty of a handful of greedy animals feeding on the soul of a great nation."

Baker is speaking from the heart and from personal experience. His experience, according to the bailout watchdog's most recent report, is not unique. "Small business credit remains severely constricted," Elizabeth Warren's bailout watchdog report concludes.[5] "Unable to find credit, many small businesses have had to shut their doors, and some of the survivors are still struggling to find adequate financing."[6]

The small business lending bubble is still popping, and like everything else, good people and their solid business models are sometimes caught in the downdraft.

Here's what happened.

For years, lending standards spiraled ever lower in this country. Money was free and easy and cheap for consumers, small companies, and big firms alike.

Now, after the financial crisis, banks are increasing their cash reserves to set aside for loans that go bad, and they are without a doubt lending money more judiciously.

That means fewer loans, smaller loans, and more conservative loans.

The problem was something called the secondary market. Banks for years would make a loan, and then sell it to someone else to be packaged with other loans and sold to investors. Those investors would collect the interest or small payments on the packaged loans, and could trade them like a stock or bond depending on how they felt the security would perform. Every time one of these individual loans was sold off the original lender's books, it freed up capital to make more loans. (Banks sold off mortgages, small business loans, and commercial loans—just about anything that could be packaged up and sold to an investor.)

This practice allowed more loans to be made than ever before. But when loans started to go bad, the secondary market nearly froze. That meant banks had to keep the loans they made on their books, and with it, all the risk that a borrower would default. As the economy got worse, the more borrowers fell behind in their payments, and the more cash the banks had to set aside to cover potential losses.

Thankfully, the market freeze that clogged the money flow is thawing. A secondary market for these loans that was all but dead in 2008 is moving again. That is good news. And regional and community bankers insist they are working hard to find viable small businesses to loan money to—but they admit that the profile of the businesses they are looking for is more conservative than a few years ago. Something as simple—and common— as a personal credit score in the low- to mid-600s might mean a business owner can't get the capital he or she wants to expand. Many small business owners use their personal credit to fill the holes when business gets tough, so it's a vicious circle. Millions of small business owners have less-than-perfect credit. And that precludes them from the bank funding they need to survive the crisis or grow.

For the survivors, small business loan officers say that every single business owner must reevaluate his or her business model and mission statement for what comes after 20 years of credit-fueled prosperity.

It's too late for Jeff Baker's textile company in Buffalo.

"I CAN CREATE JOBS!"

But restaurateur Rob Redfearn has indeed survived the crisis and is determined to grow.

In 2004, he turned an old mule stable in historic, but tired downtown Lumberton, North Carolina, into BlackWater Grille, the center of local life serving what he calls low-country fare. (Think crab cakes, fried green tomatoes, crawfish stuffed shrimp, blackened catfish, steaks and chicken breast stuffed with alligator—yes, alligator.)

He's got 35 employees, a crowded bar on weekends and a dependable banquet business. He wants to expand about 60 miles north on I–95 to the city of Fayetteville. Along the strip of chain restaurants there, the wait runs 45 minutes on weekends for predictable, mid-priced chain restaurant food.

"I can hire 35 to 50 people right away and do $3 million in sales," he says, gesturing to the empty China Buffet building he would turn into another BlackWater Grille.

He's convinced that the spillover traffic alone would pay the bills and ultimately people would search out quality, fresh local fare over the same steak and blooming onion you can get anywhere.

He's run the numbers, and figures he needs $150,000.

Local branches of the big banks weren't interested in a commercial loan. Investors, no surprise, had their wallets shut after the banking crisis.

He was overjoyed in early 2009 when Congress passed a massive economic stimulus that included billions to banks to back Small Business Administration loans. The whole idea was to stabilize and preserve U.S. small business so they could preserve jobs and stay afloat through the thick of it. It was the small business bailout Main Street was hungry for. Even better, emergency funding in the stimulus would be available for small business—$35,000 in so-called ARC funding.

It's exactly what Redfearn thought he needed to expand and grow more jobs. But for one reason after another, he didn't qualify. The $35,000 emergency loans were for current operating expenses, not to expand. And even though the stimulus was passed in February 2009, small business owners waited months for the government to hammer out and publish rules about who qualifies and how. We heard from hundreds of small business owners, who were holding out for a piece of that funding, but for them time was running out.

"Virtually every day I'm calling somebody . . . to find this loan. I've looked at all the major banks, other sort of nontraditional lenders, higher rates of interest . . . I've looked for sort of angel investors, because I don't mind getting equity in the projects in exchange for just a pass to get it going."

So passionate about getting loans to small business, Redfearn wrote to the president, and to me. So I went to Lumberton to meet him and tell his story—a typical small business owner trying to get a loan in the teeth of a tough economy.

"There's an issue here. You all want to loan money and see the economy stimulated but it's not happening and there's a disconnect between Washington wanting to give this sort of loan to people like me and I'm sure there are millions of people like me who need it, want it, could use it and really develop it."

Redfearn says he could pay his loan back in a year. If Washington wants jobs created with stimulus money, he says, he can create them.

"I don't want a bailout, I just want an opening to the door. I'll walk through it myself."

So far that door is shut.

Banks are not taking chances. Loans that may have been made a decade ago are now hard to come by. Once was, a good business plan and cash flow, but less than stellar credit meant you still got the loan, only at a higher interest rate. A divorce a few years ago dinged Redfearn's credit, and the biggest local lender, BB&T Bank, said it would not lend to him. In Redfearn's case, a million dollars in sales last year and a business degree do not trump nervous loan officers.

Lee Cornelison is the regional director for the Small Business Administration in North Carolina.

"Lenders have returned to the old-fashioned lending standards, they're making loans with the expectation that all of them will be repaid. Before, maybe a lot of those loans would be resold, packaged, and collateralized, and therefore the rest was spread so widely that it didn't matter," Cornelison says.

He's talking about that secondary market for loans. The loans were bundled and sold to investors, where the risk was spread around, allowing the banks to make more loans. After the financial system crashed last fall, that market virtually shut down and has only recently showed signs of thawing. Now, even as the secondary market perks up, lenders remain leery of taking and keeping the risk when loans of all types are defaulting.

What that means for millions of small business owners is a more discriminating lender. There are fewer loans for only the most qualified applicants.

"Right now small businesses need to be careful," Cornelison says. "If you're in business now it's probably a good time to reassess your business model in light of current economic conditions."

At the worst of it, small business loan volume fell to half what it was before the recession. Now, it is slowly coming back. The SBA credits the stimulus. Bankers credit a general improvement in the environment. Unfortunately, some businesses couldn't wait that long and have folded. And only the strongest business plans survive.

"People with good ideas are getting loans," Cornelison says. But be prepared to show a good credit score, cash flow, supplier agreements, and offer collateral, at a minimum.

The good news is that a little over a year after the stimulus created incentives to lend to small business through SBA-backed loans, that lending is approaching prerecession levels. The flagship SBA loan program backed some 29,000 in the past six months, or about $7.5 billion worth.

That's a vast improvement, but those SBA loans account for less than 5 percent of all lending to small biz.

"Everyone's been shaking down their credit cards to try to pull whatever they can out of there," says CNNMoney.com small business editor Stacy Cowley. "A lot of people are turning to family and friends, going back to suppliers, seeing if they can negotiate with them for credit. Just really shaking

AVAILABLE $$$$ AND HOW TO GET IT

- Tap credit cards.
- Family and friends as investors.
- Renegotiate supplier agreements.
- Angel investors.
- SBA ARC loans, SBA-backed loans.

the seat cushions trying to see where they can get it because they're finding the banks just aren't there for them right now."

In Fayetteville, Redfearn stands in the parking lot of the empty former Chinese restaurant he wants to transform into a second BlackWater Grille. Has he ever considered that it might not be a good time to open a restaurant? Two years into a brutal recession where consumers are thrifty and banks so risk-averse?

"Entrepreneurs—and I'm one—we're risk takers by nature."

On a scale of 1 to 10, how successful is he in his quest to get a $150,000 loan to expand and create some jobs?

"I would say I'm a 10. And it may not be this month or next month, but we'll get it. And it may not be this location. This location may dry up and move down the street, but I'm confident that we can do it."

SOCIAL BUTTERFLY

ROMANS'
NUMERAL

5 Years

About half of new small businesses survive the first five years. Seven out of 10 make it the first two years.[7]

Fewer still can survive a complete transformation of their industry and grow and thrive.

Mitch Goldstone beats all those statistics: His small business has been changing and thriving for 20 years.

In 1990 Goldstone had a film-developing storefront in Irvine, California. Drop off your roll of Kodak 200 24 exposure film, and his little shop would develop it for you.

Pretty simple and straightforward. But film died. Digital is king, and our shoeboxes full of old snapshots are gathering dust under the bed while we compose slideshows on our Mac Books and upload cell phone pictures to Facebook.

Mitch is in the same shop in Irvine. Only today, his company, Scanmyphotos.com, is international.

"I solved the biggest problem in photography—what do you do with those shoeboxes of photos and get them on iPhone and Facebook," he laughs. First he made money developing those pictures for you, and now he makes money converting them to digital. And because anyone can find him online, he gets shoeboxes of snapshots from all over the world to scan, correct, and download. (He does it fast. They scan boxes of photos the day they receive them and put them back in the mail the next day. When I interviewed him, he was doing a victory lap for turning around an order from Australia in three days.)

His best marketing is free. Goldstone is a prolific user of social media like Twitter, and uses it well. He's not always there simply pushing his company. He's become part of the photography conversation and shares interesting and helpful links and tips.

He has more than 10,000 followers on Twitter and has spirited running conversations about scanning photos and slides, photo labs, digital photography, and sometimes politics. When he's not talking all things photo, he's railing against credit card company transaction fees. It all serves to make Scanmyphotos.com relevant and visible in a sea of digital human communication.

All this, from a 1990 photo-developing shop.

He explains his online presence this way: "Personalize, humanize, and become the local evangelist for everything photo."

"Today because of technology even the smallest business can be international," he says. With sales now topping a million dollars, he calls himself "an emerging entrepreneurial business." Emerging, because even though he has been in business for 20 years, social media allows him "a smart way to fish out new customers."

It's something many small business owners resist. They don't have the time or the tech-savvy to embrace social media. They prefer a Yellow Pages ad and an old-fashioned presence as the neighborhood store.

Many industry groups and small businesses have told me they don't know how to "monetize" social media. It just isn't worth their time.

The flip view is that you can't afford *not* to embrace it. It's like not having a phone number. It's much more than just advertising or marketing. "It's much more than that. It's fun and it's essential. You don't have time *not* to do it," Goldstone says.

Goldstone says that Twitter is as transformative for finding customers as digital was to film.

SMALL BIZ AND SOCIAL MEDIA

- Don't be boring or overshare.
- Don't endlessly promote.
- Do share helpful links.
- Give free tips, or coupons. People respond to money.
- Define your online personality and be consistent.
- How do you monetize social media? Wrong attitude.
- You can't afford not to. It's as essential as a phone number.

Small business owners can't afford not to be part of a conversation that is swirling around them, especially when these social media sites are actively and quickly sharing information—and disinformation—about your industry. Consider this: Facebook did not even exist six years ago and today there are more than 500 million users around the world. The average person on Facebook has 130 friends and shares at least 70 pieces of information or messages each month. In one click, one person can share something about your company to potentially reach thousands of people.

It has the potential of a $3,500 Yellow Pages or traditional media ad, at little or no cost. That's *if* you learn how to use it.

"It's going to continue to grow and you need it to stay connected to customers," Mitch Goldstone says.

An audience of small theater owners recently asked me how they could monetize Twitter, Facebook, MySpace, Foursquare, and others. They worried they were spending valuable employee time on these media sites but not realizing increased revenue. Their focus was still on subscription sales to devoted theatergoers. Many had determined that this new trend was not applicable to their industry. Others were determined to figure it out, but weren't sure how. (This is the struggle of every manager or business owner right now using these new communication technologies, I assure you. No one has the perfect prescription for how to do it, and even if they do, it is changing literally by the week.)

And then, out of the middle of a New York City snowstorm in February, came an epiphany. Roads and bridges were shut down, airports empty, the Northeast was hammered by more than a foot of snow, and a tweet was born. "Snow Day Special: Mamma Mia! Has $31.50 tix for tonight's perf @8 pm. Visit the Winter Garden Theater Box Office for tix – NO ID required." That tweet was retweeted again and again, (I received it from the NY blog @newyorkology) and it spread like digital word of mouth. On a day when the theater should have been empty, the line for tickets was around the block.

That's exactly the right way to use Twitter for your business. Say something only when you have something to say, when it matters to your customers, and when you think your followers will retweet it to others and spread the word of mouth.

I guarantee you—that short tweet meant money. Find ways to use it spontaneously for your biz. It's a slow afternoon at the Iowa pizza parlor, tweet to your local followers a large pizza and 2-liter Coke special and see if you draw in some evening business. You're a small Brooklyn dress shop with 12 size-2 blue smocks. Put your size-2 dilemma on Facebook.

Comedian Hal Sparks put it best when he told me a tweet is "a tap on the shoulder." It's not meant to sell your whole line of products. He uses it to tease his upcoming comedy shows and keep a funny or edgy conversation running between shows. It's working, he's got more than 16,000 followers. He can tap their shoulder and get them to give him a look with little effort. The key is to do it in a way that connects with your audience, doesn't irritate them.

SHOP LOCAL

$68

ROMANS' NUMERAL

Spend $100 at a locally owned shop and $68 directly benefits the community. Spend it at a big box retailer and less, $43, does.[8]

Here's the rub for small retailers: At the same time consumers want more value with their money and want to spend each dollar in a way that matters to the world around them, they are also pinching pennies and more likely to head to a big box retailer for staples. The big guys have tremendous leverage with their suppliers to hold down costs and can even offer items for sale at a loss to draw in business. How can a Main Street shop compete with giant sales and deep discounts at the big retailers?

Shopkeeper Kelly Del Rosso owns *semplice*, a housewares and home store, named after the Italian word for simple. She lived through one tough holiday season and was bracing for another one.

"It's been a difficult year," Del Rosso says of 2009. "People are not shopping for sport anymore."

And for her, it means working harder to get customers in her New Jersey commuter town to drop into the shop.

Del Rosso decided it was time to band together with the other Main Street shops she competes against, and together, she says, start thinking like a mall in order to survive.

"It's such a big message nationally that you know if stores get together and realize you know—what if your neighbor closes on your right and on your left—you are not an island," she says.

She got 60 local businesses together—technically rivals—and brought them together on a group web site. She sent out fliers and coupons, got on Facebook and Twitter, and linked up with something called the 3/50 Project, a national movement that encourages people to buy local. The group operates from Arizona to Alabama to Illinois. Look around your own neighborhood and you can see the small 3/50 Project signs on notions stores, green grocers, and hardware stores. The idea is resonating and giving Main Street some tools to compete."

"We're not telling consumers to stop going to big boxes or to stop going to chains and franchises because it's unrealistic," says 3/50 founder and retail

---

LOCATION, LOCATION . . .

Spend $100 at local business . . .
$68 stays in the community.

Spend $100 at a chain . . .
$43 stays in the community.

Source: Civic Economics.

expert Cinda Baxter. "It's about remembering . . . that not all things have to come from a big box."

Over the holidays, it worked for the shop *semplice*. "I think the sense of community has been unbelievable," owner Del Rosso says. "There are so many customers who come in here and say, 'I'm here to shop local.'"

But the next challenge for *semplice* and its small competitors comes with a big retailer not down the highway at a strip mall, but across the street in the form of a new Anthropologie store—a national chain with deeper pockets than its new neighbors and a corporate cushion until the economy recovers.

On the one hand, it speaks volumes about what a big national chain thinks about a recovery coming here. It could mean valuable spillover to the small shops. On the other, the small retailers will have to work even harder to promote their buy-local message if consumers spend their money first with the big guy, leaving less for them.

It's a reminder that once a smart small business has survived and come out the other side of the economy, the new normal will look a whole lot different than the go-go days of spendthrift consumers and easy credit. Every one, no matter what size, is vying for the same consumer dollar.

CUPCAKE SISTERS

In the case of sisters Sophie Lamontagne and Katherine Kallinis, that consumer dollar is not $1, but $2.75 to be exact.

That's the cost of one of the Georgetown Cupcakes. They think that a small and sweet purchase is all a recessionista needs to feel satisfied. And one cupcake at a time, they are building their own little empire.

In 2007, they shocked their parents by announcing they were going to quit their jobs in venture capital and fashion, and open a cupcake bakery.

"Our parents thought we were crazy," Sophie says.

Leaving good jobs for cupcakes in a recession?!

They went to the banks to see if there was loan money available. Loan officers failed to see the timeliness of the business plan, "They were like, 'Really girls, just cupcakes?'" Sophie laughs. "We kept explaining we wanted to be a niche bakery that does one product and does it well—best in class for cupcakes."

The banks took a pass, so the women took every penny they had—their entire life savings—and maxed out all their credit cards. All told they spent about $80,000.

They secured a tiny storefront in Georgetown, a tiny neighborhood in Washington, DC, not far from an established upscale food emporium Dean and Deluca. They scrubbed floors, painted walls—"we installed the toilets ourselves," Katherine says. "We were in Home Depot every day."

Friends and family pitched in. Opening day was Valentine's Day 2008. There was no advertising, no public relations team, no big rollout. Just two sisters, one husband, their friends and their grandmother's cupcake recipes.

Sophie: "Our only advertising on opening week was a poster from Kinko's that was $80. My husband freaked, we were on such a tight budget."

They baked 500 cupcakes for opening day.

The line was out the door and they sold out in two hours.

The little location tucked just off M Street was the only thing like it in DC, and word of mouth spread.

"We couldn't afford any advertising, we just focused on doing one thing and doing it well. Making the cupcakes fresh every morning with the best ingredients and selling them at a low price point," Katherine says. ($2.75 each or a dozen for $29.)

The people kept coming and they turned a profit after just three months.

The first time they tried to raise money, the banks didn't believe in cupcakes. The second time they tried to raise money, the banks were in distress.

Finally, a small regional bank is helping them expand, opening two new shops each baking 5,000 cupcakes a day.

Last year, their main location did $2.5 million in sales and now they are expanding to four shops. They employ about 100 workers and worked closely with FedEx to design a shipping box to overnight their cupcakes anywhere. A dozen costs $55 including shipping, with special themes for a birthday, Mothers' Day, baby boy and baby girl. Again, they are appealing to the person who wants something special for their money—it's cheaper than flowers and more unexpected.

A clue here about where your own small business passion may lie: These sisters were baking cupcakes with their grandmother when they were little girls. They always had a sort of childlike fantasy about having their own bakery. But each comes to the kitchen table with complementary skills. Sophie knows a thing or two about business—she worked in venture capital for molecular biology life sciences investing. And Katherine knows a thing or two about what's in style and what people want—her career before cupcakes was fashion.

Because of their skills, their laser-like focus on making one thing and making it better than anyone else, and where they fit on the consumer spectrum, they are growing fast. In a way, their business is oblivious to the headlines about a skittish consumer, in part, because what they are selling is something dainty and sweet and stylish that makes those skittish consumers feel a little less blue about the economy.

The risk is that cupcakes are a fad—that the popularity of shows like Cake Boss and the allure of the "sweet little dessert shop that could" fades. Already, designer cupcakes are popping up in cafés, grocery stores, and coffee shops across the country.

Katherine doesn't see it that way. Imitation is the sincerest form of flattery, she says, and proof that they really were on to something. And she maintains there is plenty of room for more cupcakes in the U.S. experience. Just look at ice-cream parlors. They do one thing, do it well, with a lot of competition.

Because the sisters only make one product doesn't mean they can't find new markets with that product, either, they point out. With their elegant little cupcakes, they've stumbled into the lucrative wedding business.

"You can get a lot of cupcakes for $300 dollars," Katherine says. The sisters supplied cupcakes for seven weddings every weekend last May. "Because of the recession a lot of brides chose cupcake towers. . . . The brides have been pretty creative, using them as individual wedding cakes, takeaway gifts and favors."

It's an example of how quickly they adapted to a niche within their niche, and capitalized on it.

Still, it's not a cakewalk, especially with soon-to-be four locations, 100 employees, health-care reform changes, and competition from other cupcake start-ups.

"You just can't put your name on it and walk away," Sophie says. "You own it."

Their recipe for success—home-baked for *Smart Is the New Rich* readers?

> ### CUPCAKE RECIPE
>
> - Do what you love.
> - Know your customer and stay focused on that niche.
> - When your customers have a good idea (e.g., cupcake weddings), profit from it.
> - Take small steps and work hard.

Sophie: "If you have a passion for it go for it and take small steps and put in a lot of sweat equity."

Katherine: "Do something that you love. It is easy to look at what other people are doing and copy [but] people who are in it to make a quick buck won't make it . . . do what you love, and be the best at it."

They plow every penny back into the business, with a disbursement to themselves here and there to pay the rent and their own bills. Even as they grow quickly, they are leery of "founderitis" as Katherine calls it, where they don't step aside and let the company grow under the direction of a seasoned CEO. "We need to get to the point where we need to bring people to grow the business further."

Many a small business has been undone because the founders can't let go of control, or the business matures and can't find a new path.

Those challenges are still ahead. Right now, these sisters are in the sweet spot of small business. They are making money, having fun, and filming a TLC reality show about their bakery and what it's like to be sisters and 50/50 partners.

YES TO CARROTS

Ido Leffler and Lance Kalish know all about founderitis. They took a tiny company in Israel with 6 products in 16 stores and turned it into the second largest natural beauty brand in the United States. They've made mistakes, learned from them, made great moves, and now have just hired for their business a professional CEO who has 15 years' experience in the consumer world.

These guys are relentlessly optimistic—perhaps appropriate for a company whose name is "Yes To . . ." as in Yes To Carrots, Yes To Tomatoes, and Yes To Cucumbers. (Their natural base ingredients include beta-carotene, thus, the vegetable tie in.)

The two took over the brand in 2006 and moved it to the United States, and the big break came a year later in 2007 when Walgreens decided to plant their veggie-inspired line of natural beauty products in its stores all over the country.

It was, quite literally, every small business's dream. The big shot at the big retailer and access to all those shelves. But it was one shot—and it had to succeed.

"We really saw this as a dream come true," Leffler says. "When they first placed their first order, the quantities in itself" were huge. "When you go from 16 stores to 5,800 stores. . . . That was our first pressure."

But in the $8 billion natural beauty business, it's not getting on the shelves that counts in the end. It's getting off the shelves and into shopping carts that really matters.

"Walgreens, like most retailers here in the country, have a simple philosophy—if it doesn't sell, they can return the stock back to you," Leffler says. "At stake was the entire company."

Leffler and Kalish bet everything on traditional advertising—an entire marketing budget spent on a national magazine campaign, but the spike in sales never came.

"We had committed the vast majority of our cash into this promotional campaign, and it wasn't moving the needle," Leffler says. "It nearly got to a stage where we didn't have money to pay our salaries."

Sleepless nights, a company on the brink, money running out, and a marketing campaign that wasn't working—so much for the big break. So Yes To got creative and launched an interactive marketing campaign.

Critical to its success was a social media presence that cost nothing. Leffler says small business has a phenomenal new tool to compete.

"This is the first time in the history of brands that the smaller guys are able to take on the bigger guys on a very level playing field, and I think it's worrying the bigger guys in a very significant way. Today you don't have to spend any money at all to set up a Facebook fan page. You don't need a huge marketing fund to set up a Twitter account. You need zero," he says.

Leffler says that young brands can leverage this new media and their own young identity to relate to customers in a way that is entirely fresh and exciting.

Leffler and Kalish created a social media contest to be the face of the brand and attracted 150,000 fans, started a forum for customer feedback and passed out a million samples outside Walgreens stores.

And the seeds, pardon the pun again, began to sprout.

"Using the small little funds we had left paid significant dividends, it was phenomenal," Leffler said.

Sales doubled in six months and Yes To has grown since, reaching 28,000 stores in 30 countries.

That's where the founderitis comes in. Having struggled—and triumphed—and grown so large, they know that someone with experience running a bigger company is best at the helm. It's a good problem to have, deciding to hire an outside CEO.

Ido Leffler recounts advice from one of the company's mentors that he says resonates for all business owners who are trying to figure out what mix of skills and decisions will make them one of the few companies that survive five years as a small business.

"It's 20 percent hard work. *Hard work*. And 80 percent luck. We worked very hard, and we were lucky."

JUST SAY YES TO . . .

- Patience.
- Face to face meetings.
- Getting on a plane and making it happen.
- Partnering with suppliers and key accounts.
- Meeting everyone (you never know what may come of it).
- Relentless optimism.
- Switching gears.
- New ideas.
- Embracing social media.

When did he know they'd made it? The day he found himself on a plane sitting next to reality star Kelly Osbourne. As they were chatting about business, she reached into her bag and pulled out a "Yes To" lip balm.

FIND THE MONEY

ROMANS'
NUMERAL

95 Percent

Self-employed Americans who are "completely satisfied" or "mostly satisfied" with their jobs.[9]

So you can work hard and you're willing to try your luck. You have an idea, or an inspiration and it's time to get it out of your head, onto a business plan, and into the real world. Bravo. People who decide to start a business or venture out on their own are significantly more satisfied with their jobs than other employees. They are more likely to work because they want to and they love what they are doing, and not necessarily for the paycheck. But they have to find the money first.

Investors are justifiably nervous about funding small business start-ups. Banks are lending with the expectation that they will be paid back in full—that means that they are making fewer loans with more conservative terms. And your business partners or parents are strapped.

That doesn't mean that smart start-ups aren't finding interesting ways to raise money. There are always the tried and true—and expensive—credit cards. That is, *if* they haven't cut the credit lines or closed them on you altogether. Indeed, starting a business on credit cards is infinitely harder today than even two years ago when the Cupcake Sisters were starting out. Here are some other ways.

P2P Loans

Peer-to-peer (P2P) lending is essentially borrowing money online from strangers. Popular for small businesses that need smaller amounts (and for paying off credit card debt) lending sites like Prosper, Lending Club, and Virgin Money connect lenders with borrowers. P2P is like online dating to borrow or lend money.

Columbia University professor Ray Fisman studies the trend and calls it "Ebay meets Match.com." You set up a profile saying how much money you want to borrow. Individual lenders who are looking for a better return than they are getting on their money elsewhere typically kick in $50 to $100 each.

"In a sense it is an auction on interest rates that matches lenders to borrowers," Fisman says. "These are perfectly rational borrowers that are putting up pictures of their three cute children and two furry puppy dogs because there's evidence that actually gets you a better deal on your loan."

Tommosso Trionfi is one of the investors. He's looking to diversify and decided to lend $5,000 on the peer-to-peer lending site Prosper. "In my savings account I was getting 1¼ percent so basically nothing. And compare that to Prosper, on average, if you can fine-tune a bit, you're going to have a much better return." For him, he says it is 12 percent. So far, he is starting slowly, but if he likes the experience, he's willing to lend $50,000 eventually.

Like many lenders, he makes small individual loans online, to diversify in case some of the borrowers fail.

It certainly doesn't replace the loan volume that the banks have reeled in, but it is a viable option for some small business owners who want to get creative. It is a tiny segment of the business loan market, but it is growing, from $118 million dollars in loans in 2005 to an estimated $5.8 billion in loans this year.[10] Rising rapidly enough that the Securities and Exchange Commission says it is monitoring these sites and may regulate them in the future.

Peer-to-peer lending gets all the glowing press, but there are a few other interesting lending innovations for start-ups looking for cash. Again, none of these replaces the billions of dollars sucked out of the small business–lending environment over the past couple of years, but for creative entrepreneurs with good ideas and gumption, you just might have luck.

Y Combinator

It calls itself "a new kind of venture capital firm specializing in early stage start-ups." This start-up incubator focuses on technology and software firms, particularly Web applications—it's run by hackers, for hackers.

(No not *those* hackers—for the tech-savvy it means someone who is skilled at manipulating code.)

These investors provide the seed funding (rarely more than $20,000), in exchange for a 2 percent to 10 percent stake in the company. Y Combinator funds start-ups in batches, two each year. Entrepreneurs then go in groups to three-month-long training sessions, where they teach you how to pitch to investors, seal the business deal, and get your company incorporated properly.

So far Y Combinator has helped launch 205 companies.

Kickstarter.com

Called "crowd-funding," this site is a funding platform for creative endeavors.

If you want to make a brand of artisanal cheeses, produce a film, or design a line of handbags, Kickstarter can help. Users propose a project on the site (Kickstarter vets for quality and appropriateness), and set goals in terms of time period and dollar amount (e.g., $5,000 over 60 days). Then people make contributions toward that goal. If the project does not reach its target, no money changes hands; Kickstarter has an all-or-nothing funding model.

In exchange for funding, entrepreneurs promise something (a novelist looking for funding promises a book; a jazz musician in New Orleans might offer to cook gumbo for you and your friends). Investors do not get a stake in the company and there is no long-term return on investment.

Here's one example: A man in Portland, Oregon, who branded himself, "The Ethical Butcher," got a Kickstart for his brand of flavored bacon in the spring of 2009. A former chef, the butcher uses only the most sustainable sources as he custom-cures pork and lamb bacon in everything from rhubarb to watermelon.

TechStars.org

TechStars.org is a mentorship-driven investment program for "the next generation of technology companies," which provides up to $18,000 in seed funding. It's selective—hundreds of companies apply and about 10 get accepted in each of three cities—but if you're in, they hook you up with mentors and connect you to other entrepreneurs.

When TechStars is screening applicants they "focus primarily on the team," says founder David Cohen. "We have to love the people and they have to be very talented technically. Then, if they're in a market that we're interested in and that is growing, shrinking, or changing in some way, that's even better. But the focus is heavily on the team and their talent as demonstrated by their early execution."

One team that fits the bill was a couple of ex-Wall Streeters who quit finance right before the industry collapsed, and traveled the world for a year. When they came back, they decided to start a web site to help other travelers document and share their experiences. Using TechStars, they created Everlater.com.

The founders of Everlater, like everyone who goes through the TechStars program, attended their three-month small business boot camp. In going through training, entrepreneurs refine their business ideas and develop a prototype. At graduation, or "Investor and Demo Day," TechStars gives them the chance to pitch their product to venture capitalists and angel investors. In exchange for start-up help, they take a 6 percent equity stake in the new company.

Of the 39 companies TechStars has helped launch since 2007, 28 are still active. Some of the others have been acquired for more than $2 million, one was spun off into another company; only five have failed. Most are Web-based or software companies. About 70 percent of TechStar's trainees have gone on to raise outside funding after the program, or bootstrap to profitability.

Most of these creative-funding tools favor tech start-ups or tech ideas and are not appropriate for the established business struggling through the recession. They are incubators of ideas, and the seed money isn't much. But good ideas are being funded, and it's incredibly important that innovation continue despite credit trends. To heal the economy and build the future, we must connect the people with the ideas with the people who have money. It's as simple as that.

THE PAYOFF

Make no mistake, it is rough out there for small business owners. For starts-ups, the always troublesome scramble of finding
the money is harder. But if you know you have a good idea, a
solid business plan, a niche in the community, don't give up. Harness social
networking. Cut your costs, listen to your customers, and try new things.
And hope for that 80 percent *luck* you need to make it.

CHAPTER

11

Government

68,000 Miles

How far one trillion one-dollar bills stacked on top of each other would reach into the sky. (Nearly one-third of the way to the moon.)

Before any analysis of the government and your money, it's useful to have a gut check on just how big a trillion dollars is. For years, the big numbers started with a B. The crash of 2008 brought America into entirely new territory—the trillions.

Here's how much $1 trillion is. It's got 12 zeros. ($1,000,000,000,000!)

In the heat of the bailout drama, Republican Senator Mitch McConnell put it this way: "To put a trillion dollars in context, if you spent a million dollars every day since Jesus was born, you *still* wouldn't have spent a trillion dollars."

He's right. I checked his math with noted mathematician John Allen Paulos. "A million dollars a day for 2,000 years is only three-quarters of a trillion dollars," Paulos says. "No matter how you slice it, it's a big number."

So let's slice it another way.

One million seconds is 11½ days.

One billion seconds is 32 years.

One trillion seconds is 32,000 years.

Think of that the next time you hear bailouts, loan guarantees, and bank profit figures tossed around casually. After a $700 billion bank bailout, an $862 billion economic stimulus package, and several trillion in Fed and other government debt promises, the world is swimming in very big numbers. So big, they are almost meaningless to comprehend. Million, billion, the national debt now tops $13 trillion, have we become numb?

"The word 'number' itself can be parsed number or numb-er," Paulos emphasizes the "b" the first time, keeps it silent the second. "Maybe in this case the latter is a better pronunciation."

It almost makes you feel like Dr. Evil in the Austin Powers film when he put his pinky to his lip and demanded "one meeellion dollars."

It's just not what it used to be. Times have changed.

Back in 1993, President Bill Clinton stood before Congress and asked for something bold and audacious.

"I call on Congress to enact an immediate jobs package of over $30 billion." He was fighting the effects of a nasty recession but Congress wasn't so willing to spend such big dollars. Thirty billion dollars for a job-creation package? That was serious money. In the end, he got closer to $16 billion.

In 2008, President George Bush embarked on an historic jobs package and stimulus of his own, an enormous $168 billion in tax rebates and tax breaks for businesses. Even that wasn't enough to stave off the economic tsunami hitting the United States. Just a year later, the $787 billion Recovery Act passed by Congress and signed by President Obama in February 2009 turned out to cost, in reality, $862 billion, dwarfing the Bush stimulus five times over.

Supporters of such big stimulus spending point out that the huge size of the U.S. economic engine warrants big spending. When the size of the economy is $14 trillion, the spending is in context, supporters say.

"We do have a big economy that may not be as strong as it was but it is still a powerful economic engine," Paulos explains. "Knock on wood, we'll see what happens."

We'll see what happens indeed.

For now, all the measures seem to have pulled the economy back from the brink. The U.S. economy has grown for at least three consecutive quarters and many economists believe that the recession ended sometime in late summer 2009 or in the fall. Jobs creation has lagged, but corporate profits and the stock market have rebounded sharply. The oxygen has started to flow in the economy again, overnight lending has returned to normal.

UNITED STATES OF BAILOUTS

ROMANS'
NUMERAL

40 Million

Number of Americans on food stamps, as the stimulus expands the social safety net.

The history books will write the story of how the rescue fared. But what is clear even today is that the scope of the rescue is unfathomable. All told, the bailouts, loans, guarantees, housing rescues, and temporary liquidity programs amounted to $11 trillion—almost the size of the entire economy. Those were the promises made—promises that convinced investors and the world that the United States would not let its economy slide into a second Great Depression.

Just what did we spend all that money on? Cash for Clunkers, unemployment benefits (up to 99 weeks of jobless checks for some laid-off workers), loans and cash injections to insurance giant AIG, a quarter of a trillion injected directly into the big banks, billions to take over failing banks, student loan guarantees, purchases of mortgage debt, Fed purchases of dollars and foreign currency swaps to maintain money in the system, $26 billion for Bear Stearns, auto industry financing, the list goes on and on.

IndyMac, Bear Stearns, Lehman Brothers, AIG, Citigroup, GM, Chrysler, TARP, Fannie Mae, Freddie Mac and stimulus. Each word rife with political drama, human tragedy, and taxpayer angst.

All these bailouts were reviled by many, endorsed by others, and debated among academics who fretted they didn't go far enough. Most people think of the bailout from the crash of 2008 as the bank bailout—the Troubled Asset Relief Program. In the end it was $250 billion directly injected into the very banks whose risk-taking helped bring the economy to its knees. In reality, the massive rescue was bigger and much broader than the banks.

But for better or for worse, when the U.S. public thinks of the government bailing out the economy, they think of multimillionaire bankers heading to Washington with tin cups, filled up by clueless ex-banker bureaucrats and bought-and-paid-for politicians with money from taxpayers.

From the moment the bank bailout was first conceived in the chaotic hours of September 2008, it was contentious and hated.

Even the man who designed it hated it.

The former Treasury Secretary Henry Paulson is a free-market guy who never in a million years imagined his legacy would be forever associated with the largest government intervention into the markets in the history of the country. As part of his own book tour for *On the Brink*, a play-by-play of those bailout days, he sat down with me for 40 minutes of intense questioning about what he was thinking at the time of the crisis, who he was talking to (his old friends at Goldman Sachs?), and whether it worked.

He says he sleeps at night. He knows what was averted. And he's glad Americans have come to hate bailouts. He hates them, too.

President Obama in his 2010 State of the Union address said that Americans hate bailouts like they hate a root canal. I told Paulson that statement means that he is the dentist.

"I was the dentist having a root canal without anesthesia at the same time," he said.

The whole country had a root canal without anesthesia, and then got a big bill.

THEY GOT IT WRONG

ROMANS'
NUMERAL

70 Percent

How often Alan Greenspan says he was right in 21 years of public service.

That other 30 percent was a real doozy. It's instructive as we move forward to recognize just how wrong the assumptions were of the past 10 or 15 years. Citigroup may not have become too big to fail if not for financial deregulation under President Bill Clinton in the 1990s. His advisers counseled that complicated derivatives need not be regulated. Key players (in both parties) trying to reform financial market regulation today are the same people who for years pursued deregulation, lower lending standards, and record homeownership.

The conventional wisdom held by successive presidents, Congresses, and two Federal Reserve Chairmen, was that homeownership was a political policy to be pursued vigorously, at about the same time that financial market deregulation was championed.

Federal Reserve Chairman Alan Greenspan was hailed as the Maestro when interest rates were low and the economy boomed. He made some key assumptions that turned out to be faulty. Among them, he thought people didn't have to have as much savings in the bank if they had wealth in their home. And he thought that the housing market was too big and strong to be taken down by poor borrowers who couldn't pay their bills.

The official commission conducting the autopsy of the crisis (called the Financial Crisis Inquiry Commission) later asked Greenspan what mistakes he had made and what he could have done differently. He told the very people chronicling the debacle for history that looking backward is "futile."

"When you've been in government for 21 years as I have been," he said, "the issue of retrospective and figuring out what you should have done differently is a real futile activity because you can't in fact in the real world do it."

Greenspan went on to explain, "I think . . . I mean my experience has been in the business I was in, I was right 70 percent of the time but I was wrong 30 percent of the time. And there are of lot of mistakes in 21 years."[1]

The "business" he was in was the economy. It was your livelihood and mine. Is it any wonder CNN's polls show record low satisfaction with government and elected officials? More than a few viewers—many of them former fans of Greenspan—commented that in their jobs as plumbers, doctors, trash collectors, and auditors, if they got it wrong 30 percent of the time, they'd be out of a job.

Greenspan's legacy is clearly a little more than tarnished. But he's not the only one.

How wrong did they get it? Remember, these are the smartest people, the intellectual and economic elites who make the decisions about how to run the country and fix its problems.

The seeds of crisis sprouted and grew like weeds for two years. In December 2006, Goldman Sachs noticed 10 days straight of losses in its mortgage division and immediately began getting "closer to home," as the bank put it, selling its long real estate positions.

By early 2007, homeowners with subprime mortgages began defaulting en masse on their bills. We began covering homeowner rescue sessions in big hotel ballrooms and church basements and met thousands of homeowners in danger of losing their properties. They had no idea how to read their mortgage documents or what they meant and were anxious to figure out why their mortgage payments were exploding. Debt experts lined folding tables and people waited patiently for hours to get advice. Consumer advocates began warning that something dangerous was brewing.

For the first time since homeownership became widespread, the bank owned substantially more of the house than the homeowner did. In fact, most Americans owned far less than half their homes, with some owning nothing, thanks to exotic mortgages that weren't really building any equity or home equity loans that allowed people to drain the money out. In Cleveland, Ohio, in Modesto, California, in Phoenix, Arizona, the foreclosures were beginning.

But the economy was booming and stocks were at record highs, eventually hitting above 14,000 in the Dow. Again and again, the Fed chief, the treasury secretary, the president, and bank CEOs told me and other reporters, essentially, don't worry.

Even well into 2007, the economic leaders of this country were downplaying the mortgage crisis and saying that the economy would remain strong. It's not like they missed it. They saw the subprime crisis brewing but said it didn't matter to the overall economy.

Their own words tell the story best.

Every night as I told another "War on the Middle Class" story at 6 P.M., the treasury secretary was saying the global economy was stellar. Henry Paulson told NPR in March 2007, "It is as strong as I have seen it anytime in my business career."[2]

The new Federal Reserve Chairman Ben Bernanke, a leading Depression scholar, traveled the country giving a similar speech to business schools, chambers of commerce, Congress and local business groups.

"We do not expect significant spillovers from the subprime market to the rest of the economy or the financial system."[3]

By October 2007, Paulson agreed with Ben Bernanke that the damage from rising subprime mortgage defaults would be contained.

"This is happening against a backdrop of an economy that is in many other respects very solid. There is very little evidence it's bleeding over into other areas," he told reporters.

A lone voice in Washington, Sheila Bair at the Federal Deposit Insurance Corporation, went public with her advice to mortgage servicers to freeze rates on adjustable rate mortgages, sensing trouble was brewing.

And trouble *was* brewing. For months gas prices moved higher. Foreclosures mounted. Americans in alarming numbers began paying their credit card bills before their mortgages just to put food on the table.

President Bush for months said the economy was vibrant and the economic system strong. Even when he finally acknowledged trouble in December 2007, he downplayed it.

"There are some—there's definitely some storm clouds and concerns, but the underpinning is good, and we'll work our way through this period."[4]

It is understandable, to be fair, that the economic commander in chief could not alarm the public and make it worse.

But by then it was more than storm clouds, it was raining, and hail was coming down hard.

By March 2008, Bear Stearns was in a death spiral, and the Fed brokered its sale and the administration. The Fed and Wall Street bankers said the worst was over.

Treasury Secretary Henry Paulson told CNN's *Late Edition* in March, "Our financial institutions, banks and investment banks, are strong. Our capital markets are resilient. They're efficient. They're flexible."

Not so much.

In July, mortgage bank IndyMac failed and for the first time in a generation, people lined up outside a bank to get their money.

"We will come through this challenge stronger than ever before. I think the system basically is sound," said the president.

As summer 2008 progressed, Americans were feeling the pinch to their wallets from rising credit card fees, sky-high gas prices, and for millions, exploding teaser mortgage rates.

All the while, the dry tinder of low interest rates, poor lending standards, nonexistent derivatives regulation, mortgage fraud, and an entire country living beyond its means smoldered.

And then the whole system caught fire.

Putting it out took history-making firefighting by the very people who couldn't smell the smoke in the first place.

Eighteen months later, former Treasury Secretary Henry Paulson gamely took me on when I challenged him about why all the smartest guys in the room didn't see it coming. Why they—and he—continued to say that the housing market and the economy were strong even as borrowers with subprime loans were defaulting in record numbers.

Paulson said he knew when he came to Washington the market was overdue for a credit crisis, he just didn't know what the spark would be.

"It's very difficult beforehand to predict these things. And I think the reason that so many experts didn't see this and the reason I didn't see it, is you look at the history of our country," Paulson said. "Ever since World War II, residential home prices have generally gone up, mortgages have been safe investment. So we haven't seen a nationwide decline in home prices."

JP Morgan Chase CEO Jamie Dimon, considered in his industry a brilliant banker, later acknowledged to the official crisis commission that he and his staff had never assumed that housing prices could fall. All the risk management and financial planning in the world folded like a house of cards because that one simple assumption was never ever entered into his bank's calculations.

Other bank CEOs admitted that they, too, got caught up in the frenzy of a rising housing market.

Only Goldman Sachs acted swiftly on internal signals that the subprime housing market was going sour, averting potentially significant losses and attracting vicious public outrage later for appearing to profit on the subprime crisis that took down Main Street.

Even as I write this, 18 months after the collapse of Lehman, the autopsy is not complete on the financial crisis. The commission charged with the definitive analysis of what caused the collapse and how to avoid it has revealed frustrations at the finger-pointing and lack of real soul-searching from policymakers about the seeds of this crisis that were sown years ago, by each party, seeds that have grown into weeds choking out our own gardens years later.

Peter Wallison, one of the commissioners, grew frustrated in one hearing on Capitol Hill, saying to former Treasury Secretary and Citigroup advisor Robert Rubin and former Citi CEO Chuck Prince, who seemed to dodge real accountability for the fact that Citi ended up a ward of the state, supported by taxpayers: "Most people were very proud of the fact, especially here in this building and elsewhere in Washington, were very proud of the fact that subprime loans were being made. Now when it turns out that these mortgages failed, everyone is running away from it and trying to point fingers at who made these loans."

Indeed, at another hearing Senator Ted Kaufman of Delaware lambasted a panel of Goldman Sachs mortgage traders. He was exasperated that the Wall Street bankers were making it seem like the crisis was a hurricane that just *happened* to them. He alleges it was a storm of their own making.

"This is what I am getting out of all this: That you all say this is a natural disaster and no one's fault, like a hurricane or something. Did you ever have any concerns in 2006 to 2007 at all that there were an awful lot of home loans being securitized?"

There were a million mistakes and missed signals. First and foremost, the assumption among the nexus of business leaders and politicians that home prices would not fall.

They were wrong.

It's a little unnerving to think what else they might be wrong about today. What is that little echo you hear after even the most confident prognostication from an economist, a politician or a pundit?

"I was right 70 percent of the time but I was wrong 30 percent of the time."

What 30 percent are they getting wrong today?

SPEND, SPEND, SPEND

$1,550,000,000,000 (That's Trillion)

How much more the government is spending this year than it is taking in.

Enough hand-wringing about the past. How about the right now? Is the fire out? Are my taxes going to rise? Are debt-ridden European economies out of the woods or could they still take down the fragile global economy?

And what about that pile of debt we have amassed for what the country has spent to avert disaster but hasn't got the money to pay for yet?

Let's tackle that last question first.

The United States government is spending vastly more money than it takes in, by the widest margin in U.S. history. It began before the Great Recession, when Clinton-era budget surpluses turned into red ink when taxes were cut and defense spending soared after 9/11.

Then came a financial collapse, and the government doubled down on debt, spending furiously to try to blunt the recession and prevent whole swaths of the economy from shutting down. Some economists fretted that we weren't spending enough. Conservatives screamed that we should let the economy fix itself and not bail out the banks. On Capitol Hill whatever was said behind closed doors by then New York Fed Chairman Tim Geithner, Fed Chairman Ben Bernanke and Treasury Secretary Henry Paulson worked and a frightened Congress spent more money faster than it had ever done in history. First a bank bailout with virtually no strings attached and then an economic stimulus that rivaled the spending in Iraq and Afghanistan, and adjusted for inflation, was bigger than the Marshall Plan to rebuild Europe after World War II.

Almost everyone tried to understand this simple little truth—that to solve America's financial crisis, we may be sowing the seeds of the next one—a debt crisis. To spend the economy back to health, we were issuing even more debt and borrowing from Japan and from China, a country with strategic differences with the U.S. (Think Taiwan, the Dalai Lama and Tibet, atrocities in Sudan, and robust business relationships with Iran and Venezuela.)

Congress has passed emergency spending bills and extensions of unemployment benefits. There is free money for insulation and energy-efficient doors. And then the normal costs of running the government— schools, defense, student loan programs, health-care safety net. Some of this spending is emergency, much is nonnegotiable. All of it is moving the needle in the wrong direction.

Where is all this spending heading?

U.S. debt held by the public will top 60 percent of the size of the economy by the end of this year. It's high, yes, but it is the path of these debts that concerns budget experts. Barring a miraculous increase in revenue and cuts in spending, our public debt will skyrocket to 90 percent of the size of the economy by the year 2020. At that point, you are paying so much interest on your debts that you have less to spend domestically.

Anyone with a pile of bills can understand that. America's credit card is maxed out. We are incredibly fortunate to pay very low interest rates for that borrowing. That can't last forever.

President Obama acknowledges what families know too well: You can't spend vastly more money than you earn indefinitely.

"It's like going through the family budget. You know, you started getting too many things you couldn't afford and you're going to start making some decisions," President Obama told a Buffalo, New York, audience on his Main Street tour this spring.

Making those decisions is not easy, or they would have been made. Do you cut military spending? Social safety nets? Does everyone work longer before they get Social Security? Do you make rich people pay more in Social Security taxes? Do you raise income taxes? And by how much? Many tax experts say that reducing earmarks and slashing waste and fraud in government will only make a dent in our debt problems. It will take drastic moves— a combination of strong economic growth, tax increases, and spending cuts to get things more balanced.

Republican Congressman Paul Ryan is passionate on this point.

"We have before us the most predictable economic crisis that we've ever had in this country. Sovereign debt crises are popping up all over the world, and we are kidding ourselves if we don't think it could come to us next."

The United States spent richly to get out of its mess, and now has to figure out how and when to unwind all these programs gently and gingerly to avoid another shock to the system. And all the while, as its debt pile grows, it takes away a little more flexibility for future policy makers.

Budget hawks who worry that the United States will suffocate under a pile of unsustainable debt want a credible plan of action to get it under control once the recovery truly takes hold.

Maya MacGuineas, president of the Committee for a Responsible Budget says that the longer the country waits, the more possibilities for something to set off a crisis. And the less flexibility we have as a nation to fix it.

President Obama has called a bipartisan 18-member panel to propose ways to curb these soaring deficits. One member, Alice Rivlin, former Fed member and White House budget director in the Clinton administration, is stark in her assessment. "We're facing a serious and perhaps catastrophic threat to the future prosperity of the United States."

There are only three options: 1) spending is cut dramatically to match how much money is coming into government coffers so that Washington is no longer spending more than it makes; 2) spending stays the same, but taxes rise to bring in more money to cover the shortfall; or 3) some painful combination of the two.

It would be incredibly helpful to all three scenarios if the economy takes off like a rocket ship, millions of jobs are created quickly, and tax revenues and corporate profits soar.

The faster the economy grows, the less pain is necessary. But you can't count on it

The president's fiscal commission won't make anyone happy in all likelihood. It has to recommend how to reduce the budget deficit to only 3 percent of GDP, down from the roughly 9 percent right now. The goal is to more closely match how much more we spend than take in to reasonable expectations for how strong the economy is. The second task of this commission is to tackle the long-term drains on the federal budget. These are the politically important promises that have been made to U.S.

citizens—Social Security, Medicare, and Medicaid. These are social contracts that politicians touch at their own peril. They are also promises that along with the interest on our debt, will account for 93 percent of all the money the government collects in taxes by the year 2020.[5]

Harvard economist Ken Rogoff is the former chief economist of the IMF and a noted expert on global financial crises.

"I think within the next 5 to 10 years, we are going to have to see big changes in our fiscal policy. I think much higher taxes, less benefits. We're talking about major changes. Our politicians have made unrealistic promises; they have not prepared the public for the belt-tightening that's to come."

A low-grade version, he says, of the belt-tightening in Greece and concern in Europe that arose this spring as weak economies, huge public-sector spending, and declining tax receipts caused investors to worry about the solvency of entire nations.

Bottom line, the Crash of 2008 is behind us, the Great Recession is over, and it's about to get interesting.

What we need in government is the political will to make tough choices that might be unpopular but will be good for the United States longer-term. And we need an economy to roar back. Amid all this gloom and doom about America's checkbook, this is sometimes overlooked. Few thought in the early 1990s that we could possibly see a day of budget surpluses, but a burst of strong economic and jobs growth did just that. It's not impossible that a strong economy will give lawmakers some cover to make the tough choices they will have to make.

In the meantime, budget experts say that you and I should prepare for a more austere future. Teacher cuts as state budgets falter? Check. Higher fees and taxes. Check. Fewer benefits. Yup. The reason that the United States is not like Greece is the U.S. political system is flexible and the economic base solid. Global investors look to the United States when the rest of the world falters and U.S. debt is the world's gold standard.

But the next years will without a doubt mean big decisions for the United Kingdom, Europe, Japan, and the United States to get their financial houses in order.

THE PAYOFF

The payoff for *you* is getting your own house in order. You can't control interest rates, inflation, deflation, government spending, implementation of health-care reform, or social security. You can only control your own budget, your own planning for the future, and your own assumptions for what the American Dream will look like for your family. How?

- The first thing you can directly control is your spending. Unlike the government, it doesn't take 535 elected officials, thousands of government bureaucrats, and ever-looming election pressure for you to make decisions. You can cut your spending and reallocate your resources more wisely *today*. It might take a family meeting—and maybe some austerity measures for your children—but you can move a whole lot more quickly than the government.
- Are you a good steward of your money? Remember the advice of Ryan Mack, financial adviser, who says that the little financial decisions you make every day decide what kind of financial security and retirement you will enjoy.
- If you can't afford it, put it down. And for God's sake don't put it on a credit card if you can't pay for it when the paycheck comes.
- If you have credit card debt, strive to be debt free in three years. And remember, how well the government gets its financial house in order—and how soon—will ultimately affect your family. Will interest rates rise? Will your school district have more cuts? Will you pay more in taxes and services? Plan for the worst and hope for the best.
- Know the difference between good debt and bad debt. What is an investment for the future and what is something that will weigh you down? If you or your children are considering loads of borrowing for an expensive college degree, there is no choice but to finish, or that good debt could become bad debt *fast* and could limit your wealth for the rest of your life.
- Save for your own retirement first, before any other investments, even your kid's college education. Know how old you want to be when you'll finish working, how much money you'll need to get there.

Smart, after all, is the new rich.

Cover Letters: The Good, the Bad, the Ugly

C an you tell which of these cover letters landed an interview and which ended up in the reject pile? These are actual cover letters from job hunters, sent to career coach Brad Karsh of JobBound. We've changed the names to protect the identities of the clueless writers and the savvy job seekers who sent them. Here's a hint: The good letters have good writing, short sentences, and feel like a quick conversation or introduction. The only way to make them better would be to have an actual connection to refer to somewhere in the letter: "Jonathan Smith told me to reach out to you." (Spoiler alert: I am about to disclose the good ones and the bad ones. Skip ahead if you want to guess yourself.)

Drum roll please . . .

Joseph and Maggie's letters are short, concise, and interesting. Maggie was asked by so many hiring managers why a stockbroker would switch careers that she decided to answer the question right off the bat in her cover letter. She did it eloquently. The second two letters are unreadable. Pay special attention to Jason's prolific use of the name of the company he is applying to—almost as if he were cutting and pasting it into a form letter. Don't just regurgitate the resume, but tell your story. As Brad Karsh says, make it like a movie trailer to draw the recruiting director in. Read them for yourself to decide. And keep in mind, there are many ways to formulate a cover letter. Karsh says to shoot for clever but remember that there is a fine line between clever and irritating. Also, many younger workers are including Twitter icons and addresses and links to their social networking profiles. It's a great idea—as long as the information at the other end of those links is appropriate for a hiring manager to see. Final tip: Avoid words like facilitate, utilize, and transition (as a verb) in a cover letter. Just say what you mean in simple, clear language.

COVER LETTER 1

JOSEPH TEMPLETON
102 VANDERBILT DRIVE • DENVER, CO 89816
928.829.8611 • JOSEPH@GMAIL.COM

Gary Polecki   March 19, 2010
370001 Winson Ave.
Denver, CO 34421

Dear Mr. Polecki:

Building. It's what I do for a living.

No, not in the traditional hammer and nail sense, but in the business—whether it's building a marketplace for a product I'm selling, building a series of original products, or building a business.

Six years ago, the world of Internet advertising was unproven and untapped. I created a sales and marketing plan for this fledgling media, and ultimately built an incredibly strong client base and revenue stream that helped our company grow 500 percent in six years.

In working closely with my clients and with a project management team, I built a series of innovative programs and products that respond to an ever-changing web-based marketplace. As the technology has evolved, I've been able to adapt to the playing field.

Finally, I built a business of more than 180 clients that includes senior managers and decision makers at some of the world's largest consumer brands and advertising agencies.

I'm excited to learn more about Watta Worldwide, and I'm thrilled at the chance to build your business. I look forward to following up about the Vice-President of Marketing Services job.

Regards,
JOSEPH TEMPLETON
928.829.8611

COVER LETTER 2

MAGGIE PINTER
315 GARDEN WAY • MONROE, LA 42001
854.223.1235 • MAGGIE@HOTMAIL.COM

Richard Dale   March 19, 2010
83010 Quiet Oaks
Baker, LA 29292

Dear Mr. Dale:

Why would an established stock broker give up a lucrative career and go back to school to become an editor?

It's easy. Passion.

Finding one's true calling is much more valuable than making lots of money in an unsatisfying career. I knew from the moment I cut my first piece of film that I made the right decision. Our first school project was to cut stock with a razor; I thought they were nuts to make us do it. Once I got started, they had to drag me out of the classroom! I was hooked, and it's only gotten better.

I know that I'm a non-traditional candidate. I know I'm going to have to work hard and prove myself over and over again. At the same time, I am supremely confident that I have the skills and the desire to be successful.

When I'm in the editing room, I'm happy, passionate, and dedicated. Nothing else matters.

I look forward to speaking with you in more detail about opportunities at Strategic Solutions. I'll plan to follow up with you in a week.

Regards,
MAGGIE PIKE

COVER LETTER 3

GAVIN RICHARDSON
123 LANE
MOBILE, AL 36608

Dear Gavin,

I think I would be a great fit for your Sales position, and there are many reasons why I should be considered for this position.

As you will see on my resume, I am currently working as a receptionist at an accounting firm near campus. I've learned how to work in a fast-paced enviroment and show great customer service. I've made only A's and B's in college, and I was on the dean's list for several semesters. I also was involved in several organizations on campus.

My contact told me that you need a salesperson. I am a really hard worker and I always show intitiative so even though I don't have a lot of sales experience, I know I could learn quickly. It sounds like this would be a great place to start my career before I go on to work with computers.

I can't wait to hear from you. Please let me know when would be a good time for an interview. Please call anytime at 223-123-2323.

I look forward to working with you!

Thank you,
TAYLOR SIMPSON

COVER LETTER 4

Sarah Holliman   March 19, 2010
Director of HR
Johnson & Associates

Dear Ms. Holliman,

I am very interested in the Marketing Assistant position at Johnson & Associates. I have learned of this job opportunity from a job posting on your web site.

I am currently a senior, graduating in May 2010 with a Bachelor of Science in Advertising and a minor in Economics. I am very attracted to this position at Bay & Associates from the description on the posting online. I am looking to work for a company that has a positive outlook in business for its clients and employees. I hope to learn from passionate, motivating people in my career. I believe that the creative, fast-paced, and innovative culture at Johnson & Associates is one in which I would fit into and thrive from.

As you can see from my attached resume, I held many potions in college that make me well suited for a position at Bay. I was the Vice-President of Programming for the Marketing Association where I was responsible for bringing in speakers to help educate our members on careers in marketing. I also held an internship at Windy City Fieldhouse where I spent the summer working in the marketing department. There I had the opportunity to sit in on many meetings that discussed marketing and growing the business. I also participated in a brainstorming meeting where we were looking for different ways to fix our web site.

Finally I have held a job at Blue Sky Chicago where I gained experience and strengthened my skills in communicating with professionals, completing projects and in research, and planning. These positions have strengthened my interest in Johnson & Associates.

Additionally, I completed several team projects in college and am able to enjoy working with a variety of individuals. I believe that I succeed in a positive working environment where I can learn from my peers, and my strong work ethic and ability to work with others would be a great asset to Johnson & Associates.

An opportunity at Johnson & Associates would allow me to brainstorm new and innovative marketing techniques, while utilizing my creative, communication and leadership skills. I am very passionate about learning new ideas and working with people, and I believe that is what Johnson & Associates is about. Please review my resume attached to this application. Thank you for your consideration and I look forward to hearing from you regarding my application. I'll plan to follow up in a week's time.

Sincerely,

JASON SOMITH

(815) 555-1212

Web Resources

CHAPTER 2

National Foundation for Credit Counseling (NFCC): NFCC Budget Worksheet	www.nfcc.org/FinancialEducation/ monthlyincome.cfm
Mint	www.mint.com

CHAPTER 4

AnnualCreditReport.com	www.annualcreditreport.com
FinAid: Income-Based Repayment Calculator (10%)	www.finaid.org/calculators/ibr10 .phtml
FinAid: Income-Based Repayment Calculator	www.finaid.org/calculators/ibr .phtml
FinAid: Save-and-Borrow Calculator	www.finaid.org/calculators/ save-or-borrow.phtml
Fastweb	www.fastweb.com
Scholarships.com	www.scholarships.com
Collegeboard: AP Credit Policy Information	www.collegesearch.collegeboard .com/apcreditpolicy/index.jsp

Standard & Poor's: Projected Retirement Expense Calculator	fc.standardandpoors.com/calculators/ jha/prex/calculator.jsp?toolid= 000634
TreasuryDirect®	www.treasurydirect.gov
CNNMoney.com	www.CNNMoney.com
Rutgers University: EconKids	econkids.rutgers.edu/
Cool Works®	www.CoolWorks.com
SnagAjob	SnagAjob.com
Teens4Hire	Teens4Hire.com

CHAPTER 8

National Academy of Elder Law Attorneys, Inc.	www.naela.org
Eldercare	www.eldercare.gov
National Association for Home Care & Hospice	www.nahc.org
Consumer Consortium on Assisted Living	www.ccal.org
National Association of Professional Geriatric Care Managers	www.caremanager.org

Notes

Chapter 1   Reset, Repair, Recover

1. "2009–2010 Remodeling Cost vs. Value Report," Remodeling magazine. © 2009 Hanley Wood LLC. Complete Cost vs. Value data is available at www.costvsvalue.com.
2. Treasury Secretary Henry Paulson, NPR, *All Things Considered*. March 2, 2007.
3. Fed Chairman Ben Bernanke, Speech. "The Subprime Mortgage Market." Federal Reserve Bank of Chicago's 43rd Annual Conference on Bank Structure and Competition. Federal Reserve Bank of Chicago, Chicago. May 17, 2007.
4. Paul Volcker, "Volcker Says Fed's Bear Loan Stretches Legal Power," Bloomberg News, April 8, 2008.
5. *The 2010 Retirement Confidence Survey: Confidence Stabilizing, But Preparations Continue to Erode.* Issue brief no. 340. Employee Benefit Research Institute, March 9, 2010.
6. U.S. Millionaires Grow 16 percent to 7.8 million in 2009. Spectrem Group Reports, March 9, 2010.
7. Assuming 200,000 new jobs each month, it will take seven years to reinstate 8.4 million lost jobs and still keep up with normal labor market growth.
8. Timothy Geithner. Exclusive interview, January 28, 2010.
9. GDP report, January 29, 2010, www.economicindicators.gov/Q4.
10. Christina Romer, Council of Economic Advisers, January 29, 2010, www.bea.gov/newsreleases/national/gdp/gdpnewsrelease.htm.
11. S&P Case Shiller, May 2006 to March 2010: home prices down 29.3 percent.

Chapter 2   Spending Your $$$$$

1. "Intelligent Thrift" report, *Consumer Reports*, 2009.
2. Census Bureau, "Median and Average Square Feet of Floor Area in New Single-Family Houses Sold by Location," 2009.
3. Pew Research Center, "Women, Men and the New Economics of Marriage." January 19, 2010.
4. "Marriage in America 2009: Money and Marriage," University of Virginia.
5. Reis January 2010 rental vacancy report.

6. NPD Group research, summer 2009.
7. "Conversations on the Circle," Time Warner, June 2009.

Chapter 3   Your Job

1. Bureau of Labor Statistics Employment-Population Ratio, May 2010.
2. White House statement on the employment situation, June 2010.
3. May 2010 Employment Situation Survey, Bureau of Labor Statistics.
4. Ibid., Table A-16.
5. Federal Open Market Committee Minutes, December 2009.
6. Floyd Norris, "Steep Job Losses Offer Hope for Fast Rebound," *New York Times*, January 16, 2010.
7. "U.S. Job Satisfaction at Lowest Level in Two Decades," Conference Board report, January 5, 2010.
8. 2009/2010 US Compensation Planning Survey. *More Employers Granting Pay Raises in 2010, Mercer Survey Shows. Mercer.* December 21, 2009.
9. Bureau of Labor Statistics, Occupational Employment and Wages News Release, May 2010.
10. "Job Outlook by Education: Measuring Demand for High School and College Graduates," 2004-2014, Occupational Outlook Quarterly, Bureau of Labor Statistics.
11. "Specialist Nurses Paid Higher Salaries than Family Doctors," CNNMoney.com, March 23, 2010. Merritt Hawkins & Associates data.
12. Jobs Rated 2010 Report, CareerCast.com.
13. Bureau of Labor Statistics, Employment Situation Summary May 2010, Table A-12, seasonally adjusted.
14. Ibid.
15. Association of Certified Fraud Examiners 2008 Report to the Nation, www.acfe.com/resources/publications.asp?copy=rttn.
16. Bureau of Labor Statistics, Employment Situation Summary May 2010, Table A-12.
17. Hewitt Associates database of 851 large, major U.S. employers.
18. Sara Horowitz, executive director, Freelancers' Union.

Chapter 4   Debt

1. Myfico.com. Average Credit Score: Credit Statistics. http://www.myfico.com/credit education/averagestats.aspx.
2. Creditcards.com. Credit Card Statistics, Industry Facts, Debt Statistics. *Credit Cards – Compare Credit Card Offers at* CreditCards.com. June 10, 2010.
3. National Foundation for Credit Counseling Financial Literacy survey, April 2010.
4. "Credit Karma." Creditkarma.com, April 2010.
5. Myfico.com. Average Credit Score: Credit Statistics. http://www.myfico.com/credit education/averagestats.aspx.
6. Equifax Credit Trends, April 2010.

7. National Foundation for Credit Counseling Financial Literacy survey, April 2010.

8. Myfico.com. FICO Scores & Credit Reports www.myfico.com/HelpCenter/FICOScores .com.

9. Myfico.com. Assume a borrower has a score of 780 and is 30 days late on a credit card payment. His or her score will go down to 670.

10. College Board. *College Board Brief Highlights Patterns in Student Debt. College Board.* College Board, August 8, 2009.

11. *2007–08 National Postsecondary Student Aid Study (NPSAS:08): Student Financial Aid Estimates for 2007–08: First Look* (NCES 2009-166). National Center for Education Statistics, Institute of Education Sciences, U.S. Department of Education. Washington, D.C.

12. Anthony Carnevale, National Educational Longitudinal Survey, Georgetown University.

13. *Measuring Up 2008: The National Report Card on Higher Education.* The National Center for Public Policy and Higher Education, December 3, 2008.

14. National Association of Colleges and Employers. *Starting Salary Offers to College Class of 2010 Decline. National Association of Colleges and Employers.* April 8, 2010.

15. Alexander, Lamar. Your $$$$$ Interview. October 25, 2009.

16. "Advanced Placement Program (AP)." *College Board.*

17. "Three-Year Program Cited as Model for Other Institutions." *Judson College.* Judson College, February 10, 2010.

18. Bates College.

19. Ball State University.

20. "Student Loans and Bankruptcy." SafeBorrowing.com. American Bar Association Business Law Section.

21. Joint Committee on Taxation. *Estimates of Federal Tax Expenditures for Fiscal Years 2009–2013.* Joint Committee on Taxation, January 11, 2010.

22. Fannie Mae. *Americans Still Want to Own a Home, but Are More Cautious. Fannie Mae.* April 6, 2010.

23. Zillow Mortgage Marketplace, *Despite Mortgage Meltdown, Today's Borrowers Continue to Spend Twice as Much Time Researching a Car Purchase as Researching Their Home Loan.* Zillow.com. April 29, 2010.

24. Q1 "Homeowner Confidence Survey," Zillow.com. May 20, 2010.

25. CreditCards.com: *Weekly Credit Card Rate Report.* CreditCards.com. June 23, 2010.

Chapter 5 Credit Cards

1. Credit Card Repayment Calculator. *Board of Governors of the Federal Reserve System.* Federal Reserve. http://federalreserve.gov/creditcardcalculator/default.aspx.

2. "The Plastic Safety Net: How Households Are Coping in a Fragile Economy," Demos report, July 28, 2009.

3. Economist Elizabeth Warren, Congressional testimony, and Bankrate.com survey.

4. TransUnion. *TransUnion Study Finds More Consumers Making Payments on Their Credit Cards Before Their Mortgages*, February 3, 2010.

5. "Credit Card Costs Brought Home to Consumers," *Financial Times*, February 1, 2010.

6 "Overdraft Explosion: Bank Fees for Overdrafts Increase 35% in Two Years," Center for Responsible Lending, October 6, 2009. www.responsiblelending.org/overdraft-loans/research-analysis/crl-overdraft-explosion.pdf.

7. February Data. CreditCards.com. CreditCards.com: *Weekly Credit Card Rate Report*. CreditCards.com.

8. "Meredith Whitney: Obama credit card reform makes it 'more expensive to be poor'" CNNMoney.com April 8, 2010. http://money.cnn.com/2010/04/08/news/economy/whitney_credit_cards.fortune/index.htm?section=magazines_fortune.

9. "Average Credit Score: Credit Statistics." *MyFICO*. MyFICO http://www.myfico.com/crediteducation/averagestats.aspx.

10. Interview. Craig Watts, FICO.

11. Gail Cunningham, 2009 statistics, National Foundation for Credit Counseling.

12. Myfico.com.

Chapter 6   Home Sweet Home

1. CoreLogic, February 24, 2010.

2. RealtyTrac. *RealtyTrac Year-End Report Shows Record 2.8 Million U.S. Properties With Foreclosure Filings In 2009*, January 14, 2010.

3. U.S. Department of Housing and Urban Development. U.S. Department of Commerce. *New Residential Sales in May 2010. U.S. Census Bureau News.* U.S. Census Bureau, June 23, 2010.

4. Walter Molony, economist, National Association of Realtors.

5. Myfico.com – Credit missteps—how their affect on Fico scores varies. http://www.myfico.com/CreditEducation/Questions/Credit_Problem_Comparison.aspx.

6. "2009–2010 Remodeling Cost vs. Value Report," Remodeling magazine. © 2009 Hanley Wood LLC. Complete Cost vs. Value data is available at www.costvsvalue.com.

7. Reis, Inc., February 2010.

8. Making Home Affordable. *Administration Releases February Loan Modification Report.* MakingHomeAffordable.gov. U.S. Department of Housing and Urban Development, March 12, 2010. http://www.makinghomeaffordable.gov/pr_03122010.html.

Chapter 7   Save, Invest, Retire

1. National Foundation for Credit Counseling. *The 2010 Consumer Financial Literacy Survey Final Report.*

2. Ibid.

3. Ibid.

4. *Retirement Income Adequacy at Large Companies: The Real Deal 2010*. Hewitt Associates, May 2010.

5. *Retirement Confidence Survey*. Employee Benefit Research Institute, May 2010.

6. Weller, Christian E. *Economic Snapshot for May 2010*. Center for American Progress. May 2010. http://www.americanprogress.org/issues/2010/05/pdf/may10_econ_snapshot.pdf.

7. *The Cost of the Financial Crisis: The Impact of the September 2008 Economic Collapse*. Issue brief no. 18. Pew Financial Reform Project, April 28, 2010. http://www.pewtrusts .org/uploadedFiles/wwwpewtrustsorg/Reports/Economic_Mobility/Cost-of-the-Crisis-final.pdf?n=6727.

8. *Aggregate Mutual Fund Fee Report: US IRA Accounts 2009*. MarketRiders, March 2010. http://www.marketriders.com/MarketRiders%20IRA%20Report.pdf.

Chapter 8   Family Money

1. *Charles Schwab 2010 Families & Money Survey*, February 2010. http://www.schwab moneywise.com/downloads/2010families-and-money-survey-factsheet.pdf.

2. Ibid.

3. FindLaw. *New FindLaw Survey: Young Borrowers Often Turned Down for Credit. FindLaw*. FindLaw, 8 Mar. 2010. Web. http://commonlaw.findlaw.com/2010/03/new-findlaw-survey-young-borrowers-often.

4. CollegeGrad.com. *2009 College Graduates Moving Back Home in Larger Numbers*. CollegeGrad.com. CollegeGrad.com, 22 July 2009. http://www.collegegrad.com/press/2009_college_graduates_moving_back_home_in_larger_numbers.shtml.

5. "The Millennials: Confident. Connected. Open to Change," Pew Research Center, February 2010, http://pewresearch.org/pubs/1501/%20millennials-new-survey-generational-personality-upbeat-open-new-ideas-technology-bound.

6. "Demos Economic State of Young America," April 2008, www.demos.org/pubs/esya_web.pdf.

7. "The Millennials: Confident. Connected. Open to Change," Pew Research Center, February 2010, http://pewresearch.org/pubs/1501/%20millennials-new-survey-generational-personality-upbeat-open-new-ideas-technology-bound.

8. "Generation Y's Steep Financial Hurdles: Huge Debt, No Savings." USATODAY.com. Gannett Co. Inc., 23 Apr. 2010. Web. http://www.usatoday.com/money/economy/2010-04-23-1Ageny23_CV_N.htm.

9. *Charles Schwab 2010 Families & Money Survey*, February 2010. http://www.schwab moneywise.com/downloads/2010families-and-money-survey-factsheet.pdf.

10. Ibid.

11. Ibid.

12. "Do You Think That a Person Who Is 59 Years Old Is Young, Middle-Aged, or Old?" Chart. *Marist Poll*. Marist College, April 30, 2010. http://maristpoll.marist.edu/wp-content/misc/usapolls/US100325/LMM%20AGE/LMM_Age.htm.

13. "Choosing an Assisted-Living Facility," *Consumer Reports*, January 2010.

14. "The State of Our Unions," University of Virginia Marriage Project, December 9, 2009.

15. Dew, Jeffrey. *Bank On It: Thrifty Couples Are the Happiest.* National Marriage Project http://www.virginia.edu/marriageproject/pdfs/Unions_dew.pdf.

16. Consumer Reports National Research Center. *CRMA Survey: Disorganized Financial Paperwork Is Costing Americans Money. Consumer Reports.* Consumer Reports, March 17, 2010

17. "State of Our Unions," University of Virginia Marriage Project, December 9, 2009.

18. "Off-Ramps and On-Ramps Revisited," Center for Work-Life Policy, May 2010.

19. "Lessons Learned from Economic Downturn," Citi survey conducted by Hart Associates, May 11, 2010.

Chapter 9   Health Care

1. "Fidelity Investments® Estimates Couples Retiring In 2010 Will Need $250,000 To Pay Medical Expenses During Retirement." Fidelity Investments. March 25, 2010. http://www.fidelity.com/inside-fidelity/employer-services/fidelity-estimates-couple-retiring-in-2010-will-need-250000-to-cover-healthcare-costs.

2. "Frequently Asked Questions about Health Insurance Reform." whitehouse.gov. The White House. http://www.whitehouse.gov/realitycheck/faq.

3. "Evercare® Study of Family Caregivers – What They Spend, What They Sacrifice: Findings From a National Survey." Evercare, National Alliance for Caregiving. November 2007. http://www.caregiving.org/data/Evercare_NAC_CaregiverCostStudyFINAL20111907.pdf.

4. The 2009 MetLife Market Survey of Nursing Home, Assisted Living, Adult Day Services, and Home Care Costs." MetLife Mature Market Institute. October 2009. http://www.metlife.com/assets/cao/mmi/publications/studies/mmi-market-survey-nursing-home-assisted-living.pdf.

5. "The price of excess: Identifying waste in healthcare spending." PricewaterhouseCoopers' Health Research Institute. 2008. http://www.pwc.com/en_CZ/cz/verejna-sprava-zdravotnictvi/prices-of-excess-healthcare-spending.pdf.

Chapter 10   Small Business

1. U.S. Small Business Administration. *Frequently Asked Questions—Advocacy: The Voice of Small Business in Government.* U.S. Small Business Administration, 2009. *Small Business Administration Office of Advocacy.* U.S. Small Business Administration, September 2009. Web. http://www.sba.gov/advo/stats/sbfaq.pdf.

2. American Express. OPEN Small Business Monitor. Capital Investment and Hiring Plans Show Hints Of Recovery, but Optimism about the Economy Weakens, According to

American Express Open Small Business Monitor. American Express, March 24, 2010. http://home3.americanexpress.com/corp/pc/2010/open_recovery.asp.

3. National Federation of Independent Business. Index of Small Business Optimism. *Small Business Optimism Declines in March. NFIB: The Voice of Small Business.* National Federation of Independent Business, April 13, 2010. Web. http://www.nfib .com/newsroom/newsroom-item/cmsid/51254/.

4. Clifford, Catherine. "Small Business Owners Brace for Another Rough Year." CNNMoney.com. CNN, Fortune & Money, January 22, 2010. http://money.cnn .com/2010/01/22/smallbusiness/small_business_2010_outlook/index.htm.

5. "The Small Business Credit Crunch and the Impact of the TARP." *Congressional Oversight Panel.* Congressional Oversight Panel, May 13, 2010. http://cop.senate.gov/ reports/library/report-051310-cop.cfm.

6. "The Small Business Credit Crunch and the Impact of the TARP." *Congressional Oversight Panel.* Congressional Oversight Panel, May 13, 2010. http://cop.senate.gov/ reports/library/report-051310-cop.cfm.

7. Small Business Administration, U.S Dept. of Commerce, Bureau of the Census, Business Dynamics Statistics. Note that the figures could be skewed slightly by the rare occurrence of new firms opening multiple establishments in their first few years.

8. *The Andersonville Study Of Retail Economics.* Civic Economics, October 2004. http:// www.civiceconomics.com/Andersonville/AndersonvilleSummary.pdf.

9. Morin, Rich. *Take This Job and Love It: Job Satisfaction Highest Among the Self-Employed.* Pew Research Center, September 17, 2009. http://pewsocialtrends.org/ pubs/743/ job-satisfaction-highest-among-self-employed.

10. Celent.

Chapter 11   Government

1. Alan Greenspan testimony before Financial Crisis Inquiry Commission, April 7, 2010.

2. Treasury Secretary Henry Paulson, *All Things Considered*, March 2, 2007.

3. Federal Reserve Chairman Ben Bernanke, May 17, 2007. "The Subprime Mortgage Market." Federal Reserve Bank of Chicago's 43rd Annual Conference on Bank Structure and Competition. Chicago.

4. President George W Bush. Rotary Club, Fredericksburg, VA, December 2007.

5. Government Accountability Office estimates. GAO fiscal outlook—January 2010 update.

About the Author

Christine Romans is a correspondent for CNN and co-host of CNN's *Your $$$$$*. She is the featured business reporter on CNN's *American Morning*, and a frequent contributor to CNN International's *World Business Today*.

When the financial system nearly collapsed, Romans brought 15 years of economic and market reporting to bear on the most important story for Americans in 70 years. Since the crash, she has hosted CNN hourly specials on everything from Bernie Madoff in *Madoff: Secrets of a Scandal*, to the decline of the American auto industry in *How the Wheels Came off*, and the state of the American Dream, and *In God We Trust*, an examination of faith and money in the wake of the financial crisis.

Romans' awards include an Emmy in 2004 for her work on the series *Exporting America* about globalization and outsourcing U.S. manufacturing and high-tech jobs overseas; a 2007 MADD media award for outstanding coverage of underage drinking issues; a 2004 award from the National Foundation for Women Legislators for coverage of money issues of national importance to women and government; and, from Iowa State University, the 2006 Young Alumnus award from the College of Liberal Arts and Sciences as well as the 2009 Schwartz Award for excellence in journalism.

A proud Iowa native, Romans graduated from Iowa State University with a degree in Journalism and French. She started her business-reporting career in the Chicago commodity futures pits working first for Knight-Ridder Financial News and then Reuters.

She currently lives in New York City with her husband and three young sons.

Index